Reader's Respond to The Mañana Method

5.0 out of 5 stars Great Story! Hilarious!
The Mañana Method is told with such wit and novelty that a reader will enjoy belly laughs throughout. The Mañana Method was a much-needed break for this reader who mostly reads non-fiction and for information. The book was rowdy and raucous with story after story of wild adventures and surprise awakenings. I found it to be thoroughly entertaining and quite joyful! I recommend that it be read aloud with a friend or partner. Laughter is best when shared. I highly recommend the Mañana Method. **L.H.**

5.0 out of 5 stars I was grinning as I read, front to back.
I really was. And I did not want it to end. Dangerous Dave and Tunes' adventure with The Kid and the magical roster of characters from the. road was a really fun read. It brought me back to my own Mexican (and other) adventures and filled me with a desire to do have another. My grins were real as is my praise for the good time I had in reading this tale. Congratulations, M.D., on a fabulously enjoyable read. I have waited a while for it and I'm happy I did. See you down the road. **J.L.**

5.0 out of 5 stars Adventure through Mexico in 9,000 miles, 60 days and $1,000
Flashback to the 70's and an amazing trip through Mexico in 60 days on $1K. The author is a master of adjectives and adverbs guiding you through his adventure. Funny, educational, and historical with the changes that have been done to this laid-back country of yester yore. Loved the book and now I want to hit a few of his destinations. A great read for anyone and especially us baby boomers. **Brian P. King author of Ammunition 357**

5.0 out of 5 stars The appeal of youthful adventure
The Mañana Method is the story of young men discovering the adventure and romance of exploring a new culture—replete with music, sun, and experimentation. The kind of adventure that every young man should experience before the hand of responsibilities strangles the life out of young blood. **Allen Johnson author of Athena's Piano and Pardon My French**

Copyright 2017   2nd Edition Copyright 2023

"For me there is only the traveling on paths that have heart, on any path that may have heart, and the only worthwhile challenge is to traverse its full length-- and there I travel looking, looking breathlessly." ~ Carlos Castenada

The Mañana Method

By *Michael D. Navalinski*

2nd Edition *(revised and revisited)*

Dedicated to the spirit, humor, music, and the soul of adventure left us by Jimmy Buffett

1. The Planted Seed Blooms....
November, 1978

Dangerous Dave is right. "The Northwest Washington winters, are a conga line of gray, rain-drenched oppressive malaise that lasts approximately one hundred twenty days, sometimes more, never less..."

Put a beer or three in him and off he goes, espousing in great detail about the foods, people, jungles, ruins, mystery; until the full vision of a Mexico adventure whacks you upside the head.

Dangerous, my closest and most honorable sidekick, has recently attained his bachelor's degree from Western Washington University, not in meteorology, mind you, but in psychology.

Now, degree in hand, he opts to thumb his nose at embracing the standard nine-to-five regimen, choosing to fill his seasonal gaps with an occasional well-paying framing job or two, until it comfortably supports his true passion: travel. Dangerous prefers taking his journeys, down winding, divot-pocked back roads as opposed to the well-paved highways AAA tends to recommend.

In the past decade, he has been a busy boy. He has toured Europe by bicycle and backpacked through South America. The past three winters Dave's been busy searching for paradise with an ocean view, exploring the remote, less-traveled regions of Mexico; those little dots in an Atlas which have never seen Visa cards, let alone flushable toilets. Dangerous hunkers down in hostels and dwellings made from palm fronds and sticks, where hot water is produced solely by the heat of the midday sun.

As each precious fall day grows shorter, Dave begins to hone his blueprint for flight. Sunshine tops the list of prerequisites, followed by exotic locale, economic feasibility as well as finding the right running partners to complete the package. He prefers recruiting newbies, those unfamiliar to the challenges waiting beyond their front door; the ones who potentially may be transformed by their experiences and perceive the world in a different light by journey's end.

These past three years, I have been the one he needles, badgers, and cajoles to accompany him. Each time, I manage to deflect temptation offering a handful of flimsy excuses as to why I must stay behind such as classes I need to graduate yet frankly have no inclination to register for; my part-time six dollar an hour job at the local Budget Tapes and Records and my over-exuberant passion for following Sonic basketball on a daily basis. The truth was I suffer from a lack of confidence I am sadly aware of, yet refuse to challenge to step outside my comfort zone to enjoy opportunities I may be missing.

Once again, he has started getting that itch to depart.
Late Thursday night my phone rang shortly after 10, smack dab at the peak of my final exam cramming frenzy; a level 300 level Relevance of Existentialism in Modern Society exam I hoped to manage a C-, at best, in.
I picked up the receiver on the tenth ring.
"Tomorrow night, Up & Up Tavern, 7 p.m."
"But that's Friday night, pitchers are only half price Monday thru Wednesday." I responded weakly; my mind distracted as I struggled to decipher the illegibly-scrawled mass of consciousness lecture notes scattered before me.
"Is this that existentialism class you chose because the blonde with the humongous tatas convinced you to take?"
My silence was my answer.
"I bet you the first pitcher you can't even define what the class is about." More silence. "Existentialism is the existence of the individual person as a free and responsible agent-that's you, numb nuts-to determine their own development through acts of the will. I can think of no better place to accomplish a measure amount of *development* of your aimless soul than on a trip of this magnitude. If necessary, I'll even give you an multiple choice test of my own once we're on our way home: a) Did you have a good time b) a great time, c) The best freaking time of my worthless life, or d) All of the above. See you tomorrow night, 7 p.m., We'll drown your sorrows."

One distinction our inner circle has is the nicknames we've all been given--the majority having positive designations, mind you. Dave is the architect of these monikers, yet should he struggle to deliver, he turns to me to close the deal.
More often than not, each nom de plume defines the individual considered. Amongst our brethren is Filth, Skinny Man, Polack Pete, Itsy Bitsy Betsy, and Boy-Toy Roy. On any given evening, you may find Crab Man, Sally Mander, Dorso the Human Torso, Connie Linguist, and/or Moldy Marvin hunched over our

backgammon table, cold brew in one hand, hemostats holding a fatty in the other. To a man, we all accept and embrace our alter egos.

I was initially anointed *Sir Nibbles* well-known indulgence in late night snacking, but shortly after reefer-induced evening spent thumbing through my sixteen crates of vinyl, I was rebranded *Sir Tunes*, later modified to *Tunes*. Through our many years of friendship that name has stuck. I like it.

To this day, more than a bit of self-perpetuated myth regarding the origin of Dave's nickname, or title, as he prefers, has manifested. Yes, he rides motorcycles on extended marathon runs at frightening speeds, travels through third world jungles, and mixes alcoholically lethal cocktails for his friends at celebratory gatherings. Truth be told, his propensity to embrace fireworks during all seasons with no other purpose than to hear pops, crackles, and loud bursts of Chinese-infused gunpowder when you least expect it plays a greater role than macho bravado. Henceforth, Dangerous.

It is late November, but already the rains have increased in both quantity and intensity; ten straight days and counting. Today's latest deluge was an eleven on a scale of ten. I passed the test, ending up with a D+ by good fortune acing the true and false section. Libations were in order. Time to hit the Up & Up.

Dangerous Dave sat alone at our usual table facing the front windows. Two tall frosty mugs of overpriced Heineken were already on hand. Round one was drained in lusty fashion, while we watched the quarter-sized raindrops bounced steadily off the pavement. The Up's swollen gutters, already clogged dramatically by autumn's remaining stray leaves resembled miniature waterfalls. Fall had expired, winter had arrived.

Our warm-up conversation commenced. Aware today's D+ was bound to dampen my academic momentum, Dangerous saw his chance to score and score big.

"The way I see it, my friend, this storm that's brewing is merely a taste of what old Mother Nature will soon be sending our way.

I spoke with my folks last week and Dad said the Farmer's Almanac is predicting record precipitation is on its way.

But from now until the end of February I'll be munching on fresh *Camerones*, an ice cold cerveza close at hand, while slathering on serious layers of Crema de Tortuga to prevent my bronzed flesh from burning. Wanna hear more?" Did I have a choice?

I fiddled with my coaster, and sighed. "I really can't afford to go larking about; I've got to wrap up this bachelor's degree I've been working on."

"What the hey, man? What difference will one stinking quarter off mean to a guy who's been floundering aimlessly, struggling with the rigors of higher learning for six freaking years? Hell, one quarter off might do you good. Sit on a beach. Re-adjust your goals. It's a hell of a lot easier re-defining one's priorities with the sun beating down while the waves crash in the distance than it is sitting in an artificially-lit classroom hacking up lung mold goobers with thirty-five other goober hackers?

I stumbled on to my next rationale. Work: Providing cash, essential to accommodate this moment of beer swilling, as well as funding any other potential acts of existence, such as eating paying my rent responsibly on time. And then there was music.

Since I was five years old, music has been my enduring passion. My DNA is composed of every note played by The Beatles, Buffalo Springfield, CSN, The Doors, Moby Grape as well as the Mothers of Invention. Pure Prairie League, Santana, Elvin Bishop, Little Feat, Wet Willie, and the Marshall Tucker Band. You name them, I've listened to them all; the more obscure the better.

Whenever friends drop by to hang out, they can be assured an audio backdrop of spinning vinyl will greet them. This passion pays dividends at Budget, where I get paid to assist collegians and locals alike in search of the latest as well as the greatest music of the day. Questions? Just ask that guy there at the end of the counter. He is The Man. He is Tunes.

"And regarding my employment?"

Dangerous' grin grew. "Already talked to Red and he has given this project his full approval. Told him most likely two months and he said to take as long as you like, since winter is notoriously the slow season for new releases. In fact, he's quite envious, even considering signing up for next year's expedition. Your job, as well as position of responsibility, will be waiting for you when you return."

"And if I once again choose to decline?"

"Then, my friend, you will be destined for yet another depressing self-imposed winter of malaise, from which you may never recover."

Our waitress made her rounds and we decided it was time to matriculate from frosty mugs to frothy pitcher. In time our conversation switched from hypotheticals to the bottom-line dollars and cents, or, more suitably, dollars and sense.

"Between you and me and these four walls, how much money do you have in your savings account?"

"About twenty-five hundred, I guess." My plan was to lowball the true amount but already this damn Heineken was on its way to making my lips looser than intended.

Dangerous leaned closer. "Have you ever stopped to think how much a trip across the entire country of Mexico might actually cost, let's say, sixty days in total?"

"Of course, I haven't but if I did, I would imagine...." My arguments were little more than hypothetical estimations. "First, we have transportation necessary to get there. Then lodging, evenings of entertainment, food, glorious food, and, what would an evening with Dangerous be like without shitloads of libations. Correct?"

"In most cases, yes." Dave smiled as he gained ground. "Initial game plan sees this as primarily an overland journey. We drive to Arizona, cross the border, board a train which will economically-wise take us well down the road towards our destination. From there, bus transportation should get the job done. Worst case scenario is we may need to opt for a short, inexpensive puddle jumper flight, should more prudent options be necessary. Next up, cost of trip?"

Our waitress was summoned and a ball-point pen was called into action. My initial estimations left my saving account edging into the red. "Ballpark figure looks like around two grand. Can you do better?" I asked.

He scrutinized my totals, tilted his head side to side with each revised calculation. "Amigo, I tend to differ. Two months on the road, maximum duration. An extensive tour of Mexico, coast-to-coast, no holds barred, Mexico's finest tequila, mezcal, and God knows what else we may procure, as well as a continual supply of authentic taquitos and modestly-priced indigenous cuisine should cost you no more than...." He paused and nodded, then laid the pen down confidentially. "How's eight hundred sound?"

"Dollars?"

"Maximum, maybe another fifty, one hundred if you plan on bringing any blankets, serapes, artifacts, cow heads, or trained scorpions home with you.

Add to that a very favorable rate of exchange. I think it stands currently at least at thirty pesos per dollar. If handled in a fiscally responsible manner, it should leave you living comfortably for the duration. Anything beyond that total I will be glad to cover until you can pay me back, of course. Look at that offer as travel insurance."

Great Oogly Moogly, how tempting! "You're telling me I can live like a king on your meager estimates?"

"I consider modest to be more appropriate than meager. I perceive a potential crack in your wall of resistance!"

"If you are truly not yanking my chain, I may be willing to escalate this conversation."

"And what do I need to lay before you to seal the deal?"

I was losing ground with my objections "There's still a few stones along the proposed path to turn over."

"For instance?"

"Dangerous, outside of 'si', 'no', 'tequila', 'amigo' and 'burrito', my less-than astounding vocabulary contains nary a lick of Spanish!"

"Look at you go! You're already off to an impressive start. Spanish is the most basic learner-friendly language a human can absorb through actual experience. Unlike French, there are fewer verb tenses to twist your brain, and, unlike Japanese, which is impossible to translate visually, let alone put to paper. With Spanish, once you get the vowels down, the rest falls in place quite naturally.

"Anyone, should be capable of picking up the essentials in a matter of days. We'll start by teaching you to count from one to 100 and take it from there. Start chipping away for the rest of this month and, by the time you get to the border, you'll be ready to barter with the best. Twenty pesos says that by the time we're ready to come home, you'll be a capable, well-seasoned Spanish speaking gringo."

"What about the water?" There, I had finally asked about it.

"It's as wet as it is here in the local lakes, but a bit warmer."

"No, I mean the drinking water."

"Mere urban legend. Once we cross the border, I'll introduce you to *Agua Purificada* which should negate any potential experience with *Tourista*, at least via that source."

"You mean the runs?"

Dangerous reached across the table for a hearty high five. "Come on, and you're sitting here trying to tell me you don't know any Spanish!!"

We downed our Heinekens, even ponied up for one more pitcher.

Even though I have spent many miles on the road through Idaho, Montana, Oregon, and Washington I am a tried-and-true

Northwest Washington homeboy. This is my comfort zone, my home. Yet every winter I find myself questioning why I continue to let myself spin through the wash cycle.

Gradually my self-imposed wall of insecurity came tumbling down. What the hell? Why not find out what lures my good friend into returning year after year to relish life below the borderline? No chains to hold me back, an authorized hiatus from work verified. My runway suddenly cleared for departure and the stars were aligning.

"Any personal conflicts, grudges or potential regrets which might possibly influence your decision?"

I drew a blank. "Such as, perhaps?"

"The basics: Potential romantic flames, commitments, girly shit--that type of monkey clinging to your backside?"

None came to mind.

Just then my roommate, Alex Kendall, walked in through the door, waved, and headed our way.

Alex was as cool a roommate as one could be fortunate to have. Always dependable, on time with his half of the monthly rent check and good for his share of the bills. We had been sharing a rambler on C Street for over two years and experienced little or no turbulence in our relationship.

Tonight, his demeanor bordered on aloof, quite the opposite of his usual easygoing self, as he pulled up a chair. Something was certainly on his mind.

Dangerous carried the ball as I eased out of Mexico contemplation mode. "Care to join us?"

"Actually, I was on my way down to the south side for dinner and a movie when I saw your Datsun out front so I thought I'd drop in for a quick howdy and, uh, give you *the news*."

"What's the matter, bro? Rent's not due for at least another week."

Andy's eyes dropped to the floor. "That's what we've got to talk about, Tunes. A golden opportunity is at hand and it looks like I'm gonna have to break up the band, Ringo. Remember Sydney Riggs, Robin's roommate?"

"Super Heifer?"

"The one and only."

"She's moving out next week and…"

I raised my hand, stealing his punchline. "Let me guess. You're gonna take her place." I shrugged, sighed, then added "Destiny calls."

"And you're okay with that?"

Another half-hearted shrug. In my suddenly overturned canoe of life, it was neither right nor wrong, it just was.

Andy smiled with relief. "I'll start moving my stuff out early next week, so you can find someone as soon as possible. I'll even cough up half a month's rent, so you won't be left in a bind, if that'll work."

He extended his paw, "Still friends?" I nodded; we shook.

And so, what a night, so far, it has been. Peer group pressure, beer bath, severed ties. Dangerous raised his glass.

Bart Lombardo, one-part accomplished philosopher, one part drug-addled curmudgeon, once pontificated 'No problem in life is so large it cannot be run away from'. At our table, there at the World Famous Up & Up, we raised our glasses, clinked, then skyward--bottom's up.

Dave rolled on. "Karma works in funny ways, doesn't it? The stars have aligned. Come on Tunester, throw the bomb, man, throw the bomb."

Outside the rain picked up its tempo.

"When do we leave?"

"January ninth, 9 a.m., from Bellingham, an overnight pit stop in Longview, then onto Tucson, Arizona. Non-stop, balls to the wall, overland by automobile. You provide the wheels; I'll cover the cost of fuel. Get yourself a dependable reasonably-priced backpack, one that won't fall apart if it gets jostled around a bit-and I'll start working on your list of essential items tomorrow."

A soul shake sealed the deal. Adrenaline-infused anticipation would soon begin to flow. There would be no turning back. The trip was on.

2. Flight

Shortly before dawn, snow began to fall. Lightly at first, but sure to increase as the day wore on.

It did not matter. I was busy dancing with the Sandman, deep in strange dreams, wandering about in jungle-like conditions. Slowly, and without any idea where I was headed, I made my way through a labyrinth of dense endless foliage. Suddenly, a clearing, where a pyramid, covered in heavy moss and early morning dew, rose at least two hundred feet into the sky before me.

I made my way to the base and began lumbering up the stone steps of the huge structure until I arrived at the top. Out of breath and sweating profusely I turned and surveyed the thick jungle below, which stretched for what seemed forever in all directions, spreading over lush emerald-green rolling hills. Far off, the echo of a wild beast, perhaps a jaguar, roared and… the phone rang.

"Ready to roll?" It was the Dangerous One. "Weatherman says nothing but blue skies once we get south of Grants Pass. Be there in less than soon."

Twenty minutes later, we were officially on our way. Goodbye Bellingham, hello Destiny.

Just when I had warmed up and fully committed to the journey, snow anxiety seeped into my pores. First instinct was to temporarily scuttle the plan, abort our mission; to say my mom just died; or that my cat Windex was giving birth to a hearty litter of seven in the laundry room; that I had just been diagnosed with severe gonococcal bacteria--any justification to postpone the intended course of adventure that was about to sweep me up. All I managed to mutter was a wimpy "Uh huh." By then Dave had already hung up.

An ominous precursor to our scheduled sunrise departure, this perverse gift of Mother Nature wasted little time in transforming Interstate 5 into a white-knuckle challenge for the majority of less than snow-savvy early birds traveling south towards the Oregon border.

As the morning moved along, the snow continued its assault, raising concern of the possibility of postponement, or even cancellation. Just as I was considering unpacking, sliding back under my quilt to reacquaint myself with The Sandman, the phone rang.

Dangerous requested first shift behind the wheel. I gratefully obliged and dropped into the co-pilot's seat, where my primary roles were keeping the tunes from the close to seventy cassettes on board flowing and making sure both driver and passenger were sufficiently medicated with skunky herb.

We were off, traveling a sluggish yet safe forty-five miles an hour, focused on remaining in the two thin right lane tire tracks free of snow and/or ice the drivers ahead had left for us to follow.

Having participated in many a road excursion with Dangerous, I have come to realize that, against all politically correct road rules, his driving skills operate at maximum proficiency with a can of beer between his knees and an index finger-sized reefer alternating between passenger and driver. A top-notch co-pilot's role was to produce quality-rolled spliffs of weed de jour whenever needed, while keeping a steady flow of tunes streaming as long as the wheels were in motion. Screw existentialism, this was one test I would not fail.

Once rolled and ignited up, I passed the herb, then counted and re-counted the thick wad of Travelers Cheques I had purchased with funds withdrawn from my account yesterday afternoon. Seven hundred dollars-worth, as Dave recommended, converted into twenty-dollar increments. Never had so much money felt like so little, and all but impossible, in my mind, to cover two months of travel

And what would be my course of action once these funds dwindled into mere pocket change? He exhaled, "We'll cross that bridge when your *huaraches* get to it." Huaraches?

As the snowfall ratcheted up I-5's northern corridor was quickly becoming a whiteout mousetrap, full of greenhorn drivers unequipped for Snow Driving 101. With neither chains nor studs on hand to help provide appropriate forward motion, their ass-ends fishtailed, while attempting to negotiate each elevated terrain encountered.

Inside the Datsun, the next thirty miles passed in white-knuckled silence, medicated as much as possible by continual herbal intake. Cruising along in this pleasant mind-altering fog, my mind continued to ponder a subliminally steady stream of potential anxieties our journey may present.

The sunny-day Latin vibes of Santana's *Amigos* reverberated through my 2x4 low-end speakers, the music's tropically-induced vibe an ironic contrast to the storm at hand. Heavy percussion and searing guitar work sent nothing but positivity throughout the Datsun as we rolled southward. Smooth. Steady. Nary a fishtail or white-knuckle as we moved on down the line…

The first leg of our trip brought us to our hometowns of Longview/Kelso, less than three quarters of an hour from the Oregon border. The remainder of that day was spent sharing quality time with our respective families; time spent offering a brief explanation of our plans, enjoying an abundance of my mom's awesome comfort food, and finally by a quick pit stop at the local Les Schwab for studded tires, a bon voyage gift, compliments of my parents.

Unbeknownst to our original plan, Dave added a third traveler to our entourage. Shortly before we arrived, he broke the news that his childhood compadre, Kid, would be accompanying us on our journey. Kid grew up next door to Dangerous. With no future goals, Kid was currently enjoying all the high life Longview had to offer in his current career role as bag boy at the Longview Red Apple Market.

Another newbie was a welcome addition to our mission; serving as someone to lean on whenever cultural adjustment overload showed up to kick my ass. Once Kid threw his pack in the trunk and slid into the back seat, our crew was officially ready to roll.

We were ready and loaded for bear: In our corner, studded snow tires fresh off the sale rack, front wheel drive, the afore-mentioned abundance of road-tested kick ass cassettes, as well as a half-ounce of Humboldt County's finest Sativa, a pleasant skunk-stinky sticky herb, guaranteed to make the many hours ahead pass pleasurably by. Potential whiteout be damned--we were getting out of Dodge on the one o'clock stage.

Having driven thousands of miles across more than a dozen states in my lifetime, I consider myself a legitimate Road Warrior, yet venturing into the unknown now has my senses working overtime. Inevitably, I will be dealing with these various states of mind over the next two months; making this a good trip or turning it into a bummer. I'd be a liar if I didn't admit to being more than a little apprehensive as to how this all will play out.

Over the years, I've encountered numerous second-hand horror stories (stereotypes?) regarding traveling to Mexico: "Don't drink the water", "Watch out for banditos", "It's a filthy country", and "When I came home, I shit like a shark for two weeks!" foremost among them. Even though I have confidence in my buddy Dave and his savvy for the road, these negative testimonials create a sense of uneasiness.

According to Dangerous, I'm holding enough loot to live like a pagan god, down there in the land of the red-hot enchilada, yet I've never been forced to live frugally. I have also been warned by our host that I would be making unprecedented cultural sacrifices. "Culture shock may occur when you acclimate to your new surroundings as well as when you return home." he warned. "The creature comforts and nuances you will be faced with along the way may contrast greatly with those you have come to take for granted."

Back in Bellingham I am guilty of spending the majority of my winter evenings plopped lazily in my over-sized recliner, escaping reality by absorbing a three to four-hour average daily dose of TV.

My passion for rock n' roll and pop culture will be my hardest vice to exist without. I'll be relying on the jukebox of my subconscious to get by a whole helluva lot once embedded in our destination. Dave assures me I will survive.

And sports... No Sonics, oh my!!!

With all this in mind, it's far too late to hedge on the deal that went down at the Up & Up.

The basic essentials required for fun in the sun made packing for this trip a breeze. Here's the breakdown: Five casual pairs of short pants, two swim trunks, three pairs of white socks and a handful of clean underwear; a half dozen sunny day shirts, toiletry kit, and a backup pair of semi-stinky Nikes. Seven rolls of film, a low-end Nikon with a built-in wide-angle lens, toothbrush, paste and deodorant; a family-sized bottle of Coppertone; six mammoth paperbacks; a mid-sized backgammon board and a jean jacket (which Dave would have frowned upon had he seen it) rounded out the essentials.

Before we embarked, Dave approved of my choices of reading material, yet offered one addition. "Have you ever heard of Carlos Castaneda?"

I told him I had, that I've been a devoted fan of all his musical efforts ever since Woodstock.

"Not Santana, wise ass, Castaneda. He's written several fascinating books dealing with the magical experiences of Mexican shamans. I suggest you go out and pick up a copy of *The Teachings of Don Juan*. Something tells me that it may provide valuable insight to some of the things which may occur along our way."

I humored him with a polite "uh huh", but, quite honestly good old escapism stood at the top of what I was after.

"I'm serious, Tunes. Some of the events bound to occur along our way could very well be influenced by what you bring to the table."

"Karma?"

"Among other things. I guess what I'm saying is that if your eyes are not open, certain experiences may slip by unnoticed and unappreciated."

"and by reading this Castanet..."

"Castaneda"

"Whatever-incredible things will happen?"

"Not necessarily. But the experiences you may have could be more meaningful and stick with you the rest of your life."

"Honestly, Dangerous, my idea of magic on this trip is to order a nice cold beer, give my waiter a dollar and get some change back. That would be magic!"

He sighed. "They're not dollars, they're pesos. Best start getting into the right mindset sooner rather than later. So, Tunes, did you find any time to prep for the trip?"

I nodded, but I don't believe I sold the lie. "Sure did."

"Did you learn any Spanish?"

"Si." Somehow this did not come off as funny as I had intended.

"Anything else?"

"Well, I, uh.... I've got one of those handy dandy abridged Spanish to English dictionaries, guaranteed to instantly translate any sticky phrases that come my way."

"How far have you learned to count?"

"I'm kickin' ass--all the way up to thirteen--no, make that fifteen!" My progress seemed not to impress my friend.

"It's essential to learn how to count by tens all the way to one hundred. Once you get there, you'll be glad you did. Anything else?"

"I've been eating lots of Mexican food to get my system prepared."

"Such as?"

"Every night for the past two weeks I've been stopping by Bargain Betty's mini-mart. They have buck-and-a-half frozen burritos that are absolutely to die for. Five different kinds, and I've tried them all!"

"Incredible job of preparation, amigo, but I'm glad we're sitting down, as I have devastating news for ya. I have been to Mexico what, four times now, even South America, correct?"

"Correcto." Another golden chance to show off my ever-increasing Español with great pride.

"I've eaten many foods, some familiar, others not. Some incredibly delectable, others intensely horrific. Yet, in all my travels and in all my meals in many restaurants, bus stations, and street corners, I have never *ever* eaten anything called a burrito in a third world country. Burritos are not Mexican, nor are they Spanish, or even Latin American. They have been conceived in Mexican restaurants this side of the border. Sorry for the bad news."

All that money wasted! The crestfallen look on my face must've been obvious.

Dave put a comforting arm around my shoulder. "Hey, noble effort. What the hell, when we get to Barra de Navidad, I'll buy you your first order of *Camerones Diablo*. That's barbeque shrimp. Deal?"

Occasionally, an offer comes along too good to turn down. This was one of those whiles. "Deal."

Kid had to pee. Not over an hour down the road and his bladder was already begging for a piss stop.

"Nerves," Dangerous assumed, watching Kid cautiously navigate the icy walkway on his way to the toilets at the rest area. "We'll have to start loading him up with as much ganja as possible until he's so stoned, he'll forget he even has a bladder."

I had never met Kid before today, but I had certainly heard many tales of his adventures, or, should I say, misadventures. According to Dave, Kid is living proof of why scientists have concluded that preteen glue-sniffing results in permanent loss of brain cells.

At first glimpse, Kid resembles a beatnik with his thin black goatee, pencil thin mustache, sandals, and light brown turtleneck. All that was missing was a pair of well-worn bongos, but wait-Kid came complete with a rubber Ludwig practice pad and 5A marching band drumsticks. Perfecto.

A quick anecdote to emphasize Kid's' nature: One time Dangerous convinced a vulnerable Kid his dorm room was haunted. Within two days, he transferred back home to Longview's community college and launched his career at Red Apple. Presently, at the tender age of twenty-seven, he still lives with his parents, where he diligently patters on his practice pad in the solace of his attic bedroom.

He, too, had reservations about joining us on this expedition until his girlfriend convinced him to hit the road. As of late, their relationship had become a bit strained and she required some space to sort this matter out. Dangerous' persuasive abilities managed to lure him into coming along for the ride.

As Kid was off peeing, I inquired as to where this dude was coming from. Dave chuckled. "Just kick back and watch his persona evolve. In a short time, you're bound to experience enough Kidisms to understand why he is the Kid."

After our brief pit stop Kid climbed back into shotgun position, and fired up the king-sized reefer that had been rolled in his honor. Little Feat's *Waiting for Columbus* hit the air, ringing through the car at volume level 8. Kid grew inspired. Midway through Spanish Moon, he dug into the side pouch of his backpack, pulled out his plastic-tipped sticks and pad and joined Little Feat drummer Richie Hayward, whacking along in synchronized southern sway.

For the next six hours, our back-street drummer sweated his way through a non-stop drum session of flamadiddles, paradiddles and triple ratamacues to each and every cassette we jammed into the deck, all the while immersed in a cloud of Mother Nature's finest. The dude most certainly knew how to chase away his blues.

The white stuff continued to stick, as my first shift behind the wheel commenced.

Snowfall of this magnitude in southwest Washington was as rare as a legitimate Sasquatch sighting, and the majority of those around us continued to demonstrate their inability to function efficiently under such conditions.

As the frosty Washington landscape morphed into frosty Oregon, black ice became part of the equation. Even a fool knows you don't mess with black ice.

That bit of wisdom had not been passed on to the Cheesehead commandeering a Winnebago with British Columbia plates, thundering past us at more than sixty miles per hour. I eased off the gas, slowing from thirty-five to a more appropriate twenty-five. Once he had passed us, the clueless Canadian began doing a wicked Evel Knievel side slide for well over thirty yards in the inside lane.

After regaining control of his swaying road hog, he moved to the far-right lane, where rigs without chains or proper snow tires such as his belonged. We passed him as he slowed to take the next rest area, his face a whiter shade of pale.

Regardless of the black ice or the continual snowfall hindering our path, neither Kid nor myself suggested postponing our flight until sanity, or at the least, warmer temperatures, prevailed. We were committed to going mobile and that was that. It was time to get on down the road, even if we had to fit snowshoes on the Datsun to do so.

Now seems as good a time as any to introduce our game plan, one which has been conceived, by the Dangerous one.

We're travelling overland by auto, to Tucson, approximately three days away, where we'll leave my rig at the home of Dave's longtime friend, Linda. From there, she will drive us the short distance to Nogales, a seedy little border town of ill repute, where we will acquire tourist visas as well as train tickets.

Next, we enter Mexico via the rails; thirty-six hours down the tracks, until we reach our first destination, Guadalajara, the heartland of Mexico. Then, on to Barra De Navidad, a coastal locale, where we will acclimate, regroup and rendezvous with a familiar pair of Bellinghamites, Ted and Doris, who have already embarked on their own Mexico adventure. From there we will map out the rest of the trip, keeping several options open, foremost among them, time in Zihuatanejo, Dave's Nirvana.

This is Dangerous' sixth trip south of the border, yet he is approaching this year's endeavor with excitement and enthusiasm, feeding off the potential of turning on another pair of newbies to the magic of Mexico. He has told me his main goal is to give us such a great time that we in turn will find others to share the experience with.

He knows what awaits us and is focused on not dawdling in reaching our destination. Due to his road savvy, I shall do my best to stay positive that the chances are good he will see us through the emotional highs and frustrating lows we are bound to experience. He has his hands full as interpreter, tour guide, and spiritual guru, whenever we short circuit from an overload of culture shock. We have entrusted our lives to the Dangerous one to get us there and back, safe and sound and in one piece. He is Our Man Flint. He knows the ropes, the language, and, most importantly, how to conquer Montezuma's gnarly Revenge.

Near Salem, the snow weakened to slush. For that, it is time to celebrate.

In the passenger seat, Dangerous worked on perfecting his rolling skills, choosing up-tempo tunes as he aptly fulfilled his DJ responsibilities, then pointed out a mom-and-pop coffee stand where we could get some stiff java to help this driver sharpen his focus.

In the back seat, Kid relentlessly pattered away at his drum pad as day gradually faded into evening. It appears Kid is not a man of many words, but boy can the dude drum! The windshield wipers continued their rhythm as we made our way, mile after mile, coffee after coffee, joint after joint, down the concrete roadway towards sunny Cally-for-nigh-eh.

WEDNESDAY, JANUARY 10TH

From Salem, we forged on southward, the snow miles behind us. Dangerous and I alternated the driving chores in six-hour shifts as Kid basic back seat duties did not go beyond passing the joint after taking a toke and keeping his drumsticks in motion, as he delved deeply into percussive rudiments, patterns, expressions, and techniques upon his rubber drum pad.

San Francisco served as a brief, well-deserved pit stop. A first-class dinner at Fisherman's Wharf was followed by a drop-in at Tower Records to replenish our appetite for one final dose of new tunes.

Kid's last reefer dwindled into roach status just south of Phoenix, bringing him to the sobering reality that his time as Rasta Kid had come to an end. If he were to keep his buzz going, he would have to cross over to alcohol and join us as we joyously imbibed in $1.09 Tanqueray and Tonics and forty-five cent Michelob's in a friendly college bar we came across upon our arrival in Tucson.

These discounted spirits, alongside a sufficiently greasy home-made cheeseburger (the last taste of government-approved USDA beef I would be enjoying for quite a while) did a commendable job of extending the waning moments of 'U.S. Blues' just a smidgen longer.

In the morning: Nogales, the border, and hopefully our first glimpse of blue sky awaited we three travelers.

3. Down De Line

Still feeling the effects from yesterday's celebratory libations, we rose. as one, with the dawn.

We had arrived at Dave's friend Linda's home sometime after midnight, liquored to the gills.

Kid and I rolled out our sleeping bags and quickly became one with her dog-hair-laced carpet while Dave and our host *reacquainted* themselves upstairs.

After a welcome pot of home-ground dark roast java, Linda drove us to her favorite neighborhood diner. Here she said her goodbyes and told us were she would place the key to her door would be when we returned in late February.

As close to comfort food perfection as this meal was, the best I could do was peck nervously at the healthy portion of breakfast fare before me. Kid rode in the same boat. The two of us looked more like death row inmates partaking in their pre-execution meal than two intrepid travelers pounding down carbs as they prepared to embark upon the vacation of a lifetime.

Dangerous finished his massive plate, burped loudly and gestured towards the door. The time had come to pay our bill and catch that early morning bus waiting a few blocks away to take us the short jaunt from Nogales Arizona to Nogales, Mexico.

Dave asked the first citizen we came across for directions, and he pointed towards the south. We were off, down two blocks, moving away from what would be considered the *tourist friendly* sector part of town. After making our way down an alley full of broken bottles, and mangy feral cats feasting on overturned garbage cans, we reached our destination.

There, inside a small red booth with the word *Boletos* written hastily on a piece of notebook paper and stuck to the outside wall, sat the ticket man. No smile, no small talk, just three tickets handed through the window. We had reached our point of no return.

Unfortunately, our first of many busses boarded was not to be a Greyhound excursion.

A rusty multi-colored school bus sitting on well-worn Goodyears began revving up its engine. A line at least thirty deep had already queued up to board. The patrons, mostly Mexican, stood stone still and expressionless, breathing in the healthy fog of rich blue-gray carbon monoxide spewing from what once must have been a tailpipe. No one seemed to mind.

Already, Kid had begun turning a noticeable shade of green. This gave me a well-needed shot of confidence, knowing I wasn't the only Nervous Ned in our party.

The door flopped open and the line of bodies slowly began trudging forward. Our Mexican driver, half-burned cigarette hanging limply from dry blistered lips gave us the eye. He glared in silent disapproval at the backpacks we brought aboard, yet said nary a word as he tore our tickets and gestured us to move on.

The front of the bus filled quickly. In search of vacant seats, we shuffled down the narrow aisle way towards the rear, our lungs struggling to adapt to the thick veil of smoke hanging in the air.

Halfway to the back of the bus and still no seats. Two rows from the rear, where the haze stood thick as an after-hours card game, a wrinkled *Señora* gave me my break. Somewhat reluctantly she picked up a medium-sized wooden cage from the seat beside her containing one apparently agitated rooster and set it on her lap. She sighed, before gesturing for me to be seated.

Dangerous and Kid were not as lucky. They, along with six or seven others, had to hang on to one of the overflow poles as our bus had filled beyond capacity.

Our driver ground gears, and the passengers cheered passionately as the bus jerked forward, quivering several times as it threatened to stall, then cautiously began to roll forward. We were off.

As we pulled away a sharp, stealth spring protruding from the large tear in my half of the seat began jabbing me in my butt, but I refused to yield to negativity, even as the damn thing tore a hole the size of a quarter in the ass of my Levi's. Things were cool; I had a seat and my friends did not.

Nor did I complain about the old lady's irritated fowl that pecked tenaciously at my shirt sleeve, attempting to draw blood from the gringo who had just taken his seat. The third time the bird attacked, she noticed, and gave me a grin which showcased the dark recesses of her toothless cavern. She mumbled something in Spanish in an apparent friendly tone. I could only shrug and smile. Nogales, Mexico…. One hour away…. Let's roll……….

The hour passed and we officially crossed into Mexico, the first of many destinations yet to come. From here we would be off to Guadalajara by train. Oh joy.

Dangerous pointed to what appeared to be a bar inside a hole in the wall with no informative signage where people were staggering in and out of. He had us que up at customs while he found out where to purchase our train tickets and he'd would meet us t inside the bar for a pre-trip beer once that task was completed.

Kid and I followed directions, wading through customs, getting our tourist visas stamped by a frowning agent reminiscent of Sargent Garcia in the Zorro TV series, a staple of my late 50s/early 60s childhood.

Everywhere I looked, unkempt dirty floors and shifty-looking hombres filled my line of vision. Uneasy and more than a bit paranoid, I moved my wallet from back pocket to front and moved cautiously towards the dark, semi-boarded up cantina where we had agreed to meet.

We chose the only seats available, around a three-and-a-half legged wobbly card table. There we waited for our amigo to join us. While we anticipated Dave's arrival, we were entertained by two dozen fat juicy flies performing a Mexican Hat Dance around our coasters free of charge.

A waitress arrived and, I may only presume, asked us what we would like, in Spanish. Kid and I squirmed uncomfortably as she stood patiently staring at us, her pencil and pad poised for our reply. A hundred yards or less across the border and we were already in dire straits, as neither of us could conjure up the Spanish word for beer. Only Dave's timely arrival spared us further embarrassment. *"Tres Cerveza, por favor."*

. When the warm Tecates arrived, Dangerous pointed to the bottle and repeated *"Cerveza."* We nodded, then repeated the phrase.

Like the good student I needed to become, I scratched this handy phase down in my notepad. I had just officially recorded the first of many words/phrases essential for situations ahead.

"Si." Kid spoke up for the first time of the day.

Dave nonchalantly swatted at the pesky flies, busy making new friends upon our table, then continued with this initial language lesson by pointing at a bottle of Coke across the way *"Refresca.... Comprende?"* Kid and I nodded in unison, although I was suspicious that were now operating in the Monkey-See-Monkey-Do mode.

"What's the word for bathroom?" Kid needed to get a little something off his mind.

"*Baños*." Dangerous offered. We both chuckled silently, as Kid struggled with this new two syllable word puzzle until, after repeating it stiffly several times, he mastered proper delivery. Freshly full of confidence, he left his seat to go practice on the real world.

He tapped our waitress, then offered feebly "*Ban-yosa, poor favoro*." She pointed down the hallway towards the obvious. Off he went, through the first door he came to, a man on a mission. Unfortunately, he had chosen '*DAMAS*' as his destination.

The waitress hollered at him, to no avail, and Dangerous began laughing. "All right, Kid! This is going to be interesting. Our boy just went into the women's toilet!"

"Shouldn't we tell him?" I felt bad for our mate, after all, it could've been me making that blunder.

"Naw. Let's see if he can figure it out on his own."

As fate would have it, a chubby mama from the bus entered the cantina and headed straight for the ladies' room and our error prone muchacho. Thunder, maybe even a little lightning, was about to commence.

Within seconds, a burst of angry rapid-fire Spanish resonated throughout the cantina's four walls. Kid emerged, still fumbling to button his britches, his cheeks fully flushed with the fire of humiliation.

Dave gestured down the hall. "Try the other one, Kid."

Two minutes later he shot out of the men's room, face sweating and transformed into a combined contortion of horror and disbelief.

He sat down and quickly drained the remaining half of his cerveza. Troubled thoughts were whirring inside his overloaded cranium.

Finally, Dave had to ask, "What's the matter? You look like you've just come face to face with that ghost that used to haunt your dorm room-or at least a reasonable facsimile."

Kid finished the remaining backwash. "Worse, much worse."

Only when a second Tecate was placed before him did he finally spill the beans. "My stomach has been in knots all morning-I haven't had a bowel movement in a day and a half. So, finally things loosened up and it was time to take a number two." His face grew paler yet. "I dropped my drawers and started to sit down on the seat. That's when it happened."

"Suddenly the toilet seat, it just flew away! Flies, man, hundreds of flies--make that thousands of flies!! Laying their eggs or something--they just all flew away. I almost sat my butt on a throne of flies!!!"

He tipped his warm beer skyward and drained the contents. "No way am I crapping in that place!"

"But Kid, it's thirty-four plus hours to Guadalajara…"

He finished his second Tecate and stood up. "That's cool, man, I'll hold it until we get there."

Unfortunately, we did not score a sleeper car for our approximately 1,018-mile (or, equally as impressive 1,737 kilometer) marathon journey, yet all is not lost. For our twenty-five-dollar investment, we would be riding first class all the way to Guadalajara. No squawking roosters, toothless mamasitas or gyrating goombahs, no siree. Leg room, air conditioning, and a club car would help make the hours pass by.

We inched down the tracks, slowly at first, then finally gaining speed. My head filled with giddy enthusiasm. I was really doing this. No dream. The real deal. Holy shit!

Mucho, macho, por favor, si, gracias, que pasa and *cerveza*. Not one helluva lot of conversational Spanish under my belt to use for making amigos or impressing the natives with. Still, every time I began to feel like a stranger headed for a strange land, all I had to do was glance at Kid whose body language, facial gestures, and totally stressed-out demeanor, reassured me that I was not the weakest fish swimming in unfamiliar waters.

He hadn't muttered more than a handful of words since we boarded, his hands constantly fidgeting as he checked and rechecked the snugness of his backpack straps. This went on for well over an hour, until, finally, he pulled out his sacred practice pad, and began pounding away at the brown rubber drum head.

Most journeys, Dangerous would have chosen to ride second or third class, for economic considerations. This time, in respect for Tweedle Dee and Tweedle Dum, his tenderfoot companions, he opted for first class, hoping to soften the adjustment we both were experiencing. He pulled out a paperback of sufficient length, propped up his feet on the seat across from him and dove in. Gee, we've only thirty-three-and-a-half hours left to Guadalajara.

Outside, unexciting barren flatlands provided a vanilla panorama as we continued to pick up speed heading south, toward the

Sierra Madre Mountain range, then down towards Guadalajara. The other passengers around us, mostly nationals, tended to their own business. Occasionally they would cast a curious glance at Kid, his two flailing drumsticks, and the weird rubber apparatus he continued to whack diligently, then return to polite yet amused dialogue with their friends as he thrashed on.

Smooth sailing and an uneventful evening were the forecast. If not for the misadventures of Kid, the trip from Nogales to Guadalajara would have been less than memorable, yet night had yet to fall upon us and the fun was just about to begin.

Kid *en fuego*

No one had to twist Kid's arm for what was to come. Intent on driving out whatever demons were responsible for his current panic-stricken state of mind, he alone made the choice to partake in the foolishly massive assortment of alcoholic combinations/concoctions our fellow passengers generously placed before him.

This healing process commenced around 4 p.m. under the guidance of Raul, a fifty-six-year-old Mexican American from Klamath Falls Oregon. Bearing a smile of international goodwill, our diminutive mustachioed muchacho slid into the seat beside us, winking ever so slyly as he pulled a untapped pint of mezcal from the pocket of his wind breaker.

Cracking the seal, he proposed a toast to the good old United States of America, took a hearty swig, then handed the bottle across the aisle. Patriotic ambassadors we were, it was our duty, as southbound American citizens, to oblige his generosity.

The low-grade mezcal was warm, smoky and bitter, turning my tongue numb on contact. Nevertheless, I rose above it, sipping and rejoicing with our newfound friend. We were on the road. Raul called for a toast--God Bless America! We reciprocated--Viva Mexico! Smiles all around as the bottle circulated clockwise.

Wise men know when to rejoice more than chug while the not-so-wise tend to lose track of the prudent boundaries of moderation. Our amigo, Señor Kid, failed in his effort to balance respect those limits and approached this opportunity full speed ahead.

As daylight slipped away the Sierra Madres transformed to shadows, Kid was catching fire, the mezcal his true confidence builder. He quickly made friends with two young Hispanics sitting in front of him.

As we rode further into the evening, the trio attempted to strike up conversation. Their grasp of English rivaled Kid's meager handful of Spanish phrases, each uttered incorrectly.

Bonitas came out *bonitos*. *Perfectos* were *perfectas*. What the heck, attention to proper gender form didn't seem to matter as much as their shared passion to annihilate a grimy-looking bottle of unlabeled golden liquid we assumed was either tequila or lighter fluid. As the trio swigged their way towards oblivion Dangerous and I remained passive viewers of the activities two rows of seats away.

Kid's commitment to overindulgence overrode potential common sense. Rule number one of alcoholic consumption: One should never down hearty quaffs of any liquor on an empty stomach. Nearly twelve hours had passed since breakfast at the greasy spoon and he had eaten very little. Trouble lurked right around the corner, yet Kid was not to be denied.

Conversation continued. Kid grew excited, chattering in rapid fire gibberish that he, and no one else, conceived to be legitimate Spanish while waving his arms about dramatically.

Up ahead in the next car a party was in progress. Kid and his new friends rose to their feet, promised to return, then wobbled and weaved forward until they were out of sight.

Attracted by the potential of chaos-infused frivolity, as well as an opportunity to make the long night ahead pass more quickly, Dangerous became part of the teetering human snake. I chose instead to dive into Stephen King's voluminous The Stand.

Dangerous had emphasized learning to calculate to one hundred a priority. The more phrases or words mastered, the more ease and confidence I would have bartering for goods with street vendors or at various market places.

By 9 p.m. I had officially mastered each group of tens, arriving competently at triple digits. Piece of cake. Still no sign of the boys yet so I went to work on practicing my hundreds.

Dave returned shortly thereafter, solo, laughing his ass off as he sat down beside me.

"Heads up, Kid's on fire." He gave me that trouble's ahead smile he reserved for moments the likes of which lay ahead.

"In the car, just ahead, seriously lethal concoctions have been consumed. The boys have been downing several liters of Bacardi, half gallons of El Presidente (Mexican Brandy), two or three six packs of warm Tecates and a tad bit more of nasty mezcal." He shivered for emphasis.

Kid had sampled them all and, according to Dave, began undergoing an incredible metamorphosis. Somewhere between the Bacardi and the warm Tecates, Kid began speaking Spanish fluently.

"*Passo* the *boozo, ahmeegoh*", which translated means "give me that bottle of rum so I can make a bigger fool of myself."

"*Mee-oh friendos*, we will party *on-oh* until *tomorrowo-oh*." which, in English breaks down to "Let's drink as much as we can until I pass out and puke on your boots as well as mine."

Even though both of Kid's parents were of German descent, at a glance he could mistakenly be taken as Hispanic. He maintained a year-round tan, thanks to thrice-weekly sessions at the local tanning salon. His dark, coffee-colored eyes, lightly-oiled long black hair and Billy Goat shred of a goatee make it possible for Kid to be mistaken as a third world citizen.

Dangerous and I agreed this combination had the potential to create an interesting scenario or two in the days ahead. The only redeeming aspect of his current condition was that Kid was of the harmless species of drunk; a babbler, not a fighter.

Around midnight, just as Dave and I were trying to stretch out and call it a day, what was left of Kid returned, clutching a six pack of Tecate, his twisted mouth a devilish smirk. We hunched as low as possible into our seats, feigning sleep, hoping he would not recognize us.

"*Cervasee-ohs! Cervasee-ohs* for us all!!!"

We declined his generosity, which only served to fire him up more. "Lightweights! You guys are effin' lightweights!!!" People twenty rows ahead, once deep in sleep, were now awake, turning our way, towards the boisterous source of disruption.

It was Dangerous who brought Kid a notch closer towards sobriety with a swift touch of advice. "Kid, I'm gonna count to ten, in English, not *Spanish-o*, and you better be out of my sight or I'm gonna have your *balls-o* for a *bowtie-o, comprende?*"

Bummed by our lack of camaraderie, Kid slumped into the seat directly in front of us, next to his partying amigos who had passed out a short time earlier. He turned to say something but Dave's stone-cold stare cut him off. All dressed up with nowhere to go, he decided to revive them; to share the revelry he was hell bent on.

One groggy amigo agreed to partake, unaware of the volatile pressure from unintentional shaking during transport the can of Tecate Kid had undergone. With a flip of a finger our buddy unleashed an effervescent geyser of aggravated hops.

The foam arched a considerable distance, covering the entire row in front of him as well as drenching a sleeping family of four huddled under a blanket directly across the aisle. Sticky brew dripped down from the overhead berth. Voices buzzed all around us, angry as pissed off killer bees. Kid remained oblivious.

Nasty growls and unintelligible Spanish curses grew in pitch as well as intensity. Time to change locale, so we would not be associated with *'El Drunko'*.

We moved swiftly. One last backward glance found Kid busily opening another Tecate, this one for himself. Oblivious to the fact he had opened it upside down, the contents emptied into his lap.

A beer river started flowing down the aisle towards the conductor who immediately dispatched the train's custodian to the scene of the crime. He stood over Kid, gesturing angrily and speaking rapid fire Spanish at the humbled drunk. Kid's newfound ability to speak or comprehend Spanish suddenly abandoned him and he was helpless to do anything more than stare down at his lap, unable to lock eyes with the irate train master.

Sometime before dawn, long after Dave and I finally found sleep, Kid began the inevitable--the self-inflicted ceremony known to many Americanos as *praying to the porcelain gods*. Non-stop. Full tilt. It was our first legitimate sign Karma was following along, at least for the time being, on foreign turf.

Kid's antics certainly took the edge off what would have otherwise been a grueling, monotonous first leg of our journey. During the day, the train's air conditioning was a bonafide creature comfort of first-class travel, at least until evening arrived.

Traveling through the mountains a radical drop in temperature naturally takes place as the sun begins its descent. Basic logic suggests a slight adjustment may be in order as less cold air, less the change in temperature. Not here. Tonight, no adjustment took place. The chill remained.

The air conditioning continued to blast at high velocity from every vent. Within an hour after sunset, teeth reflexively began to chatter. Those equipped with blankets wrapped themselves up tightly. For the unfortunates, such as ourselves without, invisible icicles began forming on our freezing prostates as the relentlessly cold air continued flowing throughout the night with no consideration for thermostat adjustment.

Even with the Levi jacket I had tossed in as an afterthought serving as my sole provider of warmth, this radical drop in temperature reduced us to sleeping in fetal position in order to keep as warm as possible

During the night, our train made at least a half dozen stops to take on locals on their way to Guadalajara or destinations in between. At each stop, our conductor would make his way down the aisles, waking up each and every individual, asking to see their *boletos*. Then the fun began.

Obvious as it was we were the very same passengers with the very same tickets he had validated fifteen minutes earlier at our last stop, each time the train came to a halt, Mr. Conductor systematically woke us to conduct this process again. And again. All night long, with each passenger exchange, it was tap, tap, tap, end of sleep. *"Boletos, por favor."*

Somewhere around his fourth or fifth rude awakening I wised up, clipping my *boleto* to my coat sleeve with a safety pin. Next round, he woke me again. I snarled, pointing to the ticket. He shrugged his shoulders, examined the ticket as if I was a new arrival, then walked on down the aisle, business as usual. He did not bother me the remainder of the night.

Morning came and Kid was still alive.

We had begun our ascent, climbing through the mountains. Our train worked hard, rocking and swaying rhythmically as it traversed the steep, rugged legendary terrain of the Sierra Madres. Each time this rhythm increased in intensity, Kid flew into the toilet and locked the door behind him.

Those around us woke with cheery dispositions, made brighter each time the bathroom door would pop open to reveal our man in misery. Quite naturally, Mexicans too believe in Karma

After each episode of retching, Kid returned to the seat across from us, intentionally avoiding even a hint of eye contact with those he had bathed in beer the night before. Holding onto his head as if it may crack and fall off, he peered at us through puffy crimson eye slits. "I will **never** drink again" he proclaimed, voice gravelly and barely audible.

Our pace slowed as the train made several short stops in each small town and village along the way, adding or subtracting passengers, joining us for Destination Guadalajara.

During the ten-minute stops, local women in bright colorful clothing would swarm around the train, trying to get our attention through open windows. The more aggressive came aboard, walking the aisles, cheerfully offering a wide variety of home-baked edibles, ranging from tamales to breads, taquitos to sandwiches. None bore burritos.

They asked mere pesos for these goods, yet I failed to pursue a single transaction, fearing I would botch it, as I remained gun-shy from my initial failed negotiation back in the Nogales cantina. I was also apprehensive of any potential negative after-effects these unknown international offerings may wreak, once ingested. These misgivings needed to somehow soon be overcome. I would have to summon up some gumption if I was to truly embrace our trip.

Was this hesitancy a symptom of culture shock? All around, passengers were exchanging pesos along with pleasantries as they set about gobbling down their various purchased foodstuffs. Soon the trays were empty and the vendors vanished. My stomach began to growl. Acclimate, rookie, or live with the consequences...

By mid-morning, Dangerous stepped up to show his boys how it was done, exchanging a few pesos for a tamale and three corn taquitos. It was hell sitting there watching him wolf down the tamale. The savory aroma sent my tummy grumbling, a reminder I hadn't eaten since the diner, well over twenty-four hours ago.

He finished off the last of the taquitos in near record time and the growling of my hungry-as-a-grizzly innards intensified, convincing me it was time to quit pussy-footing along and get into the swing of things.

Next stop I made a quantum leap.

I hopped off the train, and looked around for a vendor I could feel comfortable dealing with, then went to work, mentally scrolling through the basics of my new-found Mexican math.

Suddenly my security blanket, Dave, appeared behind me , watching carefully in case negotiations somehow went awry. I spied a smiling señorita, made eye contact and the deal was on. I opted for a sixty-cent (12 peso) plate of *taquitos* which appeared to my starving soul to be the biggest plate of food she had to offer.

I pointed to it, then repeated the magic phrase Dave had just whispered to me. "*¿Cuánto es él?*" (How much?). It came out sounding much more like "Kwandie ace ale", yet it got the job done. As pesos were successfully exchanged, he gave two thumbs up for a successful transaction.

I handed her a twenty peso note, took the plateful as well as my change and sauntered back to the train feeling quite the dude. Lesson one was a success. I could now order food, hand someone money, even accept change. I was elated as I chowed down on my first official plate of authentic Mexican cuisine. It was exquisite.

The ever-changing panorama which passed by during our many hours aboard the train by was interesting, yet far from awe-inspiring.

As we left Nogales we crawled along past vast zones of poverty-ridden housing and row after row of automobile junkyards, stacked sky high with rusted-out skeletons of vehicles that had all seen better days. Once Nogales was behind us, that dismal setting gave way to dry, barren desert landscape, bearing few distinguishable trees; only mile after mile of yellow-brown wavy grasslands appeared before our eyes.

There were no major cities of interest, only modest towns and remote villages, which passed as quickly as they appeared. It was mind-boggling to consider what these people could possibly do for a living, which seemed to explain the desperate bustle of the vendors, whose existence may very well have relied solely upon the hunger of those aboard each daily passing train.

Late in the afternoon we made a twenty-minute stop; a perfect opportunity to hop down off the train and play a little Nerf football. We welcomed the chance.

At first it was just the three of us, throwing, passing, and running imperfect pass patterns, yet within minutes, six or seven local *niños* joined us as we tossed the ball about. Things went well until Kid threw an errant sidearm wobbler that unfortunately fell short of its target, before coming to rest on the tracks beneath the train.

We spotted the Nerf, yet sadly had to leave it behind, for sanitary reasons. An unlucky bounce positioned the ball in the most unfortunate of locations--directly under the streamliner's toilet, which, at this very moment was discharging a massive load. Sorry, sport fans, today's game has ended in a tie.

We waved goodbye to our young teammates and hustled back aboard with a couple minutes to spare. Some of the youngsters had already forgotten our moments together and had gone back to whipping on a burro with a stick, the game they had been playing before we had distracted them with the funny pink foam ball.

We took our seats and once again the train began moving.

After an hour or so of sitting and reading, it was time to stretch. Although our conductor frowned upon our choice of activity, we would casually slip out to the space between cars where we would just hang out enjoying the view, watching the country fly by while breathing in lungfuls of fresh sage-scented air.

Whenever anyone official spotted us, we would be quickly herded back inside. Through animated conversation, those in charge tried to convince Dave it was not safe to stand between cars. They were concerned that someone might get clumsy and tumble off.

We would return to our seats until they moved on, into the next car, then we would slither ever-so stealthily back to our viewing post outside to appreciate the sage-bearing topography fly by. After a half hour or so, they would return and once again we would be ushered back to our seats. This game went on throughout the day, both sides getting what they wanted: Us, the ability to get some stretching time in, them, the power trip of making us retreat without confrontation.

An hour short of Guadalajara, the train began slowing to a crawl as we approached the outskirts of the vast and bustling city. Thirty-six hours had passed. In that time, we had experienced a wide variety of terrain, transforming from desert to mountain, back to desert again and now as we approached, civilization; Guadalajara, one of Mexico's largest cities and cultural centers. Miles of slum-like dwellings similar to those left behind in Nogales greeted us as we crept along. Our anticipation heightened and once again the adrenaline began to flow.

The closer we came, the greater the level of carbon monoxide rose, seeping in through the air conditioning like floodwater slipping through cracks in a sandbagged wall. Up to this point, we had grown accustomed to clean, country air. Suddenly, pollution-plus brought about unwanted results in.a big-league migraine settling in. It was not a pleasant feeling at all.

A somewhat revitalized Kid looked at us and laughed. "You suckers are turning as green as I was this morning." I was fine with my faltering condition making him feel better, but I was not pleased with the flutter in my stomach and the woozy buzz ringing in my head as the train finally came to a stop. Guadalajara here we come.

'Come on boys, grab your packs. We're here." was all Dave said as he made his way briskly down the crowded aisle. He hopped down first, leading us out into the mass of humanity; brown, unfamiliar looking people, hundreds of them. I suddenly realized the obvious: "I am in a foreign country." No longer did I have the home-court advantage in the game of life, and that, my friends is a damn humbling emotional feeling to experience for the very first time.

Negative gremlins took over: Pollution assaulted my senses. Insecurity held sway. The possibility of getting separated from Dave in this strange, overwhelming foreign culture left me one step short of panic mode.
Get separated from my friend and I would be screwed. Big time.

Dangerous turned and motioned for us to quit dallying and pick up the pace. My pack felt loaded down with a bucket of rocks. My shoes filled with cement. Come on man, move!

Right here, right now, Mexico seemed to me to be the crummiest place on earth a man like myself could possibly venture.

4. Brief Bummer

Initial impression: Guadalajara sucks. There, I've got that off my chest let me come to grips with my anxiety monkey raising havoc with my soul.

We have arrived and I should be excited; cranked up like a monkey let out of his cage, and thoroughly stoked about this opportunity to engage, discover, and embrace what this major Latin American city has to offer. Instead, all I feel is overwhelmed, and inclined to curl into a ball and sleep until I can wake up in a better state of mind, or at least on a bus to Barra de Navidad.

It may be possible to chalk my vibes up to the magnitude of thirty-six hours spent in a seated position, going clickety clack down that railroad track. Tacking on two more days of overland by auto certainly belongs in that equation as well.

Arriving in the early-evening bustle of a foreign city, packed with wall-to-wall incessantly honking automobiles that are spitting forth an appalling amount of pollutants isn't helping sort my shit out. This funky uneasiness is making my skin crawl. Kid's body language, his inability to utter a single word in English is feeling the same vibe and his tense nervous facial twitching reinforces I am not in this boat alone.

I desire nothing more than getting a room, closing the door behind me and lying lower than low until it's time to proceed to the coast.

I am approximately 4,500 miles from my couch and remote control, standing on a street corner in a city of nearly a million people, the majority of which speak nary a lick of English. I shall continue to work like hell to process this unfolding scenario as all around us, the early energy of a Saturday night in the big city has begun to kick in.

The train depot is located on the fringe of the central area, or *Centro*, so we were off to track down the bus station, check the departure schedule and hopefully obtain tickets for the next available bus to Barra.

As we moved along, lead-footed drivers whizz past, honking their horns like high school seniors on the last day of school, spewing gross clouds of foul, gray carbon monoxide from their rusted tailpipes. Back home, these vehicles, mostly Vegas, Pintos, Ford Mavericks, and half a million dented Volkswagen Bugs are on the verge of extinction; inhabitants of auto salvage graveyards. In Guadalajara, they have found new life. Prime time way-cool vessels of propulsion.

Tonight, they are jammed together, filling up every square foot of city road space alongside an armada of early 1970s style red taxis. In seemingly devil-may-care fashion both species weave their way across multiple lanes without the slightest use of blinker light or hand single. Here in *Centro* it is every man for himself, driver and pedestrian alike.

Moving with the flow of the masses, my senses were continually bombarded by a thousand and one new, unfamiliar, yet often exciting aromas rising from the grills of the busy street vendors. It had been almost twelve hours since I had finished off those scrumptious taquitos. Hunger was beckons, but Dangerous pressed on. My eyes remain glued to his backside as getting lost in Guadalajara was the last thing I intended to let happen tonight.

Kid and I watched as Dave politely inquired with a local as to the location of the bus station. The man nodded, smiled, pointed west, then moved on. Unfortunately, his directions were less than accurate. We were headed towards dwellings with no train station visible for as far as we could see.

After at least ten more fruitless inquiries and misdirection's, we traversed at least a dozen blocks-first north, then south, then east and then west until we ended up once again in *Centro*, back to the street vendors we had observed fifteen minutes earlier.

Sweating profusely, they grilled sweet-smelling meats of a wide variety which, when finished, were laid upon homemade corn tortillas in generous portions. Their patrons then customized their plates with fresh cilantro, pickled veggies, and grilled onions. A variety of hot sauces provided the final touch.

Their grills sizzled nonstop, questionably grimy and appeared more than a bit unsanitary-looking. Gobs of fat dripped from their racks, feeding the flames responsible for the tantalizing odiferous smoky essence which was making my stomach growl yet we did not participate. Our mission was not yet complete.

Cheery, melodious Mexican music filled the air. All around, car radios battled with ratty distorted boom boxes. A smattering of street musicians and even a modest huddle of Mariachis scattered about did their best to compete with the dominant electronic sounds, to no avail. Boom boxes win…

Dangerous headed towards the food stand where the longest line had queued up.

Once there, he eyeballed the red-hot wares hissing and crackling on the grill. A few words in Spanish were exchanged, along with a handful of pesos. Just like that, three tortillas bulging with meat and one greasy napkin were his. Our mate attacked these items with great vigor, right then and there, before our very eye without even looking our way to see if we were inclined to participate.

I asked what he was devouring. He shrugged and continued to chew vigorously. "I dunno, cat-maybe rat. It's too chewy to be dog or armadillo meat." My famished appetite quickly retreated to the back burner. Hunger? What hunger?

Feast consumed, fearless leader wiped the oozing remnants off his cheek with a scrap of napkin, then smacked his lips. "Damn good stuff." Starving as I was, lucky, brave, or fearless I was not. Perhaps another day.

We moved on. Around the next corner our destination appeared. *AUTOBUS ESTACION.* Bingo!

Still barely early evening, many had already hunkered down for the night on the station's skinny wooden benches, a day's worth of goods bought or traded for by their sides. Others had declared squatters' rights to a few precious feet of unoccupied tile floor by laying out blankets and/or other items to define their territory. Here they would spend the remaining hours waiting for the early morning bus to take them back to their homes outside of Guadalajara.

Dave inquired about any *directo* busses bound for Barra, our next destination as well as headquarters for the next couple of weeks.

We were directed to the Tres Estrellas counter. According to Dave, Tres Estrellas was the Greyhound of Mexico, and probably the only direct first-class bus to Barra De Navidad.

The cashier handed over three tickets for a modest amount of peso notes and Dangerous turned to us. "I've got good news and bad news, so here goes: I got us all seats, first class, for a six-hour ride."

Kid spoke up, the first time since our arrival. "So, what's the bad?"

"We missed today's last bus but we are locked in for the first bus out tomorrow....at 3p.m. So, lads, you get the full-on experience of spending a night in Guadalajara." I would have done a back flip but my backpack was much too cumbersome.

He handed us each a ticket. "Boletos. For God's, or better yet, *your* sake, don't lose them. Until we convert some of those Travelers

Cheques into Mexican money I'm starting Dangerous Dave's IOU Service, comprende?" Both stooges nodded.

"It's Saturday night and the Bancos are all closed until Monday but they're bound to have a money exchange around here somewhere, keep an eye out, cause the meter's running."

"What's my bill so far?" I inquired.

"Three bucks, give or take a quarter or two. Can you handle that?"

Three bucks sounded extremely thrifty so far and Kid wasn't whimpering either.

"You guys want to spend the night here or should we go look for a room near the town square?"

Far from prepared to embrace adventure head on, Kid and I preferred the lodging option. What the heck, it would cost us a bit of money but we had been extremely thrifty so far in our endeavors.

"I don't want to harp on this but--friendly reminder to you both--the duration of this trip is dependent on how long our money holds out. When the last precious peso is cashed in, kiss the sunshine goodbye. So, grasshoppers, any time a choice must be made, be shrewd, prudent, and willing to step outside your comfort zones." We both nodded.

"Of course, you're only going to fully grasp what I'm talking about when or if your well runs dry; when you're on that train heading back to Nogales. Then and only then will you regret pissing away that twenty bucks, the equivalent of two extra days in paradise."

Wise words, no doubt. Sheer insight; but screw it, amigo. Tonight, I want to sleep in a bed, not on a cold hard tile floor.

We were still reeling from the magnitude of road miles already behind us. Forty-five hundred miles traveled in less than five days can have an overwhelming effect on most mortals and we were no exception.

Kid appeared to be simulating a Sunshine acid trip with his silent, distant and eerily uneasy presence. Yours truly was not far behind.

The previous day, as we watched the miles fly by from our train, Dangerous Dave brought up an aspect of travel he deems 'the pleasure and pain factor.'

"Every journey I've ever taken, no matter how incredible your adventure may unfold, there is always a handful of formidable obstacles one has to rise above, somewhere, sometime, along the way.

Remember this: Whatever you put into the experience; the road gives back tenfold."

He assured me this concept would become clearer with more road time accumulated under my belt, and, if and when I adhere to the required principles, the journey will become less stressful, more enjoyable and, he stressed, highly insightful

Blank stare time. Kid's acid trip appeared to have contagious ramifications. Dave picked up on my state of mind.

"Sometime soon, something is bound to happen that will test the limits of our patience and ability to go with the flow without freaking. It may be a flat tire on a bus in the middle of nowhere, or perhaps, unexpected endeavors, such as tonight's delay.

"Whatever it is, go with the flow; keep your composure; be cool. Everything will even out. The value of that experience will greatly outweigh any obstacle temporarily causing your stress, *comprende?*"

Kid had been quietly perched atop his backpack absorbing this dialogue when his self-imposed hunger and silence strikes abruptly ended. "I'm hungry."

Time to move on, find food, shelter, take three deep breaths, and get ready for Barra.

We located the local currency exchange and traded a fifty-dollar American note for a thick wad of multi-colored denominations of cash. Thanks to a generous rate of exchange, I was holding about twenty pesos for each dollar cashed in.

"Let's first get a room, and then stuff our faces with outrageous Mexican delights, rookies!" Dangerous certainly had the right idea.

With each passing hour I began to acclimatize mentally, albeit at snail's pace, to the circumstances before me; toddler-like first steps down the wobbly path towards becoming a bonafide road warrior.

As we navigated Guadalajara, I followed closely behind Dangerous, taking mental notes of his method of interacting with the citizens. No panic when misadvised. Keep moving, ask someone else. Patience, not anger or frustration was the rule. After four attempts to find sanctuary, we finally succeeded, five blocks off of the main plaza.

Even though it was not yet eight o'clock, a sleepy-looking landlord, Jose, greeted, then led us to a basic, inexpensive room consisting of two wobbly box-framed mattresses masquerading as beds and a solar-powered shower and a seatless toilet. Air conditioning was provided by two windows overlooking the narrow streets below, still thick with bumper-to-bumper horn-honking tin cans.

Dave enlightened us with the news that hot water showers are a luxury in Mexico, even in the more expensive habitats you choose to occupy. Most homes as well as hotels get their hot water from large iron water tanks located on their roofs, heated solely by the daytime sun's torrid touch. No hot water? Get over it.

Since there were only two beds for a party of three, a coin toss took place to decide who got the box springs and who got to share the floor with the house cockroaches. Dangerous flipped a peso with Kid giving him a "Heads I win, tails you lose. "option. Kid called tails and was soon spreading his sleeping bag atop the musty spare mattress on the wooden floor with nary a whimper.

Now officially situated, we agreed it was high time to indulge or at least access Guadalajara's culinary delights. Still one step removed from starvation mode, neither Kid nor myself felt confident enough to sample street cuisine. No sir, we needed to… *acclimate…* there's that word again, at a slower rate than Dangerous preferred.

We passed down many streets searching for the perfect local restaurant; one acceptable to all, yet each time Dangerous offered a suggestion, Kid and I exercised our Finicky Gringo veto power. "Looks too dirty," "No one's there," "The food must not be very good," even the very weak "Too dark-looking inside." Finally, Dave had his fill. "The hell with it guys. I'm tired, hungry, and eating right here."

Dave sauntered inside *Mamasita's*, where food was steadily coming from the kitchen and a large. energetic Saturday night crowd sat drinking and laughing as they waited for their orders to arrive.

We two guppies remained hesitant, still trying to come up with valid reasons why this bustling restaurant did not fulfill our needs and/or specifications. Our waiter arrived and handed us menus completely in Spanish! Nervously I scoured the listings, yet nothing clicked. I passed. Kid did the same. Dave ordered in rapid-fire Spanish, after we sheepishly declined our waiters prompt to order. He shrugged and headed back to place our table's lone order. Lord, if only burritos were on the menu…

Ten minutes later his cuisine arrived. Wide-eyed we could only watch as Dave unwrapped, then worked over a gigantic *tamale* before plowing into the cheese-blanketed *Enchilada Grande* which dwarfed the large hot plate. As he wolfed down the entire plates-worth, I gave myself a severe mental kick to the butt for being such a spineless guppy.

When finished he unloaded belched wholeheartedly. "God, that was awesome! Now I've got enough strength to walk around with you gutless gringos until you find a McDonalds, Skippers or whatever it's gonna take to make you girls happy."

Two blocks later, a miracle occurred. The huge red *S* of the one and only Sheraton Hotel stood glowing upon the Guadalajara skyline.

Destiny was ours.

This time *we* led the way. Dangerous followed along, shaking his head in disgust. A gold-toothed English-speaking server led us to a table by the pool. No meals from a dim, dark, greasy spoon such as *Mamasita's* for these boys. This was the right choice.

We ordered meals from a menu conveniently printed in English as well as Spanish. Kid ordered a sirloin cut while I chose a Chef's Salad and fries.

As soon as our order had been taken, an unexpected wave of guilt rolled over me. I had let Dangerous down. Right then and there I vowed that from this point on I would suck up every bit of gumption necessary and respectfully indulge elbow to elbow with the nationals and eat nothing but the local cuisine. The time had officially arrived to get my act together.

We were seated poolside, where a brisk yet warm wind whipped around us, and off through the periphery, where shadows were detected, I noticed something quickly scamper past, moving right to left.

It was something brown and very quick that scurried past the fountain, between the lights, then off behind the hedges on the back side of the pool. Three other tables of gringos seated around us continued with their meals, oblivious to the presence on the move. Shortly, it reappeared, peeking out from the far end of the hedges.

At first glance our visitor could've been mistaken for a large well-fed feline, perhaps the hotel mascot, but it quickly become apparent it was a rat. Oh, what a grandiose specimen it was!

Larger than your average poodle and with a tail half the length of an antennae, *Señor* Rat pulled up less than ten yards from our table, stood on its haunches and sniffed.

I could only emit little more than a raspy proclamation of disbelief. "I think – I – just – saw a rat."

At that moment, our meals arrived.

Three bites into my Chef Salad the unwelcome rodent reappeared. *Señor* Rat had come by to say *Buenos Noches*, welcome to Mexico. He rose on his back paws, an arm's length away from our seats, and once again began sniffing the air, lobbying for a handout, however small, from Kid or myself.

My reaction to its proximity was reflexive, swift, nowhere close to out of line. I dropped my fork with a clang and shouted, "Holy shit, it IS a rat!!!"

Kid leapt from his seat. Silverware flew and water glasses emptied on our table. Either frightened by the decibels of my proclamation or the sight of flying cutlery, our rodent friend exited, stage left, in the direction of the outdoor wet bar.

The mustachioed bartender on duty took in our state of chaos with merely a smirk, continuing to wipe down the counter in front of him in a dutiful manner. I pointed behind him, in the direction the furry pest had vamoosed, feebly emitting a squeak "A rat!" He continued nonplussed by the situation at hand.

Thinking, perhaps, a language barrier stood between us, I carried on, resorting to hand gestures in order to communicate. "Behind you! This big!"

He put down his rag, lit a cigar, then produced an ominous-looking baseball bat from behind the wet bar which he slammed down on the counter for emphasis. *"No problemo, amigos, no problemo,"* then continued cleaning glasses as the rat scurried beneath his feet. He and our waiter seemed entertained, laughing at this intrusion as if the joke was on us.

It certainly was. Famished as I was, my Chef's Salad suddenly lost any and all appeal.

Kid's appetite had gone south as well, and he hadn't even taken bite one from his steak.

Both abandoned meals ended up being shoved across the table in front of Dangerous Dave who had already decided they should not go to waste. We sat there, two dudes literally in shock, four eyes peeled and searching for the return of our uninvited guest who apparently had found better things to occupy him elsewhere. Dave finished stuffing his gullet. We paid the bill. Time to head back to our room. So much for doing' up Guadalajara, Americana Style.

We tried to sleep but found that function all but impossible to accomplish. Outside our window, a non-stop cacophony of car horns honked and hooted long after midnight.

A half dozen loud explosions picked up where the horns left off. With each blast, festive cheers rose from the heart of the city, keeping us awake and slightly on edge. Each concussion rattled our windows, blast after blast.

In the morning, landlord Jose explained what we heard was just "PRI celebration bombas", yet none of us chose to ask just what Mexico's ruling political party was celebrating from 1 until 4 a.m. in the morning.

Sleep deprived and struggling once again to fire up my inner engine due to the previous evening's post-midnight revelry, we crawled out of the covers around 9 a.m.

While Dangerous was the sole participant in a less than lukewarm shower, Kid and I packed our belongings, anxious to get back on the road to Barra. Dried off, refreshed and revitalized, Dangerous informed us we would kill about three hours of our down time perusing Centro's grandiose outdoor market place; Guadalajara's claim to fame.

Thousands of Mexicans, from the city as well as countryside, rely on Guadalajara's immense market to buy, sell or trade their wares, handmade as well as farm grown. Dangerous warned us mentally might very well be our first opportunity to barter aggressively for goods of any sort we feel a need to acquire for the road ahead.

He convinced me to work on my numbers from now to when we arrive so I may wheel and deal with confidence for a pair of huaraches, as I planned to ditch my tennis shoes as soon as possible. "Comfort is of the utmost importance. Walking in the sand in Adidas will get cumbersome, awkward and a pain in the ass if you regret to take this opportunity."

Off we went.

The closer we drew to our destination, the greater the numbers of street vendors we came upon, setting up shop, hawking their wares. Native women from grandmothers to near-toddlers offered us homegrown products, primarily produce, fruit, and spices, many the likes of which I failed to successfully identify. Magnificent orange, red, and green peppers were stacked to the sky in amazing quantities.

Hundreds of exotic and unusual vegetables, peppers foremost, took up space alongside mounds of bananas, which varied from green to overripe in maturity.

Once inside the entrance leading into the main marketplace, best be prepared for the vast number of high-energy vendors, hucksters and hagglers who await; anxious yet patient, desperate yet congenial. The market is their livelihood and their families' existence depends on how many pesos good fortune provides daily.

Row after row after row, booth after booth after booth, an incredible variety of handmade goods are on hand to boggle one's mind. Just close your eyes and smell…

After foods, one comes upon a seemingly unending array of leather products; home crafted dresses made of every material, color, style, and size conceivable. A large area was designated for cheap toys and inexpensive dime store rejects kids were digging through in joyous delight. Finally, we came to row after row hand-crafted sandals and cowboy boots, there alongside dress shoes for both sexes, adult, or child, in every conceivable style under the sun. A strong show of leather assured you these were the real deal.

Where did one start to find the right pair of huaraches? Dave's rule was to cruise and peruse, check out as many as possible until you find the perfect style and price, then try to remember just where in the heck they were located.

After perusing what appeared to be all the potential *huarache* vendors, Dave and I negotiated with a shop owner for what we considered the sturdiest-looking pair the market had to offer. Dave did the bargaining while I took copious mental notes on the fine art of bartering.

It took my amigo roughly five minutes to close the deal. After a handshake and a smile, I handed over $7.50's worth of pesos, down from the $12.00 originally asked for. A steal for solid, handcrafted leather with tire-treaded soles which, if properly taken care of, should last me for several years to come.

On we trundled, past a dazzling array of indigenous edibles giving off new and wonderful scents.
One butcher shop specialized in row after grisly row of smiling pig heads, hanging on metal rods, alongside sacks of severed chicken claws. Both were accompanied by the sour stench of slightly overheated carrion.

This area of the market sent Kid weaving to the far side of the aisle, head turned in denial, eyes trained on items as far as possible, away from the macabre smiling piggies.

Just when we thought we had seen all there was to offer, we turned a corner and came to more booths of gorgeous handmade clothing, items of every weave imaginable, alongside rugs, rug makers, more shoes, and, of course, more shoemakers.

Each area we came to seemingly bore its own sounds as well as energy. Walking down each row, we were bombarded by exuberant Mariachi music competing with the animated vendors, yelling, and waving in rapid fire Spanish as they try making eye contact with all passerby's, each eager to make a sale.

We turned another corner and came upon a central open-air plaza where we were greeted by the oh so welcome melodies of The Beatles, playing above the din. Next corner, Mariachis once again which served to remind us where we were. On it went; eyes, noses and ears, all treated to total stimulation. What a treat it was!

A short time later, intoxicated by bartering fever, I tried my hand with a hat vendor and came away with a nifty white Panama hat for three dollars. I was satisfied with my first attempt at wheeling and dealing, yet Dangerous only awarded me a B+, estimating I got burned by about a buck twenty-five. As time goes on, I will master this game.

Fortunately, as the growls from our stomachs began to match the volume of the Mariachi music we came upon a vast food court, dedicated to many family eateries with just about every style of Mexican dish I could ever begin to imagine.

Dave polished off a large bowl of Mexican soup called Pozole. I took on an cheesy enchilada the size of New Jersey and Kid pecked ever so half-heartedly at a chicken taco Dave ordered for him.

The three hours' time we were planning on killing past by swiftly--awestruck spectators to a Guadalajara day in the life, caught up in its flow as we waited for three o'clock to arrive.

Slightly after 2 p.m., we hustled off to the bus station. Soon, very soon, we would be sun gods of the southwestern shores.

A slight miscalculation in direction found us arriving at our destination minutes after our scheduled bus headed off to Barra. After friendly, yet desperate negotiations, we were allowed to trade our tickets in for the next bus leaving at 4 p.m.

We followed the pungent odor of diesel fumes to Gate B where we waited patiently for our exodus from the belly of this city of noxious fumes. Dangerous warned that if I thought this pollution was intense, wait until we get to Mexico City. Oh boy.

Tres Estrellas number 57, our ride, arrived on time.

Jorge was the driver of this iron lion; a proud professional with a first-class machine. His dashboard deco consisted of an 8x10 framed color print of Jesus, nailed rather gruesomely upon the cross, above a statue of Mother Mary, arms by her side, her tear-stained face a study of serenity as she stands upon a serpent, crushing its head. Welcome aboard, gringos! All sinners to the back of the bus. Christmas tinsel and twinkling miniature Christmas lights framed the entire front window. *Jorge*, in cursive script, was etched into his rear-view mirror and his gear shifter was a modified four iron.

Dangerous and I plopped our butts down into the seat directly behind Jorge while Kid shuffled a few rows farther towards the rear. "Welcome to The Death Seat" Dave informed me, "None of the locals prefer to sit here because they are afraid to see what may be coming their way." I found this to be an awesome location and vowed to give it my best to snag this view whenever bus travel was required.

Bus travel is the major source of transportation for a large portion of the Mexican populace, especially those in the villages surrounding the many major cities too poor to own an auto.

On our way out of Guadalajara, Jorge would stop every few miles to let off a few passengers. They would step down cautiously, struggling with arms loaded with goods purchased or traded for at market. Dangerous called this tedious portion of our ride The Milk Run because of these frequent stops.

With my access to music-on-demand a non-reality I was finding a new sacrifice--pot withdrawal.

Often, my craving to smoke a joint is influenced primarily by little more than sheer boredom, the logic being if I'm going to have to be bored, I might as well be *stupid* as well. Without ganja available to medicate my malaise, it seems for the next two months odds are I shall be forced into participating in activities such as swimming in the ocean, intelligent conversations with fellow man, walking great distances instead of pushing the pedals of my trusty Datsun, and enjoying reading the many books stuffed into my backpack. This behavior may even result in turning my body back into a temple once again, instead of the pagoda I have sadly let it deteriorate into. What a radical adaptation this will be!

Even with all these intermittent stops, we covered the distance in just over five and a half hours. Jorge negotiated each hairpin curve with precise skill, shifting the four-iron down, then back up as the windy road dictated. He bombed down the straight stretches nearly ninety miles an hour--we know that, for a fact, having been able to watch the needle rise from our vantage point there in the Death Seat. Twice we avoided near head-on collisions by what seemed to be a matter of mere millimeters.

As darkness crept upon us, the terrain outside our window magically morphed from barren tundra to tropical jungle, as grove after grove of coconut and palm trees became evident, silhouettes against the half-moon's glow.

Jorge eased up on the speed as concrete turned to cobblestones. We had reached the nearby town of Melaque. Now less than five minutes away, Barra de Navidad awaits.

As we rolled slowly down a bumpy dirt road, the low-key lights of the town of Barra de Navidad came into view. The bus ground to a halt and, as the door opened, we were greeted by exceptional tropical warmth and the sound of surf slapping the shore nearby.

We gathered our senses and nodded appreciatively to our driver for getting us there safe and sound. Stepping down, a gringo wearing a flowery Hawaiian shirt and struggling with a very cumbersome suitcase stood waiting to board. "You guys just getting here?"

We nodded.

"Good luck finding something to do. There's absolutely nothing going on in this boring hole."

I smiled, saying nothing. Isn't that why we've come here?

We stood by patiently as Jorge pulled our packs from beneath the bus. As I lifted the aluminum frame to my shoulders, I felt, for the first time, that perhaps the long, ugly journey might very well be behind us. Brimming with optimism we headed down the dimly lit road into the modest heart of Barra de Navidad. Time for a few cheeseburgers in paradise.

5. Barra de Navidad

Once off the bus, my senses start working overtime. Well after 9 p.m. Slight warm breeze and the conditions are humid, balmy, and somewhere still in the low eighties at this time of night. Ten steps from the bus the first droplets of sweat begin to form between my shoulder blades, wandering down towards the base of my spine.

Close by, off towards the west where the cobblestones turn to dirt, the roar of the Pacific churns on, even while remaining cloaked in darkness. The essence of saltwater heavily embraces my sense of smell while the seductive cadence of the surf throws a baby blanket atop any residue off angst I may be still begrudgingly be holding onto. It is a most wonderful feeling; one we have traveled so many miles to experience.

Growing up around the Northern Pacific Coast I've never had the good fortune to experience the warmth of Southern Pacific waters. My childhood summer ocean vacations consisted of testing the Northern Pacific Ocean's bone-chilling salt water and ice- breakers; water so cold, it felt as if you were getting creamed by an icy sledgehammer as it crashed down upon you.

The waters of Mexico are quite the opposite, so warm and tropical you hasten to return to shore until long after your skin begins to shrivel. For that very concept, I am more than ready.

Our backpacks removed from the undercarriage, Jorge's machine rolled off down the brick roadway, to its next destination, wherever his night's schedule is meant to lead.

Backpack in place, Dave is off, following the music of waves smashing the shoreline. The dimly lit main street of Barra lies directly ahead. It is a stark contrast to the streets in Guadalajara. No carbon monoxide or honking taxis. No bustle of humanity surging around us.

Dangerous veers right, away from Centro, off in the direction of sand and surf. Kid and I follow, several paces behind, unsure of his intent as he heads down towards the shoreline. The tops of the mid-calf breakers are visible, illuminated solely by starlight as they touch the shore, then roll back out again.

He relinquished his backpack, plop, in the sand, then made his way down to the waterline. Kid and I pulled up, watching as our amigo regressed, back in time, to sometime approximately around age ten.

Dangerous didn't bother to remove his huaraches. He peeled his tank top off in mid-stride, chucked it on the shore, then dove into the bashers with a howl of triumph that echoed the length of the coastline.

"Come on in, you guppies!!"

Guppies we were and guppies we were bound to remain--at least until tomorrow, when daylight would allow me to see just exactly what the hell I was swimming in or into.

Watching him bob about in the sea caused me to recall a recent front cover of one of those newsstand tabloids, strategically placed by the check- out counter; something about aggressive killer sharks popping up closer to west coast shorelines than ever before, feeding upon unsuspecting surfers.

Kid had parked his posterior in the sand with no intent of joining fearless leader in his salt water folly. His body language was stiff, twitchy, and exuding a high level of anxiety. "What are we gonna do if a shark gets him?"

I felt it necessary to defer to the power of positive thinking. "Right now, I'm hanging onto the thought that if we don't allow our minds to travel to the dark side, it will decrease the chances such a shitty and unfortunate occurrence will ever take place. Ya know?"

Kid sat, still as a stone and rigid, eyes pensively locked on Dave, now barely visible in the moonlight as he floated on his back like a contented seal. Still in Johnny Positive mode, I assured Kid that there was nothing to worry about, absolutely nothing at all.

Kid's what ifs continued. "What if the undertow sucks him out past the point of no return?"

The soft breaking waves, little more than knee deep, convinced me Dave truly knew what he was doing.

"What if it's not legal to swim here after dark? He may get arrested and then what would we do?"

I headed down to the shore, leaving Kid to continue his what if speculation session all by his little old lonesome.

As I left him behind, he whimpered weakly, "You're not going in, are you?"

No way was I joining Mr. Spontaneity, but I was all for getting closer to the action; to suss out the saltwater, maybe scrutinize the phosphines or whatever the heck those sparkly little shore-break critters were called.

"Come on in, Tunes, this is heavenly!!" Dangerous sounded so sincere, dammit anyway.

Everybody appreciates a bit of heavenliness, so carefully, ever so cautiously; I dipped the toes of my right huarache into the salt water. Just the toes.

Pure bliss! Warm water! Words worthy of repetition. Warm. Water.

Barra's sultry evening air tickled the beads of sweat on the nape of my neck. Common sense conceded to impulse. Time to give those bad ass *Enquirer*-bred sharks something tasty and edible to gnaw on. Tally ho, into the ocean I go; I didn't even bother to take off my shirt.

Self-imposed guardian of the backpacks, Kid sat solo on the shore, still as a Buddhist monk meditating atop a misty mountain. He viewed my salt water baptism silently, legs crossed, eyes straining in the darkness to pick up any shark fins approaching our vicinity. What a pal.

Ten minutes of salt water ecstasy followed before Dangerous and I returned to shore. Sopping wet, it was time to get down to the task of finding quarters for the evening. Dave was the first to rise from the sand. "Come on guys, we're off to find Scorpion Heights."

During his previous visit, Dave had found economically suitable sanctuary at a two-tiered structure constructed entirely of cinder blocks he christened Scorpion Heights. It was neither the Sheraton or Motel 6, yet tonight was our lucky night. We scored the only room available.

A middle-aged Señora shuffled along at a pace slower than molasses as she led us to our upper-level dwelling. She twisted the stubborn key into the locks, then uttered a few select choice words of profanity in Spanish until it yielded with a groan. There was our domain, an eight by fifteen cement fortified bunker complete with seventy-watt bulb and four six-foot-long cots, each with wafer-thin mattresses atop squeaky yet reliable springs. A scratchy wool sheet was folded atop each cot. Pillows? Who needs em?

The room had one screened window for ventilation, enough space to store our belongings, and two AAA-sized cockroaches in the corner who we assumed were our new roommates. A single solar-heated shower and outdoor toilet were there to be shared with all other hotel occupants.

All these creature comforts came at a more than reasonable price-a mere 150 pesos per day or $5.50 per day in American capital.

Once again, Dave stressed the importance of making the most out of our bankroll whenever possible. "Visualize this more than reasonable investment as a game: Say perhaps Monopoly meets the Game of Life. Do not forget, the more money you save, the longer you get to bask in the sunshine, roast on the beaches, and drink dirt cheap beer.

To Dangerous, our arrival in Barra was a ceremonious event; therefore, a Dirty Mother Bash was in order.

Imagine this combustible yet tasty blend of hooch whacking your taste buds: Two overflowing shots of tequila, matched with a comparable application of Kahlua, both poured upon a glassful of fresh ice topped by a splash of half and half. If administered properly, the dairy product should crackle and curdle as it drops upon the cubes. If your upper lip turns slightly numb upon contact, you've poured this concoction correctly.

WARNING: This drink has proven to be quite tasty, yet lethal. Those unfamiliar with the consequences of choosing excess in lieu of moderation, those imbibing could find themselves in dangerous waters which, more often than not, results in an unfortunate pernicious swoon. Kid has already waded into those waters…

400 pesos purchased a bountiful booty of booze. We returned to Scorpion Heights with a liter of Cuervo Gold, two fifths of Kahlua, some leche and a gigantic bag of ice. With Dangerous hankering to live up to his nickname, the party was on.

All in all, Scorpion Heights currently houses nine occupants inside its five cinder-gray quadrants. Our first acquaintances were our new next-door neighbors, Denny and Teresa, a recently married couple from Southern California, and Jocelyn and Michael, students from Evergreen College back home in Olympia, currently attending school in Guadalajara. We immediately connected with the two, whose suntans, athletic bodies and chill demeanor made me envious of the sunshiny environment they called their temporary home.

Denny informed us that our landlord, or rather 'land-Señora', keeps a low profile inside her home at the far end of the lower tier. Cleaning, checking tenants in and out and all odds and ends related to tenants' needs were handled by Angelica, her glowingly beautiful daughter. Not a day older than twenty, Angelica was the boss. From the moment she handed us our spare room key, Kid fell instantly in love; an infatuation destined to go unnoticed as well as unrequited.

Ours was a successful gathering. While we drank, made conversation, and generally had a great time bonding with these new neighbors, Kid sat in self-imposed silence, mapping out his game plan to steal Angelica's heart.

Since Kid converses solely in English and Angelica, strictly Spanish, he had his work cut out for him. He made a noble effort to master key phrases, yet continually keeps inverting gender tenses. Objects that are masculine, he consistently mispronounces in the feminine form. Instead of saying *Señor*, he offers "*Señora*". Dave suggested Kid return to his note pad to draw up a better game plan.

Down to the last inch and a half of Cuervo, good fortune brought us to the ultimate fringe benefit of residency at Scorpion Heights--outdoor movies.

By day, the spacious courtyard next door serves as a laundry area. It's a large, vacated lot where the many local women of Barra gather to wash their clothes. Once cleaned and rinsed, colorful clothing of all sorts is strung on a crisscross maze of sturdy nylon lines to dry in the afternoon sun while the colorfully-garbed housewives pass the time, laughing and sharing casual conversation.

"Each day, after siesta, the lines come down and out come the wooden chairs--about seventy of them" Denny explained, "then-- Voila! The laundry area transforms into outdoor cinema. The movies change about every third day. So far we've seen a young Charles Bronson western no gringo here recalls, a complete Santos serial--all ten black and white cliffhanger episodes worth--and an obscure British sixties comedy, The Wrong Box, crudely dubbed into Español.*"*

Tonight's feature had already begun and every seat was filled. We made our way across a sturdy pair of 2x4s to our prime viewing seats, twelve feet above the courtyard, atop the Scorpion Height's baños.

For the next hour and a half, we took in a true Italian cinematic classic, *Hercules and the Captive Women*. Sitting cross-legged with an unobstructed first-rate view, we finished our stout drinks while the mesmerized locals seated below smoked and chattered, sipping away at libations brought in and concealed in brown paper bags.

We quickly found ourselves caught up in their exuberance as they cheered heartily for every paper mache boulder the buff yet (in tonight's version) beardless Hercules threw, as well as the demise of every monster he muscled into oblivion.

While we enjoyed the film, Kid stayed behind, composing a letter of early trip exploits to his parents and bearing down on the list of Spanish phrases Dave thought might come in handy in his quest to court Angelica.

Hercules successfully dispatched Atlantis back to the ocean floor and our adventure came to a close. We made our way across the 2 x 4s of death, which led us back to our rooms for a well-deserved nightcap. As the last of the liter met the bottom of the solo cups, two solid raps rattled our door. In stepped an hombre Denny introduced as Willy who had detected our ruckus from his room below and wanted to be part of the action.

Willy can best be described as an over-stuffed bean bag chair of cellulite, perched on thin stilt legs.

He sported zero percent body tone and wore dilapidated sneakers that gave off a fungicidal stench, quickly noticeable in close quarters. His rapidly-receding hairline gave way to shoulder length dishwater-blonde curls. Crooked John Lennon-style glasses drooped down his greasy ski-sloped nose.

"Disk-ko-tekka time." He muttered, bloodshot half-closed peepers fluttering as he spoke.

We all declined his invitation. The Dirty Mothers had successfully pummeled our new friends and Dave, myself, and Kid were weary from our mega-marathon bus ride.

Willy spotted an unfinished plastic cup and sniffed the contents. "Dirty Mothers! You guys never even called me--master mixer and greatest damn bartender in the entire western hemisphere!!!"

"If you guys are looking for a real kickass drink, tomorrow night I'll make you MY specialty, The Famous Ramos."

Willy lit another Camel, dropped his spent match into his cup before biding adieu. With that, the party broke up.

Wednesday, January 17th

Barra de Navidad is a small, slow-paced coastal wonderland whose moderate surf rolls in serenely while the mosquitoes nip with a passion once the sun makes its way beyond the horizon.

Dave's major criteria for choosing Barra as our initial destination: To chill, adapt, indulge in great foods for quite moderate prices, and to acclimatize at a casual, comfortable pace.

Major tourist destinations such as Mazatlán, Cabo, Acapulco, Puerto Vallarta and Manzanillo appeal more to the high-rolling dollar-waving gringos. In all of these above locales, creature comforts such as air conditioning, hotel pools, and resort-made meals are par for the course and part of the package. Our game plan is based on the opposite end of that spectrum. Locales such as Barra, Melaque, and Zihuatanejo are the spots we shall be seek out.

The heart of Barra begins where the road into town changes from dirt to cobblestones. The town is approximately four blocks in length, ending at a jetty, or gravel spit that looks across at a lagoon as beautiful as it is uninhabitable. From this jetty, one looks east towards several fishing boats, charter as well as private, and a communal dock where boats belonging to gringos as well as charter fisherman are moored.

In between, there are five restaurants to choose from, two modest grocery stores, a pair of discos which are the centerpiece of the town's two major hotels, The Capri and The Sands. A large church, presumably Catholic in nature, anchors this community that has provided over a century's worth of worship. Centrally located, the church is the hub of Barra, its many rows of oft-occupied pews visible from the streets as its tall doors always remain ajar, inviting any and all to enter.

Atop the church's peak, a large bell, God's local alarm clock, begins tolling each morning at 5 a.m. sharp, without fail; a loud metallic clanging, heard from every direction, that seems to go on much longer than it actually does.

In Barra, there are no jet skis, parasail rides or culturally stimulating activities. There are scads of fishing excursions available. On a good day, Marlin, Dorado, Sailfish, or Tuna may hit your line and justify that long hot day out on the bay and the inevitable sunburn.

A vast majority of the inhabitants speak little or no English. Your food must be ordered in Spanish and street transactions require you to be able to communicate.

We have begun a nice, casual routine. Each morning the church bells serve as our wake-up call. Once fully awake and coherent, we roll into the Hotel Guadalajara to begin our day with a hearty stack of hotcakes.

On our way back to Scorpion Heights, we stop at a small plywood shed located on the beach side, across from our residence for our daily Licuado, a fruit drink squeezed while you wait.

There, for the equivalent of a quarter, you get a half-dozen oranges or a half pineapple, chopped, then tossed into a Hamilton Beach to be blended thoroughly with ice and/or leche. Dangerous and I have dubbed these concoctions the *holy rejuice-venator*, and find them an integral necessity, crucial for launching our day properly.

We visit the marketplace a short jaunt to Melaque, daily where, amidst the many stalls, we chanced upon a bookstore. There alongside the latest Spanish novels, newspapers, and smoking accessories was a shelf full of writing accessories such as blank journals, reams of typing paper, and a wide variety of pens.

Dave asked if I had considered keeping a journal of our trek. I had not. He smiled. A short while later, he handed me a daybook of about a hundred pages and a pair of pens. "You never can tell, this might be an epic," He smiled again, then headed off towards the many small restaurants ahead. In return, I sprung for the Pozole. That journal became a part of my everyday ritual.

I dedicate an hour or so to reading and writing. A short ladder and a hatch at the far end of Scorpion Heights takes you up onto the roof. With a card table and chairs, I have officially made this my space. It is my happy place. My Valhalla.

Valhalla offers a bird's-eye perspective of main street and any activity of merit taking place, as well as a prime view of Barra's shoreline, stretching out in a four-mile-long horseshoe, all the way to Melaque.

After writing, it's down to the warm sand where we hang out from approximately 11a.m. until 3 p.m., when one is forced to retreat from the sun's intensity when directly overhead. Too hot to attract casual customers, the local shops and restaurants close their doors. Welcome to *siesta* time.

The streets remain quiet and free of foot traffic. Around 6 p.m. when the sun begins making its descent, Barra once more comes back to life. Closed storefronts creak open, people again exchange greetings and the smells on the grills lure in the hungry as well as those getting ready for the evening pleasures Barra De Navidad has to offer.

Our game plan is to hang in Barra until Ted and Doris, two more of Dangerous' friends from Bellingham, rendezvous with us. Then, party of five, we will head further south, to Zihuatanejo, Dave's ultimate paradise.

Our daily doses of sun have started working their magic. Once pale torsos have transformed from new-arrival pink, into beach bum brown. This conversion demands daily applications of Crema de Tortuga, an excellent inexpensive moisturizer made from the oil of turtles.

Outside of the Scorpion Heights crew, we've come across only a random handful of gringos, roaming through Barra. Most visitors seem to be Canadians hailing from British Columbia, noted by the abundance of BC license plates lining the streets.

Most of them are here for the deep-sea fishing; from sunrise until midday, until the peak of afternoon sun forces them to retreat to shadier confines. When the sun goes down, they eat, drink, and dance the night away at one of Barra's two discotheques until the wee hours of way too late. Then they do it all over again.

For those not involved in sport fishing, recreational options here are limited to sun worship, riding a few baby waves, and enjoying the inexpensive and wonderfully fresh abundance of seafood on hand. No glitz, no glamour, just chill.

These new faces have arrived, already operating in mellow, easygoing mode; laid back pale faces in colorful Hawaiian shirts, hoping to darken their pigments and to find a room before they get down to three days of serious deep-sea fishing. So far, they complement Barra's low-key vibe. Then there's Willy.

Barra is Willy's Margaritaville. Back home he's a bartender in Santa Barbara, an occupation made for those blessed with the gift of gab as well as the art of bullshit. In between some damn funny one-liners Willy always finds a way to work in a handful of Jimmy Buffet-isms: Favorite lines lifted from the parrot-man's songbook.

A pop music aficionado myself, I relish the company of anyone passionate and knowledgeable regarding its many artists, but I have already caught Willy paraphrasing Buffet's lyrics incorrectly at least a half dozen times. A small thing, none the less an irritant to any amiable conversation we have.

Willie's tolerable until he dips into the hooch, then he begins delving into the two subjects every good mother warns her children to avoid: politics and religion. Like it or not, Willy was in love with his voice and his pointed opinions. And, he was proud to point out, never walked away from a verbal confrontation without getting in the last word.

Two of the most difficult adjustments I've had to make are to the solar-powered shower, and the primitive procedural etiquette required when using Mexican toilets.

First, showers are most enjoyable when taken during siesta time, when one's grimy body is covered with sand, salt water, and sweat, the sun is at its utmost peak and the water tank on top of the baños is fully heated from maximum exposure to the day's rays.

Second, toilet seats are all but non-existent and the plumbing systems consist of skinny little plastic piping, not copesetic with flushed toilet paper. Failure to deposit afore-mentioned paper in the plastic bucket sitting beside use has a good chance of resulting in major cloggage to the system. Just ask Kid… We'll discuss this subject shortly.

To say that our travel mate has had a rough ride so far would be a gross understatement. Still the source of much of his angst, in this traveler's opinion, has been self-inflicted.

While Dave and I frolic daily in the surf, Kid remains seated on the shore watching us, ready to alert us both at the first sign of a shark fin. He has ventured into the ocean once, for an unsuccessful attempt at body surfing. Since the waves break close to the shoreline and rarely exceed three-foot peaks, the term body whompin is most apropos.

Day one, Kid rode his first wave like a pro, heading towards the shore with a smile and a hearty whoop. Suddenly, the bottom fell out, sending him tumbling wildly. As his ride ended abruptly, he ate an untimely sand sandwich. Except for an occasional jump in jump out cool down, this was the first and sadly the only time Kid has ventured into the warm Pacific.

He has also been spending a good deal of solo time back at Scorpion Heights, punishing his practice pad and learning (or rather butchering) key phrases in Spanish while watching Angelica go through her daily chores.

His infatuation with Angelica has resulted in little more spark than a schoolboy's crush. They have not spoken to each other, yet he feels they have a lot in common. They've only made bashful eye contact, yet Kid is certain that he is picking up the same vibes from her.

Dave gave him a quick lecture on the differences between American cultural relationships compared to Mexican cultural relationships, ending with the straightforward message: "In Mexico, young lovers don't have sex until they're married. In other words, Kid, YOU BONE HER, YOU OWN HER." This bit of reality cooled his flames of passion a bit.

For this trip, Kid brought along only one book, but lord, what a book it is: **HOW THINGS WORK**. Once, when he was showering, Dangerous and I decided to give it a peek. He was on page five, which described how to build a nuclear reactor. Page six explained how toilets worked, page seven had a nifty diagram of a combustible engine in action and page eight detailed how to make ice cream. We were both impressed with this all-encompassing literature.

Kid has also been writing mass quantities of postcards home that Dangerous continually has to help him mail. A sneak peek told us that Kid had been infatuated with the wildlife he has taken in. He wrote to his brother all about seeing a rat in Guadalajara 'the size of a wastebasket', cockroaches with 'steely eyes', and the 'black furry spiders with teeth' currently infesting his living quarters. What a long strange trip it has been for The Kid.

Ever since we arrived in Barra, Kid has eaten nothing substantial of what Barra has to offer besides fruit and sunflower seeds, which he buys in large quantities (with Dave translating, of course) at the marketplace in Melaque.

Within two days of this program, he developed a severe case of the runs. Shortly thereafter, the plumbing *problem* at Scorpion

Heights prompted a detailed reminder from Dangerous to Kid on the plumbing system's rejection of toilet paper.

We awoke the day after Dave's reminder to find three Mexican workers, armed with picks and shovels, digging a twenty-yard ditch to attempt to remedy the clog. These guys were not happy.

Dangerous held a short, animated conversation with them, returned to the room. "So, which one of you jokers has been flushing his toilet paper down the pooper?"

Kid's guilty look revealed the source of the excavation. "Huh? What? I uh…You mean you really were not supposed to wipe? I mean… I thought that you were messing with my head again."

"Look Kid, you're lucky they didn't catch you flushing that fudge paper or you'd be out there digging that ditch all by your lonesome."

Once again Dave explained proper pooping procedure, slowly and clearly. Kid still wore a look of confusion.

A solemn vow of secrecy was taken never to reveal to Willy or any of our other neighbors, the identity of the Phantom Flusher.

Each passing day Kid slipped deeper inward, always reading or practicing his gender-oriented *As and Os* in self-imposed silence. It grew harder and harder to tell what was going on in his Kid-like world. Most likely nothing more cerebral than bugs, spiders, steely-eyed cockroaches, and humongous rats, stalking their prey.

We keep a low profile. We hover just below the radar of Barra's gringo social circuit, but, have made friends with a congenial cluster of middle-aged expatriates whose company we've grown to enjoy. Each evening at sunset, this small circle gathers at Ralph's Pad to launch their evening.

Ralph's Pad lies down a quiet, lightly-trafficked side street a few blocks removed from Barra's hub, away from any beach activity. Our sixty-year-old host Ralph came to Barra via Berkley. For the past two decades heads south, spending four to six months each year enjoying Barra's bliss and shall continue to until "he is pushing up daisies in the Great Beyond."

Ralph makes a living in the jewelry business, specifically gold and silver. His partner, Cathy, is a pleasant, big-boned ex-hippie full of celestial charm, who is always on hand to greet visitors with her warm smile and sparkling eyes. In the handful of evenings that I have spent in their company, I have never heard either have a negative thing to say about any subject the crowd on hand may discuss.

Most of the expats are in their late thirties or early forties; extremely mellow Marin County natives who, like Ralph, have traded in their tie dyes and Dead accoutrements for beach-oriented attire. Overall, a laid-back bunch; yet passionate about their philosophical points of view.

Each evening's cast of characters varies, all but assuring the evening's topic of conversation avoids redundancy. We sit drinking Bacardi and Cokes while listening to cassettes of early Billy Holiday, Charlie Christian, Dave Brubeck, or Ralph's personal favorite, Willie Nelson's Stardust, all which fit the casual tone of Ralph's Pad perfectly.

When the vibe is right and the crowd has dwindled to an intimate handful, Ralph takes his clarinet from its battered leather case and plays along, cut by cut, with Willie.

On the way back to Scorpion Heights, we always make time to stop by and partake in the delightful tasty craftsmanship of the Churro Dude. Churros, the Mexican equivalent of donuts, are tasty, addictive, cinnamon-coated creations tempered to perfection in a pan full of hot, nasty melted lard. Churro Dude's finished product costs a peso. That's five-cents folks.

Every evening, a half hour before sunset, our ancient Churro master, skin tight and weathered as a mummy, goes to work. He arrives with his trusty and quite rusty wheelbarrow loaded with all necessary items, doing business, setting up shop on the street corner across from the church, there at the hub of Centro.

His work is slow yet meticulous. First, he removes an armful of dry sticks, twigs, and tree branches from the wheelbarrow which he lights and fans until they begin to blaze. For the next twenty minutes, while the sticks turn to hot ash, he chain-smokes unfiltered cigarettes while catching up on small talk with the locals.

Next, he sets a large copper bowl, much like a wok, atop the glowing remnants. Once the pan begins to smoke, he drops three fistfuls of lard into the bottom. Once the sun slips over the horizon, the grease is bubbling and ready. It is time for Churro Dude to perform his magic.

He then takes thick wax paper and twists it into a funnel, then fills this cone with dough. Churro Dude begins squeezing the funnel counterclockwise around the outer edge of the bowl, working towards the middle until it is one big coil of sizzling churro batter. When the bottom side begins browning, he flips it over, one last time.

At this point a crowd has begun to gather. The word is out tonight's churros are ready for consumption. Eager niños edge towards the front of the line, shaking their pesos in their hands. Churro Dude removes the golden-brown coil from the oil. Crowd chatter raises to a anticipatory buzz.

The still sizzling coil is laid on a large sheet of wax paper, where a generous coat of cinnamon powder is added. The final touch. He then cuts them into finger-length segments with his pocketknife.

For three pesos, I was handed three still warm segments on a brown paper towel. Before you could say "two more, please," I had wolfed them down. When his turn came, Dangerous wisely purchased five.

Thursday, the quiet, unobtrusive lifestyle we have become accustomed to shifted from low to high gear as the annual swordfish tournament, with a grand prize worth several thousand pesos, launched a three-day party. Fishermen from the U.S., British Columbia and Mexico have gathered here in Barra to compete and have a rollicking good, albeit drunken time.

That morning, after breakfast, I chose to break free from my mates for a solo excursion shoreside, towel, book, and wallet in hand. I chose an isolated flat spot away from those who had already gathered; off near the tall grass--my private oasis. It was grand.

Two hours of baking, whompin' and reading later I was ready to head off to Licuado Land. I grabbed my shoes, blanket, and ever-present Panama hat but something was missing--my ever-lovin' wallet!!!

I was certain I had brought it along; in fact, I remembered laying it alongside my book. Oh hell, was I seriously that naïve?

Someone must have popped out from behind the dune's guerrilla-style, and, seeing the gringo oblivious enjoying the surf without a care, grabbed the fool's wallet, there for the taking, then slipped off, ever-so cunningly. Yours truly was in a world of hurt.

Gone, alongside irreplaceable phone numbers and luckily only the equivalent of twenty-six American dollars, was my driver's license, social security card, and, the most crucial pieces of paper a traveler must possess, my tourist visa. I was up stinky creek without a paddle. This sudden stroke of bad luck left me in a serious anxiety-ladened funk.

Confused, pissed off, and in need of a mind-numbing mid-afternoon elixir, I dropped by Ralph's for consolation.

When I explained my plight Ralph, voice of reason he was, saw things differently. "It's not fair to assume that any of the locals are responsible. There are a hundred new faces in town right now, Mexican as well as Caucasian, who are very capable of such a maneuver. The casual routine of life in Barra we know and love is vulnerable right now and, unfortunately, most likely shall remain that way until the tournament concludes."

He went into his bedroom and returned with a piece of paper as well as a cup full of rum and fresh ice. "These two items should make you feel better."

It was a blank tourist visa form. Ralph assured me that the copy of my birth certificate I had brought along, per Dave's request, would be sufficient ID to cash my Travelers Cheques. I slugged down the Bacardi and the tempest brewing inside me cooled down considerably.

Ralph also strongly advised against informing the police. "Trust me, the paperwork and red tape they would put you through are seriously not worth the hassle for the inconvenience you have just experienced. Just be wiser in everything you do from this day forward."

In Ralph we trust.

Back at Scorpion Heights I informed Dave of my shitty plight and, as usual, he saw his chance to make me twitch a bit. "We gotta get that wallet back, man, or else they'll never let you back across that border!"

"Seriously?" Why did I even bother asking?

"As a heart attack. We have got to get you as tanned as possible as fast as possible. Don't even think of shaving off that mustache. Hopefully when we go through customs, we'll be able to cut a deal to get you a temporary work visa. I'm afraid that's the only way possible to get you back home."

My guts churned at this scenario, but I considered the source.

I decided then and there to subscribe to that *Mexico Magic* Dangerous kept bringing up--to go with the flow. I wouldn't allow myself to get bogged down by detail. I'd enjoy what's going on around me instead of worrying about shit I couldn't control.

We had many, many miles to go. I would become just become a bit more wary in my approach; avoid situations that could land my caboose in hot water. Little did I know that our next challenge was out fishing in the bay as I was tucking my new piece of paperwork safely away in the pocket of my backpack.

6. <u>The Ugly American</u>

Downtown, the Swordfish Festival had begun kicking into high gear as Barra came alive with an energy we had yet to experience.

Every shop in Centro had rolled their doors open early, owners smiling and ready, hoping to attract many of the unfamiliar faces moving about. Neighbors Teresa and Denny, whom we hadn't seen for the past few days, stopped by following siesta, hoping to drag us down to The Sands, headquarters for the tournament. Denny's invitation to "Be a part of it." was too tempting to pass up. So intriguing, in fact, even Kid joined in.

Four ten-foot-long tables ran end to end, covered on one half with hundreds of ceramic mugs filled to their rims with tequila--the devil's brew. These delightful servings of cactus juice were ours, just for the asking, compliments of Sauza, the festival's sponsor.

At the other two tables, smiling señoritas in gaily flowered ankle-length dresses were busy setting up plastic cups, full of less hard-core blends (Pina Coladas and Strawberry Margaritas) as fast as they could be poured.

Happy to be on hand, we saluted the Sauza banner that ran the length of the tables. We raised the first of the free clay shot glasses to our lips and drained their potent content in one swift swallow. Once consumed, the hostesses assured us the mugs were ours to keep. This trip just keeps getting better by the minute.

Two hours later, both my front pockets were jam-full with six souvenir mugs. Over twenty-two impressive swordfish had been weighed in, and day one's activities officially came to a close.

Suddenly, around the bend, a forty-foot, full-featured rig, *The Cognac*, came into sight, busting butt on its way towards the lagoon. I'm not well-schooled when it comes to boating, but it was obvious this upscale cruiser reeked of affluence. A grandiose flag of Texas flapped in the wind and a large blond-haired sunglass-sporting skipper stood behind the wheel.

The powerful boat sped towards shore, its huge bow cutting mini tidal waves which caused two modest boats of local fisherman to bob dangerously in its wake. The angry occupants shouted and waved their fists in his direction, but *The Cognac* continued its beeline towards the docks.

The skipper quickly disembarked, then jumped up and down, fully animated, as he barked furiously while two flustered dockhands tied up his cruiser. He then bee lined briskly to the judge's stand and began a heated discussion with the tournament officials.

Our party of five stood by, too far away to catch the actual gist of his conversation/tantrum, watching in amusement as he pointed to his watch, and throwing a tantrum more often associated with a disgruntled five year-old.

It was apparent his disagreement was in regards to the official finishing time. The eldest of the three judges shrugged his shoulders, then pointed at a reader board hanging above the sign-in table, clearly posted for all to see: ***ALL COMPETITORS CRAFTS MUST BE BACK DOCKSIDE NO LATER THAN 2:45 IN ORDER FOR DAILY QUALIFICATION*** The current time was now 3:10.

The red-cheeked fisherman twitched in frustrated anger, threw his arms in the air and screamed "Fucking cheating Beaners!!" then stomped off towards the tables of Sauza, still cursing at anyone and everyone in his path.

Our next stop was Ponchos, where, once again, barbecued Camerones were the unanimous choice for all. As we inhaled our shrimp and rice, a colorful Mariachi band, fourteen members in all, entertained a nearby table of fishermen with several traditional ballads. No matter how buzzed we were, they still sounded dreadfully off key.

Another highlight of today's festivities was the public reemergence of Señor Kiddo. He had worked himself into a period of intense isolationism, pondering his phobias which ranged from waves to sharks to scorpions to Mexican food (and who could forget toilet seats?), and had been fighting a losing battle with the diarrhea gods for well over four days.

Tonight, he decided to venture forth and join us for dinner. He was game to introduce something mellow, sans spices, in an attempt to appease his discombobulated digestive tract. Rice soup appeared to fit the bill but Kid's run of bad luck had not yet concluded.

All entrées arrived, except for the soup. We devoured our meals while Kid sat patiently waiting. As we were getting down to final bites, our waiter returned with an empty bowl, which he placed before our amigo, before informing him his entrée was on its way.

Five minutes later, he returned with the aromatic rice and broth. Before pouring, he noticed a microscopic bug wandering the perimeter of Kid's bowl. The miniscule mite was struggling to make its way back out, over the lip.

After an attempt to coax it out, our waiter crushed it with his thumb, then casually wiped the interior clean with the tip of a napkin before proceeding to pour the steaming contents, offering our friend a sheepish smile.

Kid spoke nary a word, just sat there biting his tongue. We knew he noticed the unfortunate intruder and that his rapidly beating heart was doing a double somersault into the shallow end of an empty pool. He downed two timid tablespoons before abruptly dismissing himself from the table. Dave graciously paid his portion of the tab.

Dinner behind us, Denny, Teresa, Dave, and myself, all fending off post-Tequila migraines compliments of the Sauza fest, made a group decision to wander down to the disco at The Sands, mere stumbling distance away.

We arrived to find the place bustling; a sweaty floor-full of fishermen, their mates, as well as many locals caught up in the Bump, Hustle, and Bus Stop.

We unanimously decided to join in, calling on sugar and caffeine to quell all residual delirium tremors until we were Bee Gee'd out the door on a hot Donna Summer's night.

A round of longneck Tecates arrived at our table and we quickly informed our waitress of the inaccuracy of their destination. She just shook her head and pointed across the way. "They are from Señor Cognac."

Two tables away sat the blond giant, (now without his shades but sporting a natty hundred-dollar perma press flowered shirt) whom we had watched make a fool of himself back at the docks. Smiling widely, as if addressing old friends, he raised his own longneck and saluted us with a hearty "Viva Americanos!" We had a new friend. One we did not ask for.

He grabbed his chair and joined us.

"Hey there everybody, I'm Seeeñore Cognac, from *Coh-puss Cristee*. That's in Tex-*ass*, if ya haven't heard! Pleased to meet y'all."

"Thanks for the cerveza." Denny spoke for us all. "So, you're here for the fishing tournament, I suppose."

"Hell yeah, you suppose right. What the hell else would someone come to this rat-infested dung hole for?" He spoke directly at a heavyset mamasita seated at the adjacent table. "It certainly wouldn't be to find me a wife- I like *my* women with teeth."

Ouch! We all cringed. If push came to shove, Dave, Denny, and myself could probably handle ourselves adequately in a bar room brawl but this dude was big--maybe six five, two hundred forty pounds of Texas redneck, with a voice that boomed like a cannon. "Hey Whoolio-bring us another round! Pronto! And take these back--they're getting piss warm."

Dangerous spoke up. "That's all right, it's past my bedtime." I seconded that emotion. This guy made me nervous. Like REAL nervous. Cognac's glare let us know we had offended his feelings, or rather, ego.

"Shit, and here I was coming over here with a little southern *hos-pi-tal-i-tee*, to invite y'all out on my boat tomorrow to cruise this cesspool of a bay in style."

I can't explain why, perhaps I was intimidated, but I decided to stay, drink his beer, and humor this jackass until my beer debt was paid. The Californians followed my lead, then an ever-so-reluctant Dave as well. Señor Cognac was pleased. Very begrudgingly we accepted his offer for a day on the seas.

"Meet me down in the lobby-at six thirty sharp--that way I don't have to hire any of these taco-dippers to help me reel in the twenty-five- footer I'm planning on catchin'. They aren't worth a shit unless you need em to crack open a beer or gut a chum for ya. Don't know a word of English until it's time to ask for their money."

"Another hundred soldiers at the Alamo and this here town would be part of *Cally-fornicate-a* today." We gave our best exaggerated yawns, then politely excused ourselves and headed back.

Morning church bells rang right on schedule. I awoke to a headache more powerful than if Tito Puente was playing a drum solo on my forehead.

Dave was already alive, liberally applying eye drops to his puffy baby blues. "You sure you really wanna go?"

I shrugged unconvincingly, "Sure, why not?"

"Reason number one--Señor Cognac is an asshole--times five."

"Yeah, but here's a chance to do some deep-sea fishing free of charge."

"True, but is it worth it? Tunes, this guy's an *ugly* American."

"Not necessarily my type of guy, but what the hell, it's bound to be an interesting experience and *free* is a mighty fine four-letter word to be tossing around."

Downstairs, Denny and Teresa greeted us with a silent nod, apparently suffering from the same Tequila Table flu bug Dangerous and I were attempting to rise above as we headed off to The Sands.

We arrived in the lobby at 6:30 sharp; in pain, yet exceedingly punctual. No sign of Señor Asshole.

6:45-still no Texans sauntering about. We asked the desk manager for his room number.

When Denny mentioned Señor Cognac, all eyes fell upon us as if we were in cahoots with the devil. The bellboy pointed down the hallway "*Numero* 135." He did not offer to show us the way.

As we closed in on 135, cheery Mexican music wafted coming softly from the level above, setting the tone for a wonderful morning.

Suddenly that spell was broken. "TURN THAT SHIT DOWN, FOR GOD'S SAKE!!!" That voice, unfortunately, had a familiar Texas twang to it. "PLAY SOMETHING GOOD-LIKE LINDA RONSTADT, JERRY JEFF WALKER, OR DON'T PLAY NOTHING AT ALL!!!"

I suggested we draw straws to see who the lucky one to knock on his door would be, but Denny stepped up.

Four medium soft raps on his door, then "WHAT!!??"

"Señor Cognac?"

"WHO THE HELL IS IT?"

"It's us, your crew. The beer openers." Denny was one brave dude. "WHAT THE FUCK ARE YOU DOING HERE THIS EARLY?"

"You told us to meet you here at six thirty, and it's pushing seven o'clock."

"AW, SHIT. DAMN JAP WATCHES." He coughed a pitiful lung burst, then, "JUST HOLD YOUR PALAMINOS AND MEET ME IN THE LOBBY IN ... ABOUT TWENTY MINUTOS."

That did it. The scumbag didn't even say please. Right then and there Dangerous and I decided to blow this bad dream off. I wouldn't know what to do if a deep-sea fish of any proportion hit my line anyway. And I certainly didn't feel like getting a sore thumb twisting the tops off any pompous pisshead's cervezas; taking orders all day like a galley boy while Mr. Big sat on his multimillion-dollar ass, pole between his legs, singing Long Tall Texan.

Time to go back to the Heights, pretend this was all just a bad dream. More sleep was definitely in order.

Denny and Teresa chose Plan B. They had already made the commitment to drag their hungover souls out of bed, and had no other plans for the day. What the heck? We wished them well. Dangerous and I opted to go the 'another typical day in Barra' route.

The lady at our Licuado stand told Dave today's temperature was expected to rise over one hundred. When it is hot, move slow, stay close to available shade, and don't bite off more than you can chew. With that in mind, we adjusted our daily siesta to a special three-hour edition.

That evening we were in such great spirits we even invited Willy to join us for dinner at the Hotel Guadalajara. Willy pontificated on how the U.S. Military Industrial Complex intentionally lost the Korean War, but before we could press him for details, Denny and Teresa appeared, dog- hungry and lobster-red after their long hot day at sea. Yes, they had a tale to tell. We all kicked back with a round of margaritas as our sunburned companions held court.

Denny began the tale. "We waited in the lobby until around 7:45 until a rather dour-faced Cognac finally emerged. No apologies or explanation for his tardiness was offered and we followed him silently down to the docks.

"As he helped us board, Señor made sure to use both hands to assist Teresa to reach the upper deck. Neither of us missed the fact he conveniently managed to place both paws upon her butt *for leverage*, still it was easier to overlook his sly move than make noise about it.

"We milled around uncomfortably as he threw a full-fledged tantrum trying to remember where he had put his keys. Next, he started yelling at three young dock workers working on a skiff moored alongside, accusing them of sneaking on board and stealing them. They spoke no English, so just smiled and waved. That pissed him off even more. As he was threatening to use the boat's flare gun to get their attention, he dipped his hand into his right front pocket and found them. That's where they were the entire time!

"It was now 8:15 and all the other competitors had a major league jump staking out prime fishing locations. As we motored out towards open sea, Cognac made a point of veering towards each small wooden boat in the vicinity, full of local contestants with their poles cast into the bay.

"Each time he approached, he would gun the engine, then head directly at them. Only when he was close enough to see their eyes grow wide with fear would he cut away, creating sharp rolling walls of water. These intentionally directed waves would strike the smaller crafts broadside, causing them to rock and roll precariously in our wake. To prevent capsizing, the fisherman had to drop their poles and cling to the sides for dear life.

"Señor Cognac would laugh, then point his vessel in the direction of the next boat, where he would repeat the same dastardly maneuver. Needless to say, this attitude did not make us any new friends among our fellow fishermen.

"Finally, he found a killer spot and cut the motor. Before he had even tossed his line overboard, he began boring us with tales about the oil business and the multi-million-dollar corporation he was soon to inherit from his invalid father back in *Coh-puss,* just as the mother of all swordfish leaped from the water less than ten yards off the bow of our boat.

"This sent Cognac into another first-class tantrum. He threw his pole down, went to the cabin below, only to return with a double barrel shotgun, which he pointed in the general direction of where the fish had risen above the surface."

Denny paused, took a long drink from the salt-rimmed glass in front of him, then continued.

"Have you ever heard the roar of a shotgun at 8:42 a.m. in the middle of the ocean? Gentlemen, it is a real eye-opener.

Cognac cocked and fired into the water again. He issued my first cabin-boy order of the day.

'Get down below, dammit, and get me some more shells!!'

'A please would be kinda nice' I replied as I headed below. There, wall to wall, resembling a horny college boy's dorm room, were pin-up babes, freshly removed from Mexican nudie mags, thumb tacked into the cheap particle board like a poor man's wallpaper. A video cassette recorder sat on the night stand beside his waterbed, a stack of pornos ready and waiting atop his video player.

'Where the hell are those shells?'

"Grumbling, Cognac scrambled down the ladder behind me."

'Jesus, Kee-rist, I knew I should a took some beaners with me today instead of a couple of Frisco-born granola eaters.'

"He returned to the deck and fired off all three rounds into the water before opting to try the more traditional method once again. Putting his pole back into the water.

"After that, things calmed down, including his tempestuous mood. By early afternoon our host and skipper's manners bordered on charming; Over a gigantic ice chest full of Tecate and some outrageous ham tortas, the day was nearly salvaged, his rudeness forgiven. Until the cooler ran out of Tecates.

'Hey Denny, do us a favor. Go below and bring us up another batch of cold ones, would ya?'

"He saw me off with a devilish wink. Once below, I had three refrigerators to choose from. As I grabbed a six pack from the smallest, I heard Teresa, mild-mannered soul mate that she is, conversing in an unusually angry tone with the good Señor."

Teresa interrupted. "You mean the not so good, low-life *Seenyour*. The puke tried to feel me up right there on the deck! Snuck up behind me, using Roman fingers and Russian hands, so to speak, while my darling husband was diligently bringing us more brews!"

Dangerous and I were dying for the dirt. "So what did you do?"

"I slapped his smirking dog-breathed face, right there before God, Sam Houston and Jim Bowie too! He started stammering like Porky Pig, unable to spit out an 'I'm sorry' before Denny was topside."

"Then what?" prodded Dangerous.

"Did ya slug him in the kisser?" Willy queried.

My turn. "Did you make him suck on the barrel of the elephant killer?"

Denny said no to them all. "I wasn't even aware of what happened. All I knew was that Cognac looked like he got caught whacking off in church and Teresa had that 'don't even ask' gleam in her eye. We decided fishing time was over, and started to head back."

"So, where've you two been since then? Back in your room licking your wounds?" Willy's eyes twinkled at their misfortune.

They both laughed. Denny continued, "That's the punchline. The Cognac's motor wouldn't start. He tried and tried but it was deader than a mackerel, so to speak. We tried all applicable methods to get it to turn over but no luck. Then Cognac discovered the problem. The fuel line had been nicked by a bit of buckshot when the great white hunter fired his thunder stick. Ended up with a hole the size of a dime. Is that karma or what?"

We all cheered the good guys.

"We waited for what seemed like hours for someone, anyone, to come by and give us a hand but no one wanted anything to do with us. Twice, boats came in our direction--boats the Señor had tried to capsize. When they saw who was having *problemos*, they waved and turned away, back in the direction of Barra--laughing, even cheering.

"Finally, a medium-sized skiff full of drunken Canadians drifted by and Cognac offered them a hundred dollars to tow us to shore. Their under-sized vessel made a valiant effort until the weight of The Cognac snapped their tow line.

They promised to send help once they reached the docks, and were just about to leave us there broiling in the sun when Teresa charmed them into taking the two of us back with them.

"As we pulled away, Cognac took one last shot, 'Nice effin' crew I hired.' Already, the sun had roasted him into overcooked lobster status. 'You'll be sorry you ever fucked with Señor Cognac.' We could not put enough distance between us fast enough to make me happy."

"So, what are you gonna do?" Willy lobbied heavily for retribution.

They looked at each other, smiled in their celestial Californian way and both agreed. "Let it go. Why waste any more negative energy on the bum. Besides, he's about six inches taller than me and I'm seriously allergic to pain."

"I've got the answer," Kid offered, "Go get Hercules. I'm sure by now he's through saving the world." We all laughed, then paid the bill. We split up, Willy tagging along with the boaters while the boys headed back to the Heights.

Up ahead, a severely sunburned Señor Cognac was staggering down the side street, a rowdy-looking drunken sloth; causing trouble on his mind. A diminutive local walked past him and Cognac stepped directly in his way. He cursed in the local's face, raised his hammy right fist above him as if to punch the quivering young man, then howled with laughter as the frightened boy recoiled in humility.

"Coward!! You're all stinking cowards!!" He let out a whoop as he kicked the side of a car parked alongside the curb, leaving a size twelve dent in the driver's door.

He staggered down the street, back towards The Sands, cursing and harassing every person of Mexican descent he encountered along the way.

I don't consider myself a vengeful soul but tonight I felt a burning desire for redemption. There was one stumbling block. Although not a coward by any means, I too was allergic to pain, and Cognac was a damn big creep.

Dangerous nudged me as we watched the snockered Señor from a safe distance as he precariously navigated his way through the front of The Sands. "You know, Kid might just be right after all. Hercules *just might* be the man for this job."

We headed back to the Heights to draw up a sordid plan of action. I watched as Dangerous took out a pen and note pad. He scrawled in intense silence for close to twenty minutes, then handed me the pen.

"Your turn to add your ten cents-worth." He smiled. "What the hell, make it fifty cents-worth… We both agree teamwork is a valuable asset:

Dear Señor Cognac:

You are a very lucky man - lucky to be born into affluence; to have a boat, to be a very good fisherman, and to live in America. You are also very lucky that today, I have spared your pathetic life.

For the past three days, I have been watching you from a distance and there are several things I do not like about you, your surly face or your pompous shitty attitude. I don't like your cheesy flowered shirts or your foul obnoxious mouth or that hillbilly drawl it continually turns loose on humanity. I particularly don't like the way you treat the locals of Barra as if they are dogs. I don't like your aftershave, your breath or the two-hundred-dollar sunglasses propped upon your sunburned forehead like a bourgeois ornament.

I myself, collect ornaments; like chopped off fingers, ragged pieces of torn-off ears, and, if necessary, braggart's tongues, yanked from their stems with absolutely no mercy; their roots bloody and dangling while their former owner lies speechlessly whimpering, pleading to be left alive.

My Policia friends here in Barra have been considering incarcerating you. They would love nothing more than to toss you into a cold, dank, musty jail cell to sleep amidst the starving rats and the scampering scorpions, but I have intervened and cut a deal with them. You are now mine, my friend, and I promised them, on my dear Sicilian mother's grave, that come sunrise you will be gone or you will be **gone**, if you catch my drift.

Right now, as you read this, I am watching you, along with my other friends - all five of us - big hairy bastard fishermen with real nasty attitudes and very sharp serrated fishing knives we piss on to clean them. We certainly don't like what we have seen since you have come to town.

You are extremely lucky that it wasn't my boat you tried to swamp today, or the sharks would *already be snacking on your testicles and cleaning their teeth with your bones.*

We have killed men better than you and we have killed men worse than you, with little or no remorse. We will not hesitate to rid the world of one more piece of fecal-flecked garbage like yourself.

No one here will miss you, in fact they may celebrate, even ring the bells at mid-day while the sharks chow down on what was once a giant Texan's ass.

*You have no friends here in Barra. Leave quickly and quietly and you may live to cheer on the Kilgore Rangerettes next time they perform in your redneck town. Stay here and you are mine. And friend, your end will **not** be pretty......*

Adios, Vinnie Hercules

"Too sophomoric?" Dangerous had worked up a sweat, churning out this intense effort.

"I like it" It was a masterpiece. "But what's with the aftershave bit?"

"I dunno. I guess it might make him think that this person's been close enough to smell him. You added some real nice touches yourself. When we get home, we should add this to our resumes as I hear the extermination business is always looking for a few good men."

I agreed. It was getting late, almost midnight. "Now what?"

"We get Kid to tack it to his room door, knock, then run like hell."

"What if Cognac hears him coming and snags him in the act?"

"In the shape we saw him in a few minutes ago he would be hard pressed to catch a heavily-salted slug, don't you agree?"

I volunteered to be the midnight marauder; the knocker in the night.

My hands trembled as I pinned the note, and knocked loudly four times before hustling around the corner. Casually, I did a second lap, this time pounding twice with the side of my fist before sprinting off.

The snoring ceased. Finally, the door opened, then closed. The note was gone. The bait had been taken. Mission accomplished. It was finally my turn to launch a little snoring of my own before those damn bells begin to ring again.

Señor Cognac? Call it coincidence, cowardice or your favorite applicable term, but before the bells announce the coming day, that buzzard flew the coop.

After breakfast, we did a lap down by the docks. The festive tables of Tequila, the judging stand and the Sauza banners were all gone, past history. So was *The Cognac*.

A small trawler now occupied the berth where the gargantuan vessel had been moored these past few days. The citizens of Barra were once again free to walk the streets after dark without the fear of being bullied about by Ugly Americans. Viva Vinnie Hercules!!!

7. Super Bowl Sunday, Barra Style

I have already sacrificed my passion for music to partake in this slice of paradise adventure so any opportunity to immerse myself in a dose of NFL action, let alone the Super Bowl, must be fulfilled. Let us talk football for a bit, as the Super Bowl in Barra turned out to be a memorable yet wonderfully surrealistic experience.

The past few days have been spent making inquiries with the locals as to any potential locations at which we can watch the game. All we get are quizzical looks and a shrug of the shoulders. It appears (gasp!) no one here has ever heard of The Super Bowl. At least the locals.

Upon further inquiry, we discovered very few residents own televisions, and those who do need wrap a generous amount of tinfoil around their third world rabbit ears to enhance broadcast any form of programming available.

Saturday, we met a heavily-bearded Aussie at the groceria, purchasing a large sack of oranges who informed us that Gabby's, the local hamburger shop, had a television and most likely could be coaxed into letting us watch the game, especially if we showed up in substantial numbers and with substantial pesos.

Gabby's was a medium-sized palapa-style indoor eatery. Sunday was traditionally a slow day for burger business so the show was run solely by the owner's three children, none older than fifteen.

Dangerous and I were the first to arrive, around 11:30. We set up camp in the choicest viewing seats, ordered sodas, and inquired where their big screen TV was. Tomaz, our waiter, pointed proudly to the twelve-inch black and white horizontally-impaired Brand X unit, mounted crookedly on the wall above the grill. We were destined to become legally blind or at least need binoculars before half-time.

Without newspapers or T V Guides we had no idea what time the game was to commence. Unfortunately, we anticipated kickoff to take place right around noon, Barra time.

By 2 p.m. all we had experienced was pre-game anxiety as all we could dial in was a silly Mexican puppet show, which strangely featured three balloon-breasted señoritas crooning what must've been the Latin Top of the Pops, two soap operas and a pair of overly-dramatic soap operas.

As the hours rolled by we lost confidence we would be fortunate enough to find a channel carrying the game. That level sunk even lower when we found out they only could get reception from three channels.

After much prodding, Tomaz, the eldest of today's restaurant crew, scanned all three for the NBC Peacock, the sight of one hundred yards of Astroturf, a pre-game show of any sort or the voice of Super Bowl announcer, Curt Gowdy. No luck. What the heck? Surely a game of this magnitude would be broadcast worldwide. Don't these wonderful people love football? No luck.

Damon, the Aussie, arrived around 2:30, accompanied by three Brits and a Frenchman, none of whom had ever experienced an American football game, let alone the Super Bowl. He apologized for miscalculating the kickoff time, and, after a bit of scrutiny, he was now positive the game would begin at 3 p.m., Mexico City time.

Word spread through the gringo underground and soon Gabby's was stuffed to capacity with good-natured suntanned football enthusiasts. The grill was sizzling nonstop and the beer was flowing. What an atmosphere we had created! *Solemente uno problemo*--The game had yet to materialize.

Tomaz scanned the channels again. Suddenly, soccer filled the screen. The Europeans cheered lustily. In their eyes, *this* was The Super Bowl.

Apprehension, uneasiness, concern; all we were nipping at our souls like the mosquitos down in Barra's lagoon.

. What if the two games overlapped? Dangerous and I were both aware of the magnitude and importance of soccer to our fellow revelers. The Europeans cheered louder and grew rowdier with each beer they finished. Fortunately, the action was taking place late in the third period of a match between Mexico and Israel.

Game or no game, one thing was certain: at the rate these brown bottles were being emptied today's beer sales would make today the most profitable Sunday in Gabby's history.

4 p.m. and still no Rams or Steelers. A poor-man's Ed Sullivan Show, loaded with opera-crooning geeks and junior varsity jugglers wearing bow ties and shit-eating grins, ran its torturous course on the channel we were assured was Mexico's NBC. The half-looped crowd was quickly losing their energy and focus. Several of

the Europeans staggered out into the sunlight, waving a half-hearted goodbye to those remaining; diligent to the possibility of Super Bowl Sunday.

Suddenly the crowd came to life. Super Bowl Sunday was finally on the air. Everyone cheered even louder when Doogie, a wild-eyed Scotsman, strode in the front entrance with a twenty-inch Sony TV, color to boot, under his arm.

We hooked that sucker up faster than a NASCAR pit crew changes a tire at the Indy 500. The color was a bit blurry due to less than satisfactory reception, but we all adapted quickly. By the end of the first quarter, I had grown accustomed to watching multi-colored huddles and formations take place on orange Astroturf.

As the game went on, a subtle but wonderful surrealistic moment commenced before me: Just beyond the entrance of Gabby's the sight and sound of the waves rolling, then crashing walking distance away provided a fanciful backdrop.

While natures steady marine rhythm continued its beat, fifteen sweaty bronze-skinned men in tank tops huddled around a twenty-inch TV screen, engrossed in a game none of them understood, being broadcast in Spanish, on a natural green field turned orange due to obtainable yet poorly received transmission process. For the record, tin foil was never created to aid in one's television viewing.

During the Steelers' first significant drive, a curious gecko slowly crawled across the screen, paused on third down, before finding a place upon the ceiling to oversee the proceedings. While we sat intensely transfixed our waiters sweated and bustled in their attempt to keep their customers satisfied with a steady stream of beers, burgers, fries, and all other things requested to consume.

I almost forgot to mention Dave's football pool. In the spirit of good old American gambling, we mooched a piece of notebook paper from Tomaz, divided it into a hundred squares and gave the best explanation possible to our friends as to how a football pool worked. Each square cost ten pesos with a minimum five square purchase mandatory to participate. The board was full in a matter of minutes, Dave was chosen commissioner, the man designated to dish out the payoffs.

There was to be one winner per quarter, the pot to be divvied out progressively, growing larger as each quarter ended. The winner with the correct numbers of the final score would win the grand prize: five hundred pesos.

Dangerous won the first quarter and I, the second. A grumble of suspicion began to emanate within the ranks as our wary comrades began to sense they were being swindled by the Yanks. The Scotsman, thank goodness, held the winning numbers at the end of the fourth quarter A riot had been quelled.

Dave took the thirty-minute half time show as a chance to hike back to Scorpion Heights to see how Kid was getting along.

The game ended, the Steelers winning. It was a grand day. Yet one thing was missing: the presence of Willy. Both Dave and I were sure he would be there to foul the air with a continual dose of cigarette smoke, and that he would be the first willing to make a Super Bowl wager yet he never showed up.

We had dinner and churros, yet never once saw Willy carousing on the local circuit. When we retired to Scorpion Heights, we made a point of going past his room. The door was closed.

Sometime around 7 a.m. we awoke to a half-hearted knock on the door. Kid opened it yet no one was there, only a note from Willy:

'Goodbye, good luck, *Viya Condios*……Willy'

8. Night of the Rattatas

Ted and Doris (Dorcie) Faulkner are two special friends of ours back in Bellingham. Both are in their late twenties, are mellow, patient, and fun individuals who are road-tested, having taken many trips abroad together over the past decade.

Todd owns his own construction company and Doris serves her days in education at a local grade school. Both are blessed with careers that allow them the freedom to dictate their schedule in order to follow their passion for travel.

Coincidentally they had plans for Mexico, including Barra and Zihuatanejo, so before leaving the Northwest, we coordinated our calendars in order to meet in Barra and join ranks for the next leg of the journey. They will fit in very nicely and I look forward sharing the road with them for at least the next month.

The pair arrived in *Centro* late last evening by bus; way past our bedtime and the plan was to meet that Monday morning for breakfast at Hotel Guadalajara.

Dave crawled out from under the covers earlier than Kid and I, and together they discussed an agreeable alternative to spend our last few days in this pleasant playland.

Yesterday, after mailing three more letters for Kid in the residential area's post office, Dangerous happened upon a quaint duplex for rent that accommodates five for approximately the same price we've been paying at the Heights.

After many humid nights spent hunkered down inside the drab gray cinder block confines of Scorpion Heights, sleeping atop wafer-thin army issue mattresses and squeaky occasionally protruding springs, this potential upgrade sounded too sweet to pass by.

Over this breakfast the five of us unanimously agreed to pursue this opportunity, so off we headed for a group inspection of these the duplex.

This was too good to be true: One large room where we could all sleep on box frame beds; our own bathroom complete with sink, shower and (have I died and gone to heaven?) even a toilet seat!

Martin, the landlord, made a point of highlighting the kitchen, with its immaculate refrigerator, stove, pots, and pans, even silverware. We could even cook our own meals which would help us tuck away enough pesos to perhaps extend the trip a day or two longer.

Martin even twisted each burner on to assure us that they were in working condition.

Five thumbs popped up in agreement. This was our place.

We paid him five dollars a day, in advance, to cover the next three days. That afternoon we bid Angelica and the Señora a cordial farewell. New digs and new neighbors lay ahead.

Summer carnival has arrived in town, a mere two blocks from our casa. It's a low scale affair, featuring a miniature Ferris wheel as its centerpiece. No more than fifteen feet in height, this ride is adventurous primarily for the pre-teen neighborhood niños who eagerly line up to take a turn.

In the far corner of the makeshift fairgrounds, a rickety outdated version of The Octopus spun wildly. The line of spiffed-up local adolescents stretched around the corner; boys out to flex their blossoming libidos, cuddling up with young señoritas who scream and flirt on cue. They cuddle shyly as they wait their turn for the eight-armed spinning metal contraption to whirl them into a dizzy state of exhilaration.

For the many youngsters on hand the carnival is a big-time event in those innocent years. Local parents and elders mill about the modest midway more out of curiosity than intent to participate. They were there to accompany their niños, or to gnaw on carnival staples, such as corn dogs, sticky cotton candy, churros and caramel apples as they watched the youngsters enjoy the innocent joys of adolescents.

During the heat of the day, the midway drew few customers, but, at sunset, our neighborhood began humming with activity. Early on into the first evening, we noted one drawback of our backyard carnival: The Ferris wheel was an electricity hog.

The wheel would stop about every seven minutes to change passengers and each time the miniature wheel began its rotation, the lighting in our casa dimmed from about seventy-five watts to approximately fifteen. The ride would end, and full illumination was back. Over and over this went on until the wheel shut down sometime around midnight.

Due to the low wattage, our reading time ritual was put on hold. This was acceptable to all, as we were worn out from another long day spent chasing a tan. Comfortable with our new digs, we turned in earlier than usual.

Within an hour our duplex came alive with a symphony of snuffles, snorts and snores galore. Sitting, listening to these logs being sawn in grand fashion, I had a growing sense something was slightly amiss, but what?

I sat up, not quite sure of what exactly was causing this unease. This abode was excellent; an electric ceiling fan kept indoor temperatures tolerable, a warm wooden toilet seat, clean efficient fridge to help cut back on the many visits to the corner groceria, and beds which didn't squeak and bite your backside whenever you changed position on them. What the heck was bugging me? As little as they wanted to, my gremlins made themselves known.

A subtle tinkle emanated from the far side of the kitchen- barely detectable, but a tinkle, just the same. Another tinkle, then silence. Minutes passed, and then my subtle distraction rose again, ever-so softly. I crept from my bed, light and nimble as possible, to investigate. What I came upon the small cat-sized shadow there in the dim glow of the three-quarter moon shining through the kitchen window sent my heart racing--Rat attack!!!

Our dream habitat had been too good to be true. It appears that the Barra de Navidad division of the Mexican Rat Army had already claimed squatter's rights to our kitchen, setting up their command post deep inside the stove.

Rats are my least favorite species of four-legged beasts, especially those larger than most small dogs.

I flipped on the light and got less than ten watts worth. Damn that Ferris wheel anyway! There was a rat, on its haunches, strap in its mouth, trying to work his way into my backpack—the source of my tinkle! Caught in the act, it skittered quickly around the corner, back to safety behind the refrigerator. This unexpected scenario unleashed the coward residing within.

"Rats!!!! Effin' rats!!!!"

Kid cleared his throat and rolled over. Dangerous snored, paused and farted. Ted growled for me to go back to sleep, that I was dreaming. Only Doris took heed and joined me by the kitchen door.

We stood there, still as stone yet nervous as hell, for well over five minutes. No further tinkles, rat tails or additional evidence came forth to support my case. Doris started laying the evil eye of doubt upon me when suddenly, the tip of a cautious yet inquisitive snout began to emerge from behind the fridge. Doris let out a short shrill scream and the snout shadow was gone.

All but Kid awoke. The others were apathetic to our predicament, merely suggesting that rats won't mess with us if we don't mess with them. Nice freakin' logic.

Less than an hour later they were back. How many, no one could say, but this most certainly was not a family of one on our hands.

Doris heard them first. She tried to rustle Ted into consciousness but the long day's sun had tucked him deeply into the nether world. Kid was awake and on edge, eyes wide, tousled hair skyward; moving comically as his arms twitched to and fro. Dangerous grumbled and called our bluff.

Out in the kitchen our new friends were having a heyday, chewing on the straps of my pack (tinkle, tinkle), scurrying across the floor, flaunting their presence in response to our indifference.

Only when they started chattering in high-pitched rat-jabber did Dave join the fray. Time to send those suckahs packin'...

Hamstrung by inadequate illumination necessary to identify their specific locations, the rats held a distinct advantage early in this showdown. Our side: armed with stubby half-spent table candles and one miniature pocket flashlight. Their side: owned home court advantage, utilizing the familiar nooks and crannies of the kitchen to avoid detection. Dave wielded the broom while I fruitlessly supplied the feebly-thin ray of light.

We hit the kitchen with a broom, bent metal fire poker, and two pots and pans Doris clanged loudly together. The rats scrambled. One scurried from beneath the chair I was standing on, before venturing into the bedroom/living room where it was sent back our way by a powerful shriek from Kid. Dangerous swung the broom at a swift-moving target and barely missed.

Another sleazy antennae-like tail shot past untouched; The broom swish caught only its shadow, as the scalawag scurried to safety around the rear of the stove. Amidst this confusion, I could only count tails and tonight's unofficial total stood at three. End of the raid, but only the beginning of the war.

Dangerous managed to apply broom bristles to only one of the invaders, but was bound and determined to eliminate the opposition at all costs, even if it took all night.

A spot check behind the stove revealed the source of their activity. The vermin had been pecking at a large, brown straw mat-- damn good bunker building material--so we tossed their object of interest out into the back yard.

Dave spent the remainder of the night in a self-imposed vigil, sitting silently in a chair in the middle of the kitchen, poised for the kill with broom cocked and ready.

The wattage flickered somewhere between low and lower for the duration of the night, even after the midway shut down. The deck was certainly stacked against us! I kept a back-up broom by my bed. Behind the stove, they stewed in silence. No chitter, no chatter. Perhaps they were reviewing their next course of action as well.

Tomorrow morning we would seek out Martin and demand a trap.

Dave and Ted found Martin, with a carton of eggs and two packs of Winstons in his hands and explained our predicament. He chuckled softly as he unwrapped the cigarettes and assured the duo he would send a trap our way soon.

In Mexican time, *soon* takes on an entirely different meaning. Americans are spoiled by the concept of request on demand, better known as immediate gratification. Life in most every third world country moves at a much different pace. Laid back. Slow and easy.

For example, if you think you will be hungry in the near future, best head down to the local restaurant, order your meal, kick back and go with the flow. Fast food is not a concept here. Your *comida* will be ready when it is ready.

Unfortunately, this formula also applies to acquiring a rat trap, which may arrive in twenty minutes or four or five hours from now. The ball was in Martin's court. We could only play the hand we were dealt.

Today's beach time, siesta and showers came and went, and tonight's dinner strategy was being discussed when our trap finally arrived.

A barely audible knock on our door revealed a tiny coal-eyed niña no more than seven or eight years-old. The trap she was struggling to draped across both arms seemed more suitable to hold a mountain lion. Ted and I reached out and relieved her of the cumbersome metal cage. She smiled, waved, then skipped off towards home.

High fives were exchanged around the room. Spirits soared once more. We had our trap, by gummy; one large enough to hold at least four or five of the critters. I placed one enormous hunk of cheese smack in the center of the trap while cautiously setting the trigger into place. Victory would soon be ours.

On tap tonight was a first-class workout: a twenty-minute, mile-long waterline trek to Melaque, Barra's nearest neighbor. Although we are all trending towards excellent cardiovascular condition, the walk along the horseshoe-curved tilting shoreline is arduous. The soft sand gives way beneath our feet making our pace slower and our calves cramp and burn as we continually move towards our goal.

Dangerous claims to have come upon the greatest tamale stand in the entire universe in the Melaque marketplace. To a man, we are primed for the challenge. One obstacle: he cannot seem to remember exactly where it was located.

We were hungry. Ten minutes and a dozen wandered blocks later, we chose to give up the hunt and find dinner elsewhere from the many options offered at Melaque' s marketplace.

An hour later, stuffed beyond comfort, we waddled through town, back towards the shoreline. Guess what we stumbled upon? Dave's infamous tamale stand.

Unwilling to miss this opportunity to indulge in the universe's best tamales, we order three and split them between us. At my tender age of 26 I have not yet not experienced the whole universe to deem them the best but we all agreed they were well worth any potential digestive agony yet to come. We all chipped in to pay the modest bill, and headed back down the beach towards Barra, feet now sinking much deeper in the sand than on our way in the previous direction two hours earlier.

Even though it was well past sunset, we worked up a healthy sweat as this was an exceptionally warm evening on hand. We arrived back at Casa Duplexa hoping to gloat at some caged *Rattatas,* si?

Ted slid the key into the lock and pushed open the door. Kid flipped on the light. We all groaned in unison. No luck. No POWs. No takers on the bait. The trap door was still pinned back and the cheese sat untouched on the spring-loaded rat whacker.

We entered the kitchen, where all hell broke loose.

Whether Barra-born or just passing through, the biggest rat in all North America stared me down as he strutted along the cinder block below the kitchen window. His whiskers twitched as he realized he was busted and best seek cover. In the adjacent cinder block, a second culprit casually moved backwards, trying to wiggle deeper into a crevice there between the blocks, his tail mere inches from Doris' bare shoulder.

A third rascal popped into sight. I opened my mouth but words failed to come forth. With knees of jelly, I feebly managed to point a shaky finger towards the cinder blocks. We all saw them. The jig was up.

Rat l, the big guy, set things in motion as he scurried for cover behind the fridge. Dangerous grabbed the broom but before he could elevate it for a whack of any consequence, Rat 2 shot past, faking left, cutting right; safely reaching headquarters, under the stove.

Doris and Kid leaped up from the table, revealing even more rats hanging out in the blocks. Four, five, six!!! Rat 3 skittered along the brick tile window sill, just out of Dave's whacking range. Teamwork was a priority, for rats as well as rat whackers. Distraction was essential in keeping the master whacker off guard while the other rat brothers sought refuge.

I manned a second broom. While Dave thwacked away with his, I futilely began shoving the bristles of mine under the chair, trying to flush the rodents out into the open where Dangerous could attempt to land a quality lick or two. So far, rat instinct and guile was winning the battle.

Doris or Kid screamed--or was it me? This whole scenario was going down way too fast. Rat 4 shot straight up the side of the refrigerator and over the back as if there were suction cups on its paws.

Time for a new strategy. I started poking around the back of the fridge, where the remaining pack was trapped. My plan was to flush them out, in the direction of my broom-swatting partner. Rat 2 and Rat 3 made their move simultaneously towards the fridge, the downward *smoosh* of Dave's broom striking millimeters behind their porky hind quarters. Score: Rats 3 Gringos 0.

Rat 5 zoomed past, skipping the fridge, instead passing directly between Dave's legs as he heads for home base. Rat 4 wasn't as lucky. Dangerous landed a solid blow to the body, sending him rollin' and tumblin', yet good fortune came his way as he traveled a good ten feet, back behind a cluster of large returnable Pepsi empties we had been collecting for refund pesos. A vent to the outside world behind the bottles made this Rat 4's lucky day. He was alive, most likely mortally wounded, but certainly on safer ground.

A brief high five followed this slight moment of accomplishment, and Rat 6 took advantage of our letdown, slipping through our whack attack to join his friend Rat 5 somewhere out back.

The glamour of duplex living had thoroughly lost its luster. We wanted out. Screw the balance we had paid, give me the simplicity of our old digs. We headed on down to the San Lorenzo, the hotel Martin ran, and gave him the news.

Martin listened to our story, shrugged, and even offered our money back.

Ted and Doris returned to the El Dorado. We slinked back to Scorpion Heights; back to the concrete and tepid solar showers as well as stand and squat procedure pooping; Back where gringos rooming on the cheap found solace. Back in a *ratatta* free environment.

Fortunately, in the short time we were gone, our room remained vacant, and so we hunkered down humbly, once again laying back down on those wafer-thin mattresses wondering what went wrong. The Kid took out his drumsticks…

In the middle of the night, Kid's 'big gray buckets' unloaded on us. We stayed awake for an hour or two playing backgammon as the torrid rain kept falling in voluminous proportion. When the squalls descended on Barra, life in paradise was not so romantic. Lots of down time, man, lots of down time.

.

The rains moved inland shortly before noon and the welcome sun returned. I took this chance to spend one last writing session atop Valhalla. In my absence, it seemed someone else had been hanging out on my tar-papered perch. There at my writing space sat an empty soda can, a chewed up half-pencil, a pack of playing cards and a book. The book caught my attention- *The Teachings of Don Juan*, by Carlos Castaneda. Isn't that the author Dave mentioned I should be checking out--the guy who would enlighten me on my journey?

I checked out the cover. It was dog-eared, half torn and featured a drawing of a crow watching two people, off in the distance, contemplating a wave of rolling gray mountains.

I opened it to the following passage: **"For me there is only the traveling on paths that have heart, on any path that may have heart. There I travel, and the only worthwhile challenge is to traverse its full length. And there I travel, looking, looking, breathlessly."-Don Juan**

If not for the bookmark midway through, I would have taken it on the spot. Obviously, this was a read in progress, so I left it there on the table, intent in acquiring a copy of my own. Sitting in the sand enjoying the sounds of the ocean I found myself wishing I was following Don Juan as he searches for his inner self, or whatever it was he was looking for.

Tomorrow, we bid farewell to Barra. Back to Guadalajara, for a bus transfer, then on to Zihuatanejo. Looking at a map, it would make sense to travel south instead of having to retrace our steps back inland. One problem. The highway that would have shaved approximately ten hours off our trek has not yet been completed, therefore this detour of great magnitude.

I have grown quite comfortable these past two weeks building a daily routine dedicated to embracing the principles of leisure. I will miss my *Licuados* and my daily sunset dose of warm brown-sugared churros. I'll miss licking the spicy Camerones Diabla sauce from my fingers as I watch the sun dip over the horizon with my feet deep in the sand at Ponchos, as much as our daily body whomping sessions in Barra's P-G rated surf. I will also miss my rooftop perch, Valhalla.

Dangerous recognized my state of melancholy and took me aside for a well-timed pep talk. "Remember, this has only been a warm up--getting your toes wet in Mexico's cultural waters. You can count, barter with confidence, and order food without accidentally ordering monkey brains. No more crawling, amigo, it is time to start walking. There's a ton more to see and do that will be equally as cool as Barra de Navidad, that I   promise. The best is yet to come."
. There will be a dozen more ponchos, *eskimos and* Licuados, and wait until you see the beach at *Playa La Ropa*." He mentioned snorkeling, another experience I have always wanted to try.

Ralph stopped by after lunch with an ice cold adios brew for us all. He also brought a special little treasure that had come his way the night before. It was a scorpion--dead, thank goodness, but perfectly intact.

"It hardly ever rains here but when it does all kind of interesting critters fall out of the thatched roofs palapa roofs. This little sucker was unlucky enough to land dead center in a candle I lit during last night's storm. I figure you might be able to find a use for it somewhere along the line."

He handed it to Dave on a wine-soaked slightly crinkled cocktail napkin, exchanged handshakes all around and bid farewell with a smile I have fondly filed away in my memory's vault.

Dangerous and I locked eyes in conspiratorial glee. A mischievous spark of devilish delight was born then and there. We already knew the Scorpion's ultimate purpose, its inevitable destiny.

"Where'd my drum pad go?" The trap was set, the bait was placed and the lamb was on its way to slaughter.

"I think it's over by your pillow." Kid took the bait, moving innocently toward his cot.

"You must've moved it when you were looking for your address book." I offered.

He shrugged and flopped down onto the cot. The waxed scorpion slid off the pad, coming to rest on the edge of his pillowcase. He fluffed up his feathered headrest, the dead bug now mere inches from his left ear.

"Kid, for God's sake, don't move!"

The drum pad whacker cranked his head to his left and spied the ugly bug beside him. Like a stray bottle rocket spinning out of control, he flew backwards through the air, shrieking as he landed.

"Jeeeeeesus!!! What is it?"

"It's some kind of bug, I think."

I approached his bed, doing my best to keep a straight face. Slowly I slipped the edge of a postcard underneath the bug, then held steady as I feigned an examination, "Good lord, it's a Scorpion!" then flung it in his direction, "and it's… alive!!!"

Kid paled, face gray and glazed with sweat, eyes bugging big as tennis balls. He was on the verge of stroking out.

"Get it outta here, man!!!"

Dangerous pulled the plug on our joke. "Kid, it's not alive."

"I don't care. Get rid of it or I'll keep you both up all night counting to 360 million!!!"

Dave and I belly laughed until tears ran down our cheeks. No guilt, no remorse, just a juvenile prank of the third degree; straight out of a junior high asshole's handbook--no blood, no foul. Our mirth did not subside for a good fifteen, maybe twenty minutes. Yesirree, we had pulled a good one, sending our mate over the edge.

Kid may never have experienced another good night's sleep the rest of the time he remained in Mexico. From that point on he never went to bed without shaking his covers until certain no creepy crawlies were clinging to any part of them.

From that night on he never slipped on his tennis shoes without thoroughly examining every inch, right down to the toes, in advance. Our amigo had seriously fried first gear of his clutch of life. Funny, funny, funny.

Up above, the Mexican Gods of Karma and Good Will taking note disagreed with our shenanigan and decided retribution was in order.

It was 9 p.m. and the rain once again began pounding down in bucket-sized volume. I decided to wipe the remaining tears of merriment from my eyes and read another hundred pages or so.

At 9:30, Karma came knocking on my back door, and this visit was not at all friendly, to say the very least.

9: South: The Road Redux

After spending my last night in Barra de Navidad in well-deserved misery and embarrassing physical anguish I somehow managed to survive.

It is known by many names, or nicknames: Dysentery, Montezuma's Revenge, Tourista, the Trots, Aztec Two-Step, the Hershey Squirts, the Night of the Living Dead. You name it, brother, I had it. All night long………

Here's the recipe:

2 NIGHTS OF MINIMAL SLEEP
+
EXCESSIVE RUM & COKES AND OTHER LIBATIONS
+
INNUMERABLE JOINTS
+
3 DAYS OF TOO MUCH SUN
+
5 ENCHILADAS & 3 TAMALES
+
ONE 2 MILE SWEATY MOONLIGHT HIKE TO & FROM MELAQUE
+
1 MISUSED WAXED SCORPION
(It appears Karma frowns on this type of behavior!)
=
TOURISTA!!!!!!

No one can truly say who was the first individual to proclaim "When in Mexico, for God's sake, don't drink the water!" Whoever that wise sage was had the right plane, baby, but the wrong airport.

When cultural cuisine from any foreign country is ingested in piggishly excessive quantities, an individual's immune system becomes vulnerable to potential negative consequences which may follow.

Simple equation: the more street food consumed, the greater the chance potential bacteria one invites into their body. Add that to a system whose resistance has already been weakened by night after night of self-abuse. The results often result in very unpleasant calamity. You have upped the ante; you've rolled dem cozmik bones.

Approximately twenty minutes following my *Kid meets the scorpion* shenanigan, the first wave of what was to come rolled ashore.

First symptom of the arrival of dysentery's mischievous delivery boys disguised itself as potential flu--queasiness, slight fever and the onset of overwhelming physical weakness. Soon thereafter, your intestine begins to communicate through gurgles and rumbles. The optimist may misdiagnose this stage as heartburn or indigestion—until afore-mentioned intestines take on the characteristics of ingesting a nest full of disgruntled mud wasps.

That is how my scorpion-joke payback began.

When this bacterial warfare thankfully ended, there was not one ominous toxin or measurable number of bacteria left behind for my immune system to reject. My body was ravaged and weak, yet free of impurities. Sleep became imperative and sleep I did.

From that moment forward, I vowed to be a new man. IF I survived this unpleasant ordeal, moderation would be my mantra, as I would do my best to avoid rekindling Montezuma's fiery wrath, so help me Buddha. No more scorpions, no more tricks.

The bells tolled seven times. I was still alive. While my amigos packed for our departure, I remained horizontal on my cot, wrapped up in as many blankets I could gather, shivering and shaking in fetal position as though it was mid-winter, even though the temperature was already nearing eighty degrees.

Noticing my absence around the pancake table, Ted came by and coaxed me into indulging in a very mellow melon licuado to prevent dehydration on the bus ride ahead to Guadalajara.

He convinced me to utilize the prescription of Lomatil I had wisely included in my travel kit. From past experience, he guaranteed two of the tiny pills would sufficiently take the place of a cork and get me all the way to Zihuatanejo without any messy incidents.

Once aboard the departing *Tres Estrellas* I slept the entire five-hour ride to Guadalajara.

Good news awaited at the bus station. A Zihuatanejo-bound bus was scheduled for an evening departure and we were on it. Since it was scheduled for midnight and it was only 7:28 we had four hours of downtime to venture out into the big city once again.

Ted, Doris, and Dave wandered off in search of a pre-road meal. Lacking even a minute shred of hunger I hunkered down on a bench and watched the bus station scenarios unfold. Kid stayed behind as well, working over a sack of peanuts. A thin, yet continual crowd of curious onlookers watched from a distance as he drummed on his pad relentlessly while time moved slowly on.

As we moved later into the evening, the depot's floors and benches, nearly totally unoccupied earlier, filled to capacity. Many had thrown down blankets or extra articles of clothing to mark their territory.

Once settled in, they passed the time wrapped tightly in colorful serapes and shawls which buffered them from the evening chill drifting in through the many open air bus gates. I missed the tropical evening warmth of Barra we had grown accustomed to.

By 11 p.m. floor space was nonexistent, lined with literally hundreds of travelers, the fortunate sleeping horizontally while others dozed upright, arms folded, baskets of goods most likely purchased in a day at the market squeezed securely between their legs. We shared the same purpose. We were all waiting to move on...

At 11:30 we headed towards our gate. Once again, Dangerous and I secured The Death Seat while the rest of our entourage slipped into the back to stretch out for the night. Good thing we had queued up early, as our half-filled cruiser rolled out fifteen minutes ahead of schedule.

Air conditioning and a nonstop assortment of up-tempo Latin music highlighted our surrealistic night owl voyage south to Zihuatanejo.

Our bus driver sported a broad thick mustache and devilish grin which reminded me of the late great comedian Ernie Kovacs. By his side, was a box overflowing with cassettes. Once we were rolling, he would slip one in and sing along, drinking Coke after Coke from a small ice chest stuffed between his seat and gearshift. Not too bad of a voice, either.

This trip was slated to take a dozen hours but, from sunrise on, our bus, Occidental *numero nueve* became a milk run luxury liner.

We would start up, get rolling, only to stop ever so briefly at about half-mile intervals to pick up more travelers waiting at the side of the road. They would pay a handful of pesos, then ride the route a few miles before getting off with a slight nod or mumbled "*gracias*."

This milk run phase provided a dazzling cast of characters: Poker faced lunchbox toting farmhands with skin toasted brown and weathered from years of combatting the sun; somberly headed to another day's work.

There were chicken bearers, awkwardly wrestling with oversized cages of doomed squawking fowls. Nattily-appareled tuba players and snare drummers came aboard, heading lord knows where. Aged mamasitas, whom time had not been very kind to, worked hard to fit their robust tushes into the narrow, worn-out second-class seats. The smell of bellowing diaper-filling babies permeated the air around us.

Even though we hadn't eaten since the previous evening, we passed on barrage after barrage of high-pressure taco vendors, coming aboard to display their goods whenever brief stops allowed.

I am positive, with perhaps a wee bit of exaggeration, almost half of Western Mexico got on and off that bus during our sixteen-hour marathon. We vowed that next time we would make sure ours was a *directo*, first class only cruiser.

The Lomatil performed admirably.

Around noon, we were the sole passengers left of the original bus load who had boarded back in Guadalajara. A special bond between driver and our crew had been formed. Old Ernie Kovacs generously offered Dave and I ice-cold Cokes from his stash which we graciously accepted. He and Dave engaged in a round of good-natured conversation that left Spanish ignorant Kid and me out of the loop, yet with an ear towards their conversation, just the same.

An hour or so later, Dangerous confided to me he too was beginning to fell a slight twinge of karmic dysentery bubbling downstairs in his boiler room. Shortly after four, Occidente numero nueve ground to a halt, our driver's proclamation sweet music to our ears. "Zihuatanejo."

About an hour past sunset our bus door swung open and once again we were immersed in warm tropical air surprisingly even more humid than Barra.

We thanked our driver for safe passage and bid farewell, strapped on our backpacks, and began the long trek from the bus station on the edge of town to *Centro* and the magic of Zihuatanejo which lie ahead.

Dangerous was in one grumpy mood. Unbeknownst to either Kid or myself, he was working hard to ward off an impending *Tourista* storm which revealed itself in a heavy mask of sweat, pouring profusely down his face. He was in a hurry to get into town, walking double time the entire way. The rest of us struggled to keep up as our pace quickened.

Clouds were visible across the evening horizon. Had the doozy of a rainstorm we dealt with yesterday tagged along as we moved south down the coastline? Sometimes life can be so unfair.

Zihuatanejo was larger and much busier than Barra, yet Dave gave us little time to assess our new surroundings. Our man on a mission led us directly to and through the doors of the Hotel El Dorado, where he hastily negotiated a five-hundred-peso deal with the Señora, then led us, two steps at a time, up the stairs to our room.

Once inside, Dangerous commandeered the bathroom. There he remained, well over two hours, emerging only once, to request the Lomatil. Kid and I unpacked our belongings, then sat in silence, reeling and weary from sixteen hours on the road.

We plopped down on rickety beds anchored by cockeyed box frames, silently praying our traveling companion was not knock knock knocking on heaven's door. Ted and Doris booked their own room directly across the hall. They were trying to get their bearings as well. All indications suggested that this was going to be an unexpectedly wet and crummy inaugural evening arrival.

Next door a couple settled in for some not-so-subtle early evening lovemaking, every amorous ooh and ahh aloud and clear through the paper-thin walls. Mere feet away Dave continued making his own music. I sat there, so able to relate to what he was going through, thankful that it no longer was me.

Kid settled in, once more trying to figure out *How Things Work*.

10. Report Card #1: Dangerous Takes the Wheel

Dangerous Dave here:

The primary rule, principal or credo lived by as I prepare for a road trip of any magnitude is simply this: No two trips, same location or not, bear the same fruit. No matter how pleasant or unpleasant a previous experience, let us say in Zihuatanejo or even Barra, there is no guarantee a return visit will be comparable.

I'm a travelin' fool. I've been to Nepal, stood in awe at the foot of Mt. Everest and bartered intensely at the marketplace in Katmandu. I've traveled most of Europe by bicycle and rode the rickety railways through the jungles of Costa Rica, sitting alongside a half-busted crate full of venomous snakes. I've laid down upon the soft green grass of St. Steven's Park in Dublin watching the clouds float by while tuning into the indigenous sound of street musicians, in the distance, offering a song for their supper.

It's a charmed and fortunate life, that of the long-distance traveler. And here it is, winter again, and here I am, hoofing through Mexico--Zihuatanejo, to boot.

My philosophy of life is simple: travel now, work later. I want to see it all and do it all while I am still a young man in a young man's body. I can never imagine working the road and seeing the sights I've seen at sixty years of age with aching bones and diminished eyesight. Climbing onto a bus full of seniors being chauffeured about in well-orchestrated tour groups. No sir, give it to me now. I'll become an integral part of society's work force soon enough, but not today, nor tomorrow. Maybe the day after.

One of my favorite aspects of traveling is seeking out virgin travelers, raw and oblivious to the road; individuals who have never, for whatever reason, been exposed to a trip of any magnitude greater than a four-hour Sunday drive down the Oregon Coast. My cohorts on this trip fit the criteria to a tee.

You've got Kid, my childhood next door neighbor whose roots are mired in the security of small-town life. He's a happy little Mayberry drone who is more than a bit of a basket case. At age 27, he still lives in his room upstairs at home with Mom, Dad and dysfunctional teenage brother.

His lack of motivation can be attributed to the occasional glue sniffing binges he partook in back in our junior high days, out in his dad's workshop with Red Head Riley and Crabman, his sole playmates in our neighborhood.

Quite content in his Longview world, Kid is on his way to the top, holding down a stellar three-year stint as courtesy clerk at Red Apple Market. He's comfortable earning thirteen dollars an hour pushing carts full of groceries out to little old ladies' cars when he is not busy restocking the frozen food aisle.

His major recreational activities consist of smoking joints and banging on his twelve-piece drum set in uninspired jazz quartets each weekend at the local junior college coffee shop. Someday he'll marry a generic Longview girl, have a batch of generic little Kids and slip into middle age having experienced nothing more than a sedentary Longview life cycle.

I'm hoping this trip to Mexico will inspire him, and expose him to the fact there are incredible things to experience once you drive ten miles north, south, east or west of Longview.

On the other hand, Tunes Clark is the kind of individual who should thrive on a trip of this magnitude. He's a slave to his couch and televised sports, his passion for music, and tossing backgammon bones with the stereo on. He loves the pub life and most likely will go to college for at least eight years to get that elusive bachelor's degree in journalism.

Even though he too is content with his status quo, I detect more than a glimmer of potential burning within; sparks of imagination and creativity. Exposing him to a journey of this stature is certain to start something real.

So here we are, Tres Amigos, three weeks into exploring and sampling Mexican culture. So far, the results have been a mixed bag.

Kid steadfastly remains a basket case. I brought him here to turn him on to a whole new world, full of enough fresh and exotic stimulus.

He appears to enjoy the sun and the water, although he rarely goes in, opting instead to roast, greased to the max in

Coppertone, on his blanket, doing little more than digging sand out of the crack of his ass as he watches us have a great time.

Unfortunately, the third world pitfalls one may encounter have grown larger than life in his eyes, negating any potential growth and change this experience has to offer.

Through his eyes, Mexico has been a strange and threatening world, full of monstrous bugs, foods inconceivable to consume and living conditions replicating Alcatraz. If I am more than thirty yards away, he starts twitching in fear that I may abandon him, smack dab in the middle of Mexico.

Even after partaking in our occasional sessions of marijuana therapy he steadfastly remains terse. While Tunes and I are acclimating to our surroundings, Señor Kid is not grasping even a small corner of the big picture.

I've got a hunch that sometime soon he will load up his backpack and abort our mission. If he rises up and rallies and manages to make it to the finish line, I'll give him a C-, for admirable readjustment. Right now, his midterm grade would be H, for hopeless.

The Tunester is, as he would say, rockin' and rollin'. Occasionally he is tentative about taking chances, usually whenever unfamiliar circumstances or situations catch him off guard, still he seems to have adjusted to sacrificing those vices he has left back home and immersing himself in the culture.

He's learned how to count admirably, order his own food well enough to almost always get what he thinks he has ordered, and is diligently spending time learning enough phrases in Spanish to get by. Let's give him a B.

If all goes according to plan, very special adventures may become a reality during the remainder of our journey. We'll spend only a day or two more here in Centro at the El Dorado, a real dump of a habitat, until we can find more suitable accommodations to house us all for a reasonable price. When negotiating for a room, duration of stay plays a huge factor. The longer you stay, the less the cost.

Our overall game plan is still up in the air. Ted and Doris have Oaxaca at the top of their destination list. I have never been there, so that option is enticing.

I would love to take these boys on a real mind bender of a journey-all the way to the eastern seaboard to the mystical ruins of Palenque. This would be a marathon run, a real trip topper, which once again will depend on our financial state when and if that possibility becomes reality.

If we manage to pull the Palenque expedition off, their lives will never be the same after being bombarded by a mind-boggling array of cultural stimulus, exotic terrains, and above all, worldly experiences of incredible magnitude. Enlightenment, the likes of which they have never imagined, lies just beyond our grasp.

For now, time to enjoy Zihuatanejo; tropical paradise of many beaches, hot sun and white sand. We shall move at a slightly faster pace than Barra, yet my amigos should find Z-Wat to be as charming and pleasurable an experience as they allow it to be.

It seems longer than four years since I have last been here to experience its charm. Hello again Zihuatanejo.

This was once a small, sleepy fishing village, inconspicuously tucked into the rugged tropical coast line of the state of Guerrero. Legend has it that twenty years ago, Timothy Leary, father of the psychedelic movement, led about two hundred of his devotees here to trip their acid-eating brains out amidst the nearly unfathomable beauty of the jagged jungle mountains which jut out abruptly from the Pacific.

Back then, dirt roads lead the way into the cobblestone streets of Centro, where you could share a smile and a casual tug on a bottle of Tequila with the easy-going locals you chanced upon. Four years ago, there were seven thousand inhabitants in the area. Today Zihuatanejo is home to over sixteen thousand, and that number is growing.

Last visit, one would be extremely lucky to find accommodations that featured a shower, let alone use a toilet that wasn't community shared. Hard to believe, but four years ago, electricity was shut off every evening at eleven o'clock. No fooling. Every morning, a raspy-throated rooster singing from a rooftop served as your alarm clock.

This was a lazy little paradise with run-down liquado shops run by children who lacked even the most basic knowledge in regards to acceptable standards of human hygiene. But damn those *liquados* sure tasted good. The aromas one encountered walking down any street were foreign yet appealing, seductive in their manner to entice you. But alas, the passing of time has brought about change.

To return this winter to discover many of the town's attractive particulars have become part of the past disappoints me, yet progress marches on. I have to remind myself to refer to good old rule #1, then not let these changes stand in the way of the good times and places that await us.

The first radically noticeable change is the increase in hustle and bustle going on in Centro. The once quiet cobblestone streets have become home for a horde of customer-starved vendors, overeager, in their attempts to sell you their wares. I have no need for hand-carved wooden turtles, hammocks or turquoise or onyx jewelry.

The sincere, friendly proprietors I once befriended are nowhere to be found, replaced by grease balls who man these storefronts with only the all-mighty peso in mind. Each shop has the feel of a carnival midway's aggressive pitch. I find myself constantly repeating the phrase "*Yo no tengo mucho denero.*" (I don't have much money.) My mainstay liquado and eskimo shops, known for crumbling plaster walls and three-legged stools, have been replaced by sleek boutiques built solely with the tourist in mind.

The new number one menace residing in Zihuatanejo is taxi cab drivers; madmen manning freshly-waxed yellow Chevys who shoot down the narrow streets with reckless abandon. They are hungry to snag prospective passengers before the other six cabs working the same *calle* get there first. After our time spent in Barra, these guys make me feel like I've set foot in New York City.

Why this unholy transformation? Tourism, the inevitable beast.

Ten kilometers down the road is Ixtapa, Mexican resort haven of the future. There you will find newly constructed skyscraper resorts complete with private beaches and modern nightclubs, fed and fueled by a major airport whose blacktop runways have replaced the primitive palm-treed terrain where wild animals once grazed.

Ixtapa has become *the* new hot spot with its architecturally awesome designer hotels, discotheques, shopping malls, and recreational opportunities. Windsurfing, over-inflated swordfish junkets, snorkeling, and 18 holes of golf have made Ixtapa an attractive location. With this influx of tourism comes the inevitable: a steep, lecherous rise in the cost of living, dining, and whatever other service requiring cash. This inflation trickles down to Z-Wat, as many of Ixtapa's clientele grow bored of its luxuries and board a hotel-sponsored bus for a visit to see what a charming modern day *native village* has to offer.

It is going to take these vendors a week or two to recognize that our crew is not part of the Ixtapa contingency.

It is also in our best interest to avoid Centro in the late morning, when the shuttles are most active, or we will end up paying Ixtapa prices for our meals as well as any necessities desired. It is disappointing how, around 11 a.m., those Huevos Rancheros we devoured three hours earlier have increased in price by a hundred pesos.

Around two o'clock, when the sun reaches its peak and really jacks up the burners, ninety per cent of the Ixtapa-ites saunter back to their busses, sporting new straw hats while clutching their outta-site new ZIHUATANEJO-FOR A DAY OR A LIFETIME souvenir T-shirts, strategically sold in every corner store. Once aboard, back to the air-conditioned comfort of their hundred-dollar plus a day digs, where they will spend the remainder of another romantic evening in Mexico, watching the sun set from their balconies while eating hotel made *traditional* Mexican meals.

Sorry to say, our Shangri-La has taken larger than baby steps towards bending to the all-mighty lure of the dollar. Positive move for the locals, solar plexus punch to the casual traveler. It is inevitable that many more of these sleepy little villages scattered along the coast will prosper in the years to come.

To my good friend Neil, who was there by my side as we enjoyed discovering the magic Zihuatanejo had to offer more than a decade ago on our first trip to Z-Wat, you certainly called this one, bro, when you told me to get back here quick because it was too good to last. I'm glad to have experienced this region when it was pure, beautiful, honest and unspoiled by the influence of capitalism. Good bye, old Z-Wat, what a grand pipe dream you once were.

My case of *tourista* has receded, along with the rain. It's time to take the gang out, have some breakfast and show them the town. Today's destination will most likely be Playa La Ropa, one of four local beaches we must choose from.

It's also time to hop back into the passenger seat, quit squawking about the good old days, and let Tunes once again steer you through this adventure. We will make the best out of what we have to work with, I'm sure. Now if I can only locate that doggone eskimo stand.

Cheers. The Dangerous one.

11. Nirvana's Playground

Jan 29th: Welcome to Larry Land

Dangerous rallied and was back among the living. With hair stiffly- matted in thick sweaty clumps, eighty-six hours of stubble, and eyes redder than a matador's cape, he rose gingerly from his cot to address the troops. "Let's go get some grub." With Ted and Doris in tow, we stepped onto main street in search of some tasty early morning *desayuno*.

It was early; 7:30 to be exact. The sun was already high in the sky and on its way to delivering another warm Zihuatanejo day. Centro had begun to bustle with activity. Señoras were vigorously sloshing bucket after bucket of water across the cobblestones in front of their storefronts, washing away residual funk and filth left behind by late night revelers.

Men with satchels upon their hips worked the perimeter, meticulously stuffing garbage, stray bottles, and abandoned beer cans into their bags. Further down the road, people watered overhanging flowers, then swept their respective areas clean all the while offering a smile or greeting to those passing by.

Dave had given us fair warning regarding street vendors--The vultures of Z-Wat, he had labeled them. He reminded the two of us to ignore them--to quickly muster up a 'No, Gracias' and move on.

Good fortune provided us with the last available table at Café New Zealand. We were seated by a pleasant English-speaking waiter in a brown safari suit who took our orders then promptly returned with five large urns filled with pulpy fresh-squeezed orange juice.

We inhaled our eggs, salsa, and tortillas in near world record time. Dangerous sat by, unusually somber, damn near sulking. At first I attributed his funk to yesterday's Tourista storm. He revealed the true source of his doleful state; On our way across town he had noticed that tourist-fueled capitalism and inevitable growth, factors he neglected to consider, were more prominent here in his paradise.

As our waiter cleared the table, Dangerous asked what night the local boxing matches would be taking place. Safari suit man frowned. Sorry, boxing was no longer a staple of Z-Wat culture.

In the past two years, more action began taking place outside the ring than on the actual canvas. Excessive drinking and gambling had led to way too many arguments, which eventually escalated into fisticuffs. The inevitable result—fan injuries. Last year a stabbing even occurred! This bit of news was a real bummer for Dave, as he had earmarked the matches as a must-attend highlight for our trip.

Many times, during our long train ride from Nogales, he shared wild vignettes from matches he had attended with great enthusiasm. He painted surrealistic images: sweat dripping from the walls, smoke so thick it hurts your eyes to see, intermingling with the pungent odors of alcohol, along with an adrenaline rush of occupying a seat there at ringside.

Dangerous came alive as he described the high-spirited wagering; the fistfuls of multi-colored peso notes feverishly changing hands following each bout; the occasional brandishing of pistolas, which served to bring about immediate resolution to heated arguments; the intense rivalries between those in the ring and their followers on hand and cheering in large boisterous numbers. Yet, he was quick to point out; true violence was never a consideration, let alone happenstance. Alas, these matches have become folklore and a footnote of Zihuantanejo's past.

Walking down Main Street, towards the picturesque backdrop of Zihuatanejo Bay, you come to Playa Principal. The water before us is seductively inviting until you notice the rainbow glaze created by a layer of oil and diesel skim which seeps out from beneath the scads of motorized fishing boats bobbing within the harbor.

The hub of activity in Centro revolves around a mid-sized basketball court, complete with sturdy ten-foot hoops at each end of the concrete court, designated foul lines and high intensity halogen lights for night games and social events.

Ten minutes past nine in the morning and already two local youth teams, the red jerseys vs the yellows, were lined up doing pre-game drills. A sizable crowd was on hand to cheer on their favorite squads.

Another surrealistic moment; sitting on concrete bleachers sweating at mid-morning, watching hoopsters fully engaged in my favorite sport. In the background, yards away, sea birds match shrieks with the naked niños already in the water, as they fish-dive beneath the surface between the boats bobbing about the oily harbor.

The game began. The dominant red team began firing high arching fifteen footers with impressive accuracy. The first of many whistles blew as one of two very serious young referees called a foul beneath the basket. The crowd booed the call and we joined in.

Only one element was missing. Every time someone would make a basket, the swish sound, associated with the ball dropping through the twine, was replaced by a 'schwang' instead. Here in Z-Wat, cost-effective stainless-steel chains have replaced standard netting. Even though the sound is foreign, the result remains the same. Two points.

When the town game ended, several players hung around, shooting.

I must admit, that so far I've been pretty passive traveling down the road but watching honest to goodness basketball set my jock corpuscles into motion. Longing for some of this action, I hustled back to our room, dug out my high tops from the bottom of my pack, and headed back court side. Surf and sand can wait. Right now, give me the ball, set a solid screen and get out of my way, brother.

Out on the court there was no language barrier. Action replaced words. Two of the players from the earlier game made eye contact and signaled me to join with them for some three on three. I took the court. Here we go.

Even in Mexico the fundamentals were the same: pass, shoot, play defense. Sensing this gringo had no game, our opponents assigned a chubby lad about three inches shorter to guard me.

He got the ball, whirled around to shoot. I swatted his shot back to midcourt. Several of the players on the sideline hooted. Both my teammates smiled and nodded. My teammate with Roberto on his jersey fed me the ball. I faked Chubby into the air and drove to the hoop uncontested. The metal net clanged as the ball dropped through for two. We exchanged high fives.

We played at least a half hour, beating all challengers, until the heat began to knock this gringo for a loop. Another team cued up for a challenge but I muttered "*no mas*" one of the few phrases I had managed to acquire. I crumbled when Roberto asked "*Como te llamas?*". They chuckled and pointed to the names on their jerseys. Embarrassed, I mumbled "Tunes."

We exchanged high fives, they offered "*Hasta Luego Señor Tunes*" and I headed back towards Hotel El Dorado feeling mighty good.

While I was hooping it up, Dave and Ted were busy finding long-term accommodations for the five of us. After several stops at several beachfront locations, they came up big, negotiating a two week stay at the Casa del Playa for four hundred pesos per day. In

Yankee bucks, that's a very economical four dollars per day per person!

Our new landlord, Jose, gave us the grand tour: Casa del Playa consists of five adjoining rooms and ours, Casa **numbero uno**, is the largest. Each room has its own shower, toilet, ceiling fan and beds.

The courtyard is shared by all residents, but each room had its own individual set of table and chairs perfect for taking in the animated beach activity which goes on 24-7 along the boardwalk before us.

We ditched the El Dorado and made our way to the Casa del Playa. Once inside, we turned the ceiling fan on high and reconnoitered our new digs. No stoves harboring rat headquarters, no refrigerators to entice unwanted vermin. This place was gonna be all right.

Let's do a lap. Check things out. Get to know our neighborhood…

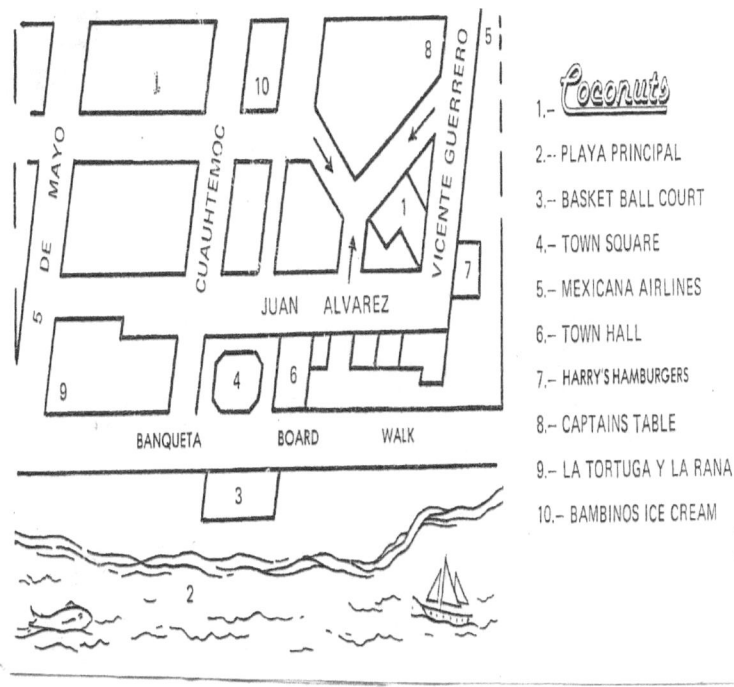

Even though teeming with moored boats of many makes and styles, Playa Principal offered a romantic snapshot of postcard quality, facing south, out towards the open seas and Acapulco. The sun setting on the western horizon cast a luscious raspberry sherbet hue upon the fishing boats, sailboats and catamarans bobbing about in the bay.

For those choosing to splash about in Principal, the shore break is PG-rated; salty and warm with breakers which peak no higher than mid-calf. Once you get out about thirty yards from shore that rainbow layer of motor oils/gasoline becomes detectable by sight as well as smell. Never fear, there are three other beaches along the curve of the bay which are free of this desecration. There you may swim, snorkel, or just float about to your heart's content with nary a fume to be found.

Z-Wat's peak temperature comes in around ninety-one, roughly five degrees warmer than the average in Barra. Even though we're sporting sun-bronzed hides, one lapse of precaution and wicked sunburns will be the consequence.

Playa Principal is the calmest of Zihuantanejo's four bays. It is the family-friendly beach, frequented primarily by locals who bring their entire clan down to the shore's edge in the early evening to cool off with a swim, clothes and all.

Z-Wat's boardwalk runs east to west. Follow the hungry pelicans down to the west end and you come to the fisherman's docks. This is the point of departure for marlin fishing junkets as well as day trips to Ixtapa Island, and skiff transports--a lazy man's shortcut, to Las Gatos--all of which can be booked for reasonable prices.

Let's do an about face heading east, away from the docks, returning to Centro. Here you will come upon tourist-oriented beachfront palapas and shops reminiscent of the ten-cent stores frequented during my childhood.

You'll also come across bins full of every style and size of seashell imaginable, alongside others full of starfish and a wealth of fragile seashell creations and crafts-keen gifts.

Across the way, tucked back behind the hedges on the left-hand side of the street, the local Policia station can be found. It's a small, dank, and unfriendly-looking complex that immediately brings to mind the classic movie Papillion. This locale stands at the top of my list of places to most certainly avoid during our stay.

Stone-faced Federales flank the jail's main entrance, giving all those who pass by their best no-nonsense scowls. They come equipped with M-16 rifles which dangle haphazardly over their right shoulder. Neither greeting nor acknowledgement is exchanged between the law and its citizens.

Their ranks are many, and can be found walking along the docks where fishermen gather, doing laps around town and even lurking about in the shadow of trees located at the edges of the shoreline. They twirl their rifles casually, as if playing with toy guns, all the while maintaining their tough guy demeanor. When a woman passes, they extend their spines and, standing a bit taller while striking a classic macho pose, chest thrust out, gut sucked in.

Step out of line, there will be hell to pay.

A stone's throw away from Casa del Playa, a modest friendly seafood shack specializes in Ceviche and Coctels de Camerones, shrimp cocktails. They are noted for their potent horseradish-laced sauce capable of searing the nasal passages of even the most hardcore and daring cocktail sauce connoisseurs.

Dave points out the rectangular erasable white board and marker--our menu--hanging above where the day's catch is listed, in English as well as Español.

"I'd be willing to bet the reason it's erasable is so, come weekends, when the largest number of tourists are on hand, adjustments are made. For instance, today, a low traffic weekday, the price for ceviche is twenty pesos. With one sweep of a cloth, that price can be instantly bumped upwards, to let's say one hundred pesos and those Ixtapa-ites won't even bat an eye."

"If we want to be treated like the regulars, it's in our best interest to spend some time and a few pesos here each day. If we get to know the owner we won't get lumped in with the tourists, which will keep our price on par with what these locals pay, *comprende*?"

Our trip down the boardwalk ends back where it started, at the Casa del Playa. If you continue east, down towards the canal, you will eventually find your way to the other north end beach, Playa Madera. This is another beach popular with locals, dotted by architecturally-dull mid-range hotels built snugly into the rocky hillside. Madera is much cleaner than Principal, and at the opposite end of the bay where the fishing boats are moored.

From here, we hike straight up a steep set of steps through a residential district before heading south along an steeply elevated two-lane paved road which leads to Playa La Ropa.

Back at our casa, Ted and Doris were deep in reading mode, Kid was crafting another letter bound for Longview and Dangerous had called dibs on first shower. I sat outside, soaking in the view from our new patio.

At the far end of the property, the screen door to numero cinco stood wide open. The gentle strumming of acoustic guitar floated on the air, chords slightly out of tune, yet the emergence of live music within earshot set me in immediate motion.

Above the doorway, a freshly-lacquered 1x4 hand-carved cedar plaque hung catawampus, into which someone had painstakingly etched, **LARRY LAND**.

A cardboard Corona case filled with upside-down empties served as a doorstop. I followed the sound of off-key B flat chords, peering casually inside.

On the couch sat a pale shirtless skinny dude, legs stretched across the coffee table as he played. He was busy assaulting his steel strings with one of his empty Coronas, using it as a slide, playing a white boy's version of bottleneck blues. Muddy Waters, Dickey Betts, Duane Allman or Lowell George, he was not.

With each chord he struck, he hummed along in a mournful tonal manner until he reached the last line of the final verse. When he realized he had an audience, he put down his ciggie and gave me a congenial toothy smile. "Yo, man, come on in, eh?"

Canadian descent easily identified. "Wanna cigarette?" Enough bad habits already on my plate, I declined.

"Wanna brew?" He handed me a Corona, lukewarm and two hours flat. I nodded in gratitude.

"I'm Larry, from Whitehorse, Canada, eh? I came here to drink beer, write compelling songs and drink beer."

This was Larry's fifth visit to Zihautanejo. I asked what magical factor or factors kept him coming back year after year.

"They've got a Corona factory just ootside of town. There I can get *the* cheapest beer in the entire world; aboot eleven cents apiece, after I return the bloody empties. That's why, come the first of December, you'll find me packing my Gibson and trusty hammock that's hanging just ootside. I throw in three or so sets of clean shirts and shorts, break my piggy bank, then head right back here, eh, to good old Nirvana's Playground."

"You like the blues?" I nodded, which pleased him.

"Got one here I wrote last night. Care to give it an ear, Van Gogh?"

He strummed a butchered C chord, then took off.

"Down at La Flamita
I met a cross-eyed señorita
Busy chewin' on a plate of raw meat-ah
But she sure thought I was cool.

Moved here from east New York
But her kisses taste like pork
And I felt like one lost dork
'Cause she made me her lovin' fool

On a plate of Rellenos
She huffed a half ounce of cocaine-o
That her ex-friend cut with Drano
Thus, she bid this world farewell

And as she laid there sadly dyin'
My eyes turned red from cryin'
It's the truth, my heart was dying'
For my sweet Flamita Nell."

He set his guitar down, finished the final inch of foam from *my* Corona, then looked up. "You've just been exposed to the French-Canadian Blues. Pretty fookin' cool, eh?"

I was speechless. A true Canadian epic. Look out world, live from Nirvana's Playground, heeeere's Larry!

"Awesome, Larry, I really liked the way you subtly managed to work all the references to culinary items into each verse. Sheer brilliance, man."

His eyes twinkled. "Thanks mate. I knocked that one oot in little over two hours." He snapped his fingers. "Just like that."

I shuddered at the thought of Larry and Kid hooking up; the two of them sitting here in numero cinco, Kid keeping the beat on his practice pad while Larry fingers off-key blues, trusty beer bottle slide giving birth to blood blisters, as they jam all through the night.

"I don't mean to be rude or nothin' but I've got to ask you to leave now." He nodded to the bed across the room. "My roommate's coming back any minute now and I've got to shower and go ooot fer dinner."

"Larry's got a lady?"

"Naw, it's my mum and she's kind of odd aboot company."

No further explanation was needed. This scenario had the potential to only get weirder. We shook hands, I thanked him for the brew as well as the tunes, then exited the way I had come.

"Hey, stop by on Thursday. It's my birthday. I'm hitting thirty-seven and, as I do every year, I'm going to drink my age in Coronas. Kind of a ritual, you know, one for every year I've been kickin' arooond, eh?"

I nodded and promised to check back into LARRY LAND. It looked like there was never a dull moment in Z-Wat, or should I say, Nirvana's Playground, eh?

12. Adventures in Paradise

Could this be heaven?

Every day we practice the *4 S's*, in no particular order: Sunshine, swimming, surfing (body, at least) and snorkeling.

The *Mañana* Method continues to weave its spell upon us. No worries, cares, or real-world commitments of any consequence to be dealt with. No commitments to bog me down or foul my mellow yellow constitution.

Here in Zihuatanejo, no newspapers printed in English are to be found. World affairs are irrelevant. Everything is flowing in a positive mode. Slow down. Hang loose. Unwind.

Add a healthy dose of basketball to my everyday routine, two hours of swimming, a plate full of succulent red snapper, Camerones Diabla or Dave's favorite--dog brain tacos and you've pretty well-defined easy living.

Don't get me wrong. We don't just lie around like lazy seals, rotating side to side each half hour to maintain an even tan. Most of each day revolves around well-chosen healthy endeavors.

It's a twenty-minute hike to and from Playa La Ropa, our daily hangout. Our legs churn up quarter-mile-long steep embankments leading to the main road. Even though we climb them every day, these hilly inclines make hamstrings burn, calves ache, and your heart pound like a drum as you reach the top.

We swim for hours in the warm salt water and, I've been told, swimming is just about the best exercise one can participate in. Salt water eliminates nasty toxins, so we've been cleansing our systems daily while logging hours of cardiovascular activity.

After dinner, when the temperature has dropped to a balmy seventy- five or so, it's hoops time. To say we are getting in shape is an understatement. It's also a fact none of us are having trouble going to sleep each night.

Even though I'm averaging about eight deep, uninterrupted hours per night, my dreams still raise a bit of havoc with my psyche.

We have been in Mexico for almost a month, far from home and friends, yet every night my dream scenarios still revolve around life and friends back home, as if I've never left.

I may give the impression that my experience has been one big bowl of cherries, yet that impression is not completely true.

Even with the amazing stimuli I have experienced, an occasional wave of melancholy, or moodiness, occasionally finds a way to creep into my psyche.

I miss my cultural necessities—music, movies and, yes, even television. I miss friends and family and hope they are all doing fine. Then I watch Kid, ever-so silent, taking no challenges, pounding that pad while the rest of us feed off this adventure we're caught up in. Then all is right once more.

Our first Saturday in Z-Wat, tourism, something we've yet to experience, came down around us The hordes had arrived. There in the majestic bay was the Love Boat, its massive girth swallowing up the majority of Playa Principal.

Welcome to a typical Saturday morning at the peak of tourist season in Zihuatanejo.

Very soon the first boat of pale-fleshed potential customers arrives, scouring main street; hungry for trinkets, treasures, souvenirs, and most importantly, a deal.

We watched from the basketball court bleachers as boat after boat was lowered over the side down into the harbor below. Closer they came; seven, eight, nine, ten boats full.

A carnival atmosphere awaited their arrival. Since most shops carry many of the same items, the art of the hustle is crucial in luring potential customers to one's business.

The streets were suddenly full of new faces, pale-skinned middle-aged men and women sporting souvenir T-shirts purchased at previous shore leaves--Puerto Vallarta, Mazatlán—they came and they conquered.

The male species came ashore wearing plaid shorts and dress shoes with knee high black compression socks pulled up high and tight as possible to hide skinny legs and varicose-veins.

Most women, middle-aged as well, arrived in festive cotton flower print dresses and new sandals. Shopping was the sole feverish agenda on their minds. They pointed, posed, and snapped their Instamatics enthusiastically, documenting their fantastic journey to share with bingo buddies Edna and Stew, back home, once their cruise returned stateside.

Before mistakenly being lumped in with the Love Boat crowd, we grabbed our gear, passed on breakfast, and headed off to Playa La Ropa.

Stretching out southward towards the mouth of the Pacific, Playa La Ropa, the most popular of Z-Wat's beaches, presents a near-mile of flat, moderately-populated sand. Choose a spot, toss down your blanket, and indulge in sun lover's bliss.

Many small palapas are found a short distance removed from the waterline. Each offers abundant shade as well as modest restaurants and each has its own personality, or niche. Rumor has it local *herb* is attainable, should one spend a few days frequenting the same establishment chatting up the regulars.

Beach vendors drift by once or twice a day at most, pestering those who make eye contact, flogging their beads, jewelry, or blankets.

Perhaps because today was Saturday or perhaps because others, seeking sanctuary from the tour boat intruders roaming *Centro* had gravitated here, La Ropa was much more active than usual. Dangerous suggested this to be the perfect time to take a hike to Las Gatas.

The southern end of Playa La Ropa fades into a small foot trail winding up along the rocks and around the bend, alternating between footpath, rocks, then back to footpath again. Those rugged enough to challenge this route eventually wind up at Las Gatas, the fourth and most secluded of the four Z-Wat beaches.

It is accessible from Centro by a short one-peso boat ride, across the bay. Being the adventuresome (as well as fiscally frugal) enthusiasts we are, we will always choose the rocky footpath to reach this destination.

Playa Las Gatas means beach of the cats, even though it was not actually named after the feline species, but rather for nurse sharks who inhabited these waters in ancient times. They were not man eaters, in fact actually quite harmless, yet bore catlike whiskers-- henceforth, Las Gatas. Just a little folklore passed along by the Dangerous one.

Las Gatas' seclusion is a major selling point, but the main draw is its man-made reef, superb for snorkeling. As the story goes, centuries ago this area was inhabited by an ancient ruler, Calzontzín, one of the last kings of the Tarascan Indians from Michoacán, who built the stone reef for his many wives to swim without worry. This reef remains intact today, still responsible for the currents which lend to excellent snorkeling conditions.

Fins and snorkels in good working condition are readily available for ten pesos per day. We rented three pairs between the five of us, then took turns making lengthy excursions along the man-made reef. Kid even participated enthusiastically in this aquatic activity without knowing that many of the small fish that swam around us were baby barracudas.

For beginners such as myself, swimming below the clear shallow surface alongside schools of tropical native fishies (which include those flesh-nibbling baby barracudas) as well as following the colorful coral that extends the length of the reef, Las Gatas is a great experience. It was safe, sane, inexpensive, and a ton of fun.

In Barra, our evening cultural resources tended to be a bit on the dull side. Here in Z-Wat our evenings require a much higher level of energy.

Last night, around seven thirty, A Ryder van backed up to the basketball court and several worker bees began unloading band equipment. Two electric guitars, bass, B-3 organ, drums and timbales, and a modest stack of amplifiers were unpacked and set upon the risers.

By nine o'clock Gruppo Shark, a popular local Latin-flavored rock band walked through a hasty yet promising sound check before nodding to their sound man. Let the show begin.

The locals have come spiffed up for a Saturday night on the town. Many of the ladies are gorgeous, in long flowing floral dresses accentuating their natural attributes, the gents, natty in dress shirts, occasional safari jackets, slacks and dress boots.

A pungent blend of perfumes and after-shave collide on the warm night air as Gruppo Shark provided an infectious groove, embraced by all on hand.

The first set concluded and I took this opportunity to wander off into Centro. Just a few blocks away I came upon a local groceria with a very impressive liquor section.

The people of Zihuatanejo appear to have a unbridled passion for brandy. Well over two dozen species of the gut-warming essence was available in dusty pints, fifths, as well as the half-gallon portion.

I was just about to take a walk on the wild side and nab a pint of El Presidente, when a voice came from behind.

"Looking for a real *ass-kicker*, friend?"

A tall mustachioed gringo with long, wavy, salt and pepper hair smiled. He wore a FISHERMEN MAKE BETTER LOVERS tank top, and his gray eyes were slits redder than a stoned tie-dyed Deadhead. Beside him stood well over three hundred pounds of burly dude who pointed at the shelf before me.

"Are you looking for socially stimulating substances or would you prefer something guaranteed to put your wagon wheels in the ditch so you can just sit and watch the stars shine for a while?

If your purpose is trolling for trouser trout, stick with sissy Tecate. It's dirt cheap and efficient. But, if you want to go the distance and end up stinkier than a skunk, go for that bottle of Anise--Tastes like licorice turds but the locals claim it's got an opium base guaranteed to kick your ass quicker than Chuck Norris."

I noticed there were two species: One, with a monkey grinning standing there waving, the other, same monkey seated in a chair. "Which carried more bounce per ounce?"

"Depends on if you want to rock or want to roll. I've been told the monkey sitting in the chair comes complete with an opium base." He winked, just like the monkey. "Ya know, ***KABOOMY!***"

I snagged the last pint of monkey in chair, offered thanks. One question remained. "How should I drink this stuff?"

"Orally, dude." Both snickered. I considered handing back a smart-ass retort until I noticed the big guy's tattoo--a dagger and skeleton head combo, which ran the length of his beefy, muscular forearm.

Time to rephrase that sentence: "Correction, how best does this stuff go down--straight or mixed?"

"I recommend on ice." Salt and pepper's burly bucko replied with a deep gravely growl some would consider gruff. "No mixer."

I nodded my thanks as I headed to the counter.

"Where ya from?" This was getting personal.

"Bellingham; as in Washington."

That earned a grin from the bigger of the two. "No shit--we live just up north. Ferndale!" He stuck out his huge paw and shook my hand like a long-lost brother.

"I'm Daryl, and this loco bastard here is Richard."

They were fishermen, hanging out at Playa La Ropa for at least one more month. Following the completion of halibut season each of the past three years, these two migrated to Z-Wat for "drinking, smoking and playing cards." Daryl explained. We chatted a few minutes more as we paid for our respective bottles, then said goodbye.

We played the 'Don't I know you from somewhere?' game until his sidekick, a wild and wavy-haired dude who could have doubled for Jimmy Buffett without the trademark flowered shirts, arrived with a sack full of ciggies, mixers, and chips.

Small world time: Both were Alaskan fisherman, as mentioned, based out of Ferndale Washington, a burg ten miles north of Bellingham.

I was just a few steps out the door when I heard, "Hey Bellingham,"

I turned around and there was Daryl, holding a large cup of ice in my direction. "Fire stoker for the monkey juice--Knock yourself out, have fun and most important of all, **stay out of the local jail**. It's noted for lice."

With one last boomer of a laugh, he stuffed his oversized body into the undersized passenger seat of the exhaust-spewing military-style mid-sixties jeep there at the curb. The shocks groaned, the clutch ground, and I was left swimming in the fog the muffler-less vehicle emitted. They were off, swerving their way back up into the hills to Playa La Ropa.

Was there any validity to Richard's claim to the contents I was consuming? He may very well have known a sucker when he saw one.

It was quite possible he and Daryl were back at Playa La Ropa, swinging in hammocks, laughing their mezcal-loaded asses off recalling the gullible Bellingham gringo they had just suckered into purchasing the awful rot-gut tasting pint.

As midnight drew near, the street dance crowd was hitting their stride as Gruppo Shark continued churning out sexy Latin rhythms. The throng of curious American onlookers had thinned out considerably. The night now belonged to the people of Zihuatanejo.

As the clock struck twelve, the energy level began to soar. The court quickly became a shoulder-to-shoulder mass of whirling sweaty bodies.

Dangerous and Kid checked out shortly thereafter, just as I was being led out onto the dance floor by a well upholstered middle-aged mamasita bent on teaching her toasty gringo partner the Meringue. We had an insanely good time dancing long into the night until sometime close to 2 a.m. when Gruppo Shark finally called it a night.

Dawn arrived and I impressed my mates by rising with nary a delirium tremor from my monkeyshines. I had a barrel of fun, yet can say with confidence, Tunes will. remain reluctant to shake hands with Mr. Monkey for the remainder of this trip.

13. Kevin's Crew

Time to introduce the rest of the inhabitants of Casa Del Playa:

You have met Larry next door in numero cinco. Most days our Canadian composer can be found snoring in his hammock, hat covering his face, a Corona just an arm's length away.

On our other side, in numero dos, resides an interesting quartet of from the Midwest, pale snowbirds, from Minnesota.

First, there's Kevin and Alice. Kevin's a diminutive guy, capable of being charming and friendly, but with an extremely jealous nature which surfaces whenever someone strikes up a conversation with Alice. We give Kevin his space.

Ray and Hank, also from Minnesota, round out the foursome. Ray, forty-one, has Multiple Sclerosis. The right side of his body has been moderately crippled from birth, yet he still has the ability to use his arms and can walk to a very limited degree.

He spends his days confined to a wheel chair, looked after by his surly nurse, Hank. Ray's speech is difficult to understand and he often loses use of his arms, yet what this man can accomplish with his feet more than compensates for his condition. His determination has resulted in seven broken collarbones due to innumerable tumbles. That same spirit has brought him all the way here to Casa Del Playa in Zihuatanejo.

Each day Ray spends an hour or two out in our shared area painting pictures with his feet. Hank will lay out a canvas, move Ray into a well-shaded area and turn him loose with a brush, palette, and paints which provide a wide spectrum of colors, then let him paint.

His technique is impressionistic in tone. To watch his diligence, and intensity completing a canvas is humbling. He has promised to send Dave a favorite from his collection once he returns to the Land of 10,000 Lakes.

Dave and Ray have struck up a warm friendship. Each evening the two of them find time to sit out at the verandah, talking and laughing like old friends. I admire the patience my friend has been blessed with.

Whenever Ray struggles with getting a thought across he uses his feet to write notes to express his thoughts. Dave sincerely enjoys their time spent together, seemingly taking more of an interest in his needs than Ray's roommates do.

In Dave's eyes, Hank puts very little passion into his job. He's snappy and surly with Ray, prone to pouting and he hasn't seemed to go out of his way to make this vacation a pleasurable experience for his patient.

Hank knows Dave would like to snap his scrawny little neck, so he summons up his best professional demeanor whenever the Dangerous one is around. Ray has already promised Dave that once they get back to the states, he's going to hand Hank his walking papers.

Thursday evening Dave and Ted took Ray to watch them play squash. They left him alone for a moment at the foot of the stairs leading to the spectator's area while they checked out equipment, all the while trying to figure out how they were going to get him up the treacherous flight of steps to watch.

They came back to find Ray already halfway up the stairs, wheelchair below. Dangerous took hold of his arm to help. Ray shook loose. "Let go, dammit!!!" They asked if he was sure he could make it and received an adamant "Yes!"

He did.

The main topic of early morning conversation at Casa Del Playa, following the street dance, focused on grumpy Kevin and how his hair-trigger temper took him on a detour to No Man's Land and the amazing transformation which followed.

Around the time I was getting out on the court getting hands on instruction on how to perform the Winkin' Monkey Mambo, Kevin and Alice were on hand taking in the festivities as well.

Shortly after 1 a.m., a friendly somewhat inebriated local invited Alice to join him for a dance. Immediately Kevin's fuse was lit. In an impulsive moment of jealously he popped the fellow right there on the dance floor.

As fate would have it, two federales were holding up a wall a few yards away. They quickly cuffed him and took him off to headquarters. To Kevin and Alice, neither knowing a lick of Spanish, this situation quickly became a nightmare. She tearfully watched the scenario unfold, all her pleas for leniency falling on uncomprehending ears.

Once at the jailhouse, our hotheaded neighbor was swiftly and unceremoniously tossed behind bars to spend the night amid the cockroaches, drunks, lost souls, and losers.

Alice hurried back to the Casa Del Playa and pounded desperately on our door, pleading for help.

Between sobs, she recounted the incident to Dave and Ted. They wiped their sleep-encrusted eyes and offered to test their Spanish-speaking negotiating skills by accompanying her back to the local station house.

Ted recommended Alice bring her purse and all funds on hand as well. He also requested my empty bottle of winking monkey, in case he needed to pull an ace from his sleeve, should negotiations take a turn for the worse. Fortunately, the bottle was still in the trash can outside our room.

They pleaded their case in fluent Spanish, still, the disinterested desk sergeant on duty merely shrugged, pretending not to comprehend their request. This forced Ted to lay down his trump card earlier than anticipated.

He produced the empty bottle of Anise from his day pack, set it before the sergeant and pleaded temporary Anise-induced insanity on the part of incarcerated Kevin.

The emergence of the monkey actually got a chuckle from the man behind the desk. He said that if one wanted to drink the monkey, he best not end up acting like one. Time for plan B.

As soon as Alice produced a five-hundred peso note, the sergeant's inability to consider leniency began to soften. She pulled out another five-hundred peso note, and, just like that, all was forgiven. Kevin was a free man. Sarge got the key, farted loudly as he sauntered back to the holding cells, then returned with Alice's humble-pie guy.

Our punch-flinging amigo was overwhelmed with gratitude, for once happy to see his casa mates. No one requested any grisly details about what exactly he had seen or been subjected to during his two hours in captivity. That sacred experience is his and his alone.

The following morning an amazing transformation had taken place. Kevin's scowling persona gave way to a Minnesotan with a smile and a warm salutation for all those he encountered.

Saturday night is movie night in Zihuatanejo. More cinema under the stars, and we were just as excited for celluloid stimulus as the locals.

Earlier in the week we passed the local theater as two young workers were pasting color posters featuring this week's feature atop last week's show. No more Hercules, Mexican mummies or B grade

Bronson flicks. No sir, we were about to be treated to a shark flick. Dangerous suggested we get their early as the typical Mexican citizen has an intense and reverent affinity for shark movies.

We arrived at seven for a seven thirty show time and queued up in a line stretching halfway down the block. Energetic chatter and enthusiasm whirled about the many animated patrons anxious to watch man get devoured by finned fiends. Dave was right--this shark stuff had them primed.

Everyone who was anyone in Z-Wat seemed to be on hand. *Niños* sat next to winos, the wealthy alongside the poor, store owners and street sweepers shared greetings as well as hearty swigs from various pints inconspicuously smuggled into this event.

The sun dropped below the hills and the projector started to roll. Dave produced a pint of rum from his pocket and started passing it down our row. I declined, kidneys and brain cells still recovering from the previous evening's workout. I passed it along to the elderly Mexican gentleman beside me.

On the screen, a monstrous mechanical shark took its first victim, tearing the leg off a screaming *señorita* caught too far from shore for her own good. She emitted one final bloodcurdling scream and the crowd cheered wildly. Five bloody attacks later, Kid got up and hustled out, leaving us a pleasant span of elbow room for the remainder of the show.

As the credits rolled, the majority of moviegoers expressed their approval by continuing to clap and cheer until the last credit rolled off the screen. What a great way to start a Saturday night.

Tomorrow we will need all the physical strength and endurance we can muster, as we are off to legendary Playa Majahua to test our mettle as we ride God's waves.

14. Majahua

Imagine the ultimate beach: Secluded, pristine, uninhabited shoreline, stretching out well over a hundred yards. Your feet are cushioned by a toasty blanket of white granules--sand that crunches beneath each footprint you leave behind. By noon it becomes so hot you must wear either flip flops or sandals in order to walk upon its delicate surface.

Majahua has remained a well-kept secret due to its remote location, and substantial hiking distance away from the heart of Zihuatanejo. Not many individuals are willing to undertake the steep laborious jaunt required to enjoy this majestic locale. Far too many other beaches are closer in proximity, yet none provide the elements which make Playa Majahua so special.

To swim or body surf here one must be aware Majahua has a rip tide more severe, even dangerous for those not paying attention of just how far from shore you are swimming, compared to the other beach fronts one has to choose from.

To say Majahua is off the beaten path is truly an understatement. Indulge in this solitude. Pick a spot and have a happy day; This pipe dream is real. Outside of a cluster of coconut trees far from shore, shade is nonexistent. Best arrive early and plan to leave before the sun hits its stride straight above. Water, or Agua Purificada, is *the* most essential item to bring with you. Bring an abundant amount, if possible. Sun screen 30 or even 50 is recommended along with a and a visor or cap to repel the fierce midday heat as well.

Here twelve-foot El Supremo waves, tailor-made for Grade A body surfing, await the more skilled surf enthusiasts. Each breaks with a thunderous roar, dropping you into waist-deep foamy landing pads when your ride comes to an end. As a result, Playa Majahua boasts the afore-mentioned powerful undertow, one which needs to be always respected by those participating.

Dangerous' last visit to Zihuatanejo ended prematurely when he miscalculated the crest of a whopper breaker. At the peak of what was intended to be last ride of the day, his wave broke too close to the shoreline. He ended up a whirling tumble bug, with a dislocated shoulder, a broken collarbone and a painfully long walk back to civilization.

Following breakfast we filled our day packs with the essentials, then were off, past the marina, over a rustic semi-swaying footbridge leading to Hotel Tres Marias, into the heart of old Z-Wat, far removed from the commercial zone. Today we were a party of seven; Ted and Doris, Dangerous, Kid and I, with Kevin and Miss Alice bringing up the rear.

We passed a large gathering of cheerful Señoras washing baskets of laundry in a small freshwater stream flowing in from the bay. They smiled and waved as they scrubbed intensely. We returned their greetings, then began our trek away from town, off towards the residential zone, home for the town's lower income population.

We walked on past rows of ghetto-like shanties, passing masses of children at play, and legions of lazy dogs, so thin you could count each rib. From here the sidewalk bent back to our left, then followed a partially paved asphalt road with a steep seemingly endless grade.

Although only nine in the morning, the heat reflecting off the pavement upped the ante by at least ten degrees and our well-conditioned calf muscles took on that tight burning associated with shin splints.

Onward we went, legs continuing to strain and ache as the uphill grade continued to escalate. Each time the earth presented an incline I anticipated the summit to be just ahead. Miracle denied

Four years ago, this asphalt pathway currently melting our tire-treaded huaraches was dirt and gravel; a footpath so narrow you were required to traverse single file. More indications progress would further alter this path lie just ahead.

Dangerous snarled and snorted, then delivered an impressive string of indignant vernacular as he spotted a long row of land survey stakes, driven deeply along the left side of the pavement.

Feverishly he began yanking up stake after stubby stake, then chucked them off into the vegetation as far as stakes were possible to be chucked. This was such an inspiring act of thumbing one's nose at progress, I decided to join in the protest.

"That should set those money-grubbing land barons back at least another decade." The Dangerous one declared once the last stake had been successfully uprooted.

Continuing uphill for another mile we finally reached the crest. Here the pavement ended. Civilization, as we knew it, had tossed in the towel. We paused for a long, well-deserved oxygen break before beginning a slight descent, down a narrow path which led into lush jungle terrain.

The trail was primitive, thinning in width with each step we took, deeper and deeper into the heavy vegetation. We had to bend slightly in order to avoid being whacked in the forehead by huge low-hanging branches whose leaves grew twice the size of any I had ever seen before.

In the distance the roar of the Pacific resounded, justifying this arduous trek. There really is a Majahua. Steeper and steeper we went, and with each step taken, the ocean's cadence increased in magnitude.

A three-foot-long lime green iguana lumbered lazily across our path, flicking its long red tongue our way before warily blending back into the tall jungle grass. No one bothered to turn a head to see if Kid, bringing up the rear, had begun experiencing massive heart palpitations.

Around the next bend a clearing provided our first glimpse of Majahua. A hearty cheer arose from all. We stood silently, taking in the white foam breakers as they rolled the length of the bay. Words cannot do justice to how magical our first glimpse of Majahua was. *You had to be there* nails it best.

Single file, we edged our way, down the tricky trail. The salty sea breeze brought potent and unfamiliar scents from exotic plants and flowers, stirring my olfactory factory with their unusual fragrances.

Once around a final bend, we had, at last, arrived. What an awesome sight to behold!

We made our way across fallen coconut trees, knee-high protruding rocks and half a football field's worth of driftwood until we reached the flat, virgin, sun bleached sand where our explorer's instincts took over.

Time to take in the many yards of pristine beach we had all to ourselves.

Sea birds watched from a large boulder at the closest end of the beach as Ted and Kid, in unusually high spirits, began chucking a Frisbee, airing it out thirty to forty yards per toss. While the Frisbee flew, the rest of us jockeyed for prime locations to throw down our blankets.

A thick grove of coconut trees ran the length of the beach, leading off into dense jungle. I was hesitant to pursue any extended explorations into its depths, not wanting to push my luck by going where I may not be welcome.

Earlier, midway up the first Hill of Death, Dave brought up a few simple do's and don'ts designed to make the most of our initial visit to Mahujua.

"Beware of the possibility of encountering banditos. It's unlikely, especially due to the size of our party.

"In the dozen times that I've been here, I've never had a bad experience, but I've heard horror stories of others not quite as lucky. Keep your wits about you and your eyes open. Even though it seems like we have the beach to ourselves there is a very good chance that we are not alone. I suggested you all leave anything of value back in the room. If you brought a watch or your wallet, don't leave them in plain sight. DO NOT offer temptation of *any* kind."

One look back at the dense coconut grove rolling off into the countryside and you understand that if someone were watching us, they would have one helluva home-court advantage.

"Since we've all brought our day packs it would be wise if one, or more of us stay back on the blankets at all times to discourage temptation."

This advice was not lost on me. As I learned back in Barra, if you turn your head for ten seconds, things can disappear very quickly.

"Finally, if any locals do show up, do your best to ignore them. We do not need to make any new friends. Don't be rude, just do your own thing and let them do their own thing. We didn't come here for a fiesta, si?"

With those guidelines in mind, it was surf time. Dangerous was already on his way towards the water, back to where this very same crashing surf had unceremoniously kicked his butt.

The surf did not disappoint. Big booming breakers roll in, one after another, each with a thundering crash and a foamy landing pad, as thick as the richest head of Guinness Stout an Irishman could ever hope to pour.

In Barra, we cavorted on three-foot baby waves. Playa Majahua's breakers roll down on you from three times that height. When the bottom falls out things can get ugly, as you are sent tumbling towards shore. Each time I get to this part of the ride, I recall Dave's separated shoulder and back out before the crest, never getting the full rush yet have a great ride just the same.

It is also important to respect potential undertow. Dave offers this hint: "Pick a spot down the beach to your left to estimate how far away from shore you are. I choose those rocks jutting out around that corner for my sight line. If I find myself inching further out than that, I'll be getting my ass back home really quick, or else."

Come mid-afternoon, "or else" was put to the test.

Body surfing is physically demanding. Between working your way out to meet a wave, finding the crest, and completing a ride, you can become exhausted in short time.

Dave, Ted, and I had just returned to shore following a vigorous session of whompin' and were getting ready to kick back for Kevin, Alice, and Kid to take their turn in the waves.

Well over three hours spent in the Majahua heat left me woozy and worn. I had just applied sun screen, drained my bottle of warm agua purificada and was considering a well-deserved siesta when a piercing scream came from the water. Alice had drifted well beyond her established boundary.

Only knee deep, Kid and Kevin showed panic and confusion. Time quickly growing crucial, Dangerous made a move. Quickly he bolted into the surf. Alice continued drifting away, growing smaller and smaller.

Tense moments followed. Dave grew closer, urging her to stop panicking and paddle towards shore. He too was drifting dangerously further away. Not yet in dire straits, Alice continued to flounder.

Finally, Dave, with Kevin beside him, reached the distraught young lady and together they began the long haul back to shore, working against the tenacious pull of the undertow with every ounce of strength they could muster until all three had returned, shaking, exhausted, and emotionally spent.

For the second time in less than twenty-four hours, Kevin felt indebted to our crew for services rendered. Alice, trembling and as close to going into shock as one could possibly be, managed endearing hugs for their efforts. It was as good a time as any to wrap this party up. Dog-tired and worn from our experience, we began the long trek back to civilization.

We left *Playa Mahujua* at that absolute peak of the day; when old Mr. Sol shows neither respect nor regard for those beneath his unrelenting rays.

Packs slung over fricasseed shoulders, we began another shin-burner, this time up the rugged beach entryway, moving slower than elephants in a conga line. The steep grade we had wound down upon arrival was now Bitch of Bitches heading back up.

At the summit, we paused to catch our breath. The most strenuous leg of our homeward journey was behind us. When we reached town, Kevin and Alice took the road to the right while we veered left. Dave said a treat for a hard day of whomping was in order so we followed behind…

The ultimate reward for a long day at the beach lay ahead, at the edge of town--a reward as highly-touted by our compadre as the infamous canceled boxing matches: Ice cold Eskimos (pronounced Ski-Moes). We made our way home in slow motion as Dangerous led us to Zihuantanejo's Eskimo stand.

More than once on the train Dave spun tales of ice cold eskimos; guaranteed to make your brain freeze and your internal thermostat purr like a kitten. He assured me that my first Eskimo would be a highlight of our trip.

"Aha!" Dangerous pointed across the street to a shadowy storefront where three idle blenders, one metal card table, five unoccupied stools, and a very bored looking young señorita waited for customers to materialize. She appeared to be on the verge of her own siesta, elbow on her chin, entertained solely by a mangy mutt lying in the shade, scratching intensely at flea infestation. This was the world famous eskimo stand?

Kevin and Alice opted to head back, so we five remaining deep-fried muchachos plopped down upon the squeaky stools. Sweaty and thirsty, we sat patiently, waiting for the rather unfriendly looking Eskimo Goddess to step forth and take our orders.

"*Eskimos aqui?*" Dave inquired.

She nodded reluctantly, as if we had interrupted her dog watching.

"*Cinco eskimos, con Rompope, por favor.*"

Rompope is a fifty-seven-proof liqueur with a Hollandaise base. The crucial ingredients are Leche (milk), Azucar (sugar) and our old standby, alcohol.

How Dave stumbled upon this concoction he refuses to reveal. But after walking several miles through prime-time heat and jungle, I was more than willing to participate in Eskimo Madness.

Our Eskimo Goddess shook her head. She had run out of Rompope, and Dave was adamant that without Rompope, an Eskimo is mere pedestrian whimsy.

He growled, then left us sitting there like four weary bumps on a log while he disappeared around the corner. Before we could debate whether to leave or hang out just a little longer, he was back with two large bottles, which he handed across the counter to the girl.

She accepted them with a surprised shrug. *"Cinco?"*

"Si" he added, ever so politely.

Then, with a touch of exaggerated drama, Eskimo King leaned forward emphatically adding, *"Señorita-necessito muy fria!"* (very cold)

She went to work, liberally adding about a quarter of the first bottle into each silver cup before sending each blender into action. Dangerous gestured it would be acceptable to add even more to the whirring cylinders. Ice thoroughly pureed, she poured equal portions into five plastic cups, then poked a straw into each before setting them before us. Five spent beach buddies sucked the ice-cold delicacies to the bottom in silence.

Suddenly, Kid crumpled to his knees, holding his head, and writhing from side to side. "Brain Freeze!! Brain Freeze!!" was all he could offer as he rubbed his temples trying to make the invisible spike sticking through his head go away.

Having experienced this agony myself, I've come to the conclusion the only antidote for Brain Freeze is resorting quickly to Zen. Both hands to your temples may help blot out the sledgehammer banging inside your cranium. After forty-five seconds the throbbing agony should subside. Now, slow down, or you will be holding your skull again.

Goddess looked at Dave with concern. Had she contributed to this poor fool's condition? Why was he lying there moaning, as if near death? And why were we all just sitting there, laughing?

A handful of inquisitive locals passing by paused to observe the Americano, on his knees, holding his head while his mates watched passively. Sometimes so cold, so uncaring, those damn Americans can be.

Dave turned and addressed their concern. *"Mi amigo esta una grande cerdo"* (My friend is a big pig).

They too laughed, then went about their business. Ted stepped forth. "Anybody game for round two?"

No one had to twist my arm. The blenders began whirling again. *Eskimos* for all-except Señor Cerdo, still busy rubbing his temples.

When all was said and done, we downed three apiece and left the remaining half bottle of Rompope with our new friend; a thank you for a job well done.

On each of the four remaining days in Z-Wat we made sure to make an Eskimo session a mandatory ritual, each afternoon, just before siesta.

15. Adios, Amigo

Thursday Feb. 8th: Kid pulls the plug.

We have spent an incredible two weeks in Zihuatanejo. It's difficult leaving this Shangri-La behind, but our timetable dictates we move forward.

"Many new adventures await," I have been assured.

Our game plan is to head south to Puerto Escondido, test the vibes, then head into the interior, to Oaxaca, for an introduction to ancient ruins and culture far removed from that experienced on the coastal fronts.

If time and finances allow, we shall push on, to the eastern seaboard and Palenque, land of mystical Mayan ruins. If we can pull that venture off, Dave guarantees an experience which will impact my life. Bring it on...

The past four days have brought continual sunshine and one big surprise. Our comrade, the Kid, had decided to throw a curve ball at our intended plans.

This past week Kid has finally emerged from his shell. Instead of following at Dave's heels like a skittish puppy, he has shed his Nervous Ned exterior and is having a good time doing things on his own. He can count to one thousand (in Spanish, as well as English) and even order his own orange juice!

Once Dangerous showed him the location of the post office Kid would tread off daily to mail epic letters he spends each day composing. We would see him on the street coming our way, yet he would pass by, groovin' in his own little world, oblivious to our greetings; truly a man on a mission.

His diet remains a carnivore's nightmare. While we stuff ourselves with the finest Mexican cuisine imaginable, Kid is content nibbling on market raisins, oranges, apples, unsalted sunflower seeds, and, once in a blue moon, cheese quesadillas.

Despite his ability with numbers, Kid struggles with basic Spanish. No matter how much coaching he's been given, he still addresses men in the feminine tense, the women vice versa. This occurs every time, even though he has a fifty/fifty chance of getting it right just by guessing.

Dave's big mistake was introducing Kid to the *Larga Distancia*, or Long-Distance office. Soon thereafter he began making collect calls to his mom, who lent a sympathetic ear to his plight. Little did we imagine these treks of independence would provide the opportunity to hatch an escape plan, let alone summon up the intestinal fortitude needed to carry it out.

On Monday, a dozen American college girls arrived in town, on break from classes in Guadalajara. Having just completed their mid-term exams we hung out with them at *Playa Principal*, and were quickly adopted as their official tour guides. We were well-suited for this job, having spent the past month dedicated to a wide variety of leisure activities.

Dealing with the intensity, magnitude, and demands of a month plus on the road, interaction with the feminine gender had been put on the back burner. Meeting these friendly and extremely beautiful young ladies quickly rekindled my desire for interaction with the opposite sex. Gracious hosts we would like to consider ourselves, the Three Amigos offered to show these ladies the town.

The evening wore on and, under the light of a bright Zihuatanejo moon, a casual chemistry began brewing between Alison, a brown-eyed outgoing Coloradoan and myself.

As everyone gathered at Playa Principal, the two of us soon found ourselves drifting a short distance away from the rest of the gang, sharing our favorite experiences here in Mexico.

As the rum ran dry and the lightweights began to disperse, my vulnerable heart began to flutter as her smile grew warmer and we sat just a little bit closer.

What was going on here? I kept trying to rationalize this scenario. Having been deprived of female companionship for so long, I didn't want to misinterpret friendliness for anything greater than good company. I maintained my calm, cool, and collected persona, even after Alison suggested the four of us--she, her constantly giggling roommate, Kid and myself--casually drop our drawers and inhibitions and go skinny-dipping right there in Playa Principal.

Common sense told me skinny-dipping was frowned upon—especially as our M-16 toting friends in the blue uniforms were certain to be lurking nearby in the shadowy recesses. Lacking the thousand pesos necessary to pay my way out of jail, I suggested we head down to the lagoon and listen to the frog's croak instead.

This was only Monday. There would be more time for potentially amorous opportunities. Unfortunately, Alison neglected to mention that their group would be moving on to Puerto Escondido the following afternoon.

We visited long after most of Z-Wat had gone to bed when she abruptly grabbed the giggler, suggested we rendezvous later in the week, blew me a kiss, and called it a day. Listening to croaking frogs suddenly lost its luster. I too called it a day.

Tuesday's dinner at Restaurante Kon Tiki introduced us to Enrique, a significant influence on our final days in Z-Wat. Six foot two and lanky, Enrique had an unusual anomaly-one gray eye, the other blue-something I'd never encountered before.

He smiled warmly as he took our order. "Have you enjoyed your time so far while in Zihuatanejo my friend?" I told him we had been pleasantly busy embracing all the town had to offer.

"Perhaps there are more pleasant times yet to come your way."

The Kon Tiki, located high on a hill overlooking the entire bay, was a bit out of the norm for us, being a three-star restaurant noted for such tourist favorites as lamb chops and filet mignons alongside exceptionally highly-touted pizza.

As Enrique refilled our water, I could not help but notice that the necklace he wore was a shiny silver marijuana leaf. As he set down Dave's sizzling plate of tamales and rice before him, the two exchanged a subtle reference to the ornament he was wearing.

More innuendoes passed between them throughout our meal. As we settled the bill, Enrique offered an invitation for us to join him tomorrow at Playa La Ropa around noon at Restaurante El Taco for a ***special treat***.

Dave and I made a point of getting there five minutes early.

Restaurante El Taco was your basic beachside snack bar; four card tables, salsa, hot sauce, and a modest bar stocked with an ice chest of various refreshments. Mariachi classics blared from a cassette recorder whose batteries were operating on borrowed time. For the record, El Taco does not serve tacos.

We had chomped our way through two baskets of chips, guacamole and two Coronas each when Enrique finally showed up. He emerged from the bay wearing fins and a snorkel, holding up a large lively lobster in each hand.

He exchanged pleasantries with our waitress, handed her the still snapping sea creatures then joined us with a fresh round of beers.

Enrique was a graduate student in medicine at the University of Mexico City, home for winter break, working to earn enough to afford an easier life in the country's biggest city. Enrique speaks excellent English and hopes someday to get additional schooling in the States.

We finished our cervezas and Enrique asked if we'd like to join him for some 'good smoke.' He grabbed a small satchel from behind the counter and we were off to the far end of Playa La Ropa-- down to the wall of rockery and the goat trail leading to Las Gatas.

Certain we were alone, he dug deep into the satchel, producing a stout, two-finger-wide, hand-rolled spliff, then offered Dave the initial toke. Minutes later with the pungent herb reduced to roach status, I realized I was extremely loaded.

"Very good, no?" Our host grinned.

We nodded, illegal smiles all around.

'Red-haired Sinsemilla, THE best smoke in all Mexico-- grown right here in the hillsides of Guerrero. Would you like some?"

Enrique dug back into his bag and produced a foot-long bud, then handed it to Dave. "This is for you, my friends."

What price was he asking for this gorgeous specimen? Enrique shook his head. "I receive this from friends at no charge. The two of you give off such positive energy I gladly offer this for your journey ahead. Use it wisely." He smiled. Somewhere up above hippy angels sang.

"Just remember when you return home, whenever someone says Mexico is a bad place--that the people are dirty, ignorant and only want your money--please inform them they are not correct."

We assured him we would do just that, even without the generous ganja we had just received. The next half hour was spent in calm repose, alone on the rocks, reveling in the beauty of the Mexican magic there before our eyes.

Looking down at picturesque Zihuatanejo Bay, this tranquility became a perfect moment; one of the most incomparable I've ever experienced.

A slew of sailboats bob about, swaying in time to the rhythm of wind and waves. Blue sky above; dominated by shrieking feathered dots which plummet recklessly, before regaining their composure to glide gracefully amidst an obstacle course of varied masts.

The background is a canvas of rich deciduous hillsides, rising taller than a giant's shoulders. Lush green and brown vegetation give way to acre after acre of palm trees stretching out as far as the eye can see.

I closed my eyes, took a mental snapshot, and filed it away for what I hope will be forever; placed inside my happy place for whenever I need to summon positive vibes.

Time to head back to town. We bid Enrique farewell and he requested we stop by the Kon Tiki before moving on, or perhaps meet at El Taco tomorrow, if so inclined.

The majority of those we have met along our way have offered us nothing but warmth and cordiality. Enrique disappearing around the bend, was no exception. We gathered our stupefied wits and headed back down the beach towards town and reality.

Wednesday morning was spent assessing my financial situation and a sobering red flag popped up. Midway through the fifth week of our trip here was the tally: Three hundred seventy-five dollars down, three hundred twenty-five dollars to go. Subtract another fifty for the train ride back to Nogales and jeeesh!

A somber cloud quickly overrode my positive vibes. I've paid heed to Dave's pre-trip advice regarding fiscal prudence and look where it's got me: Heading down the homestretch, sooner than planned, even after practicing what I consider frugal responsibility

Dave tried turning my current financial status into a positive. He assured me I have done better than most others he's traveled with, saying most last only a month on the amount of cash I've allotted. Still, I'm determined to prolong this adventure as long as possible. If handled shrewdly, our trip is far from over. Many adventures still lie ahead.

I could always have my cash reserve wired, via Western Union, but Dangerous wants this to remain a last-ditch effort; for emergencies only, as wiring money to Mexico from the States often is met with complications. International transfers may get lost or delayed longer than anticipated, resulting in the recipient being, quite bluntly, shit out of luck.

Time to tighten up, starting by skipping a few afternoon meals in the days ahead. No more Kon Tiki soirees. This whole experience is just too incredible to imagine coming to a close prematurely.

Later, that afternoon, I made a solo venture to Playa La Ropa, back to El Taco, for cervezas and hopefully another visit with Enrique.

He was already there and introduced me to Paco, from Peru, and Vinnie, a retired fireman from 'New Yawk.' I was invited to take a trip up the beach with them, up into the hills, where Vinnie and Enrique shared a condo-style beach house.

It was an open-air pad, complete with a grand ocean view, several hammocks to enjoy and a big-league sound system. Paco produced a spliff and soon we were all feeling quite fine.

Outside, a large iguana stared us down, slithering cautiously down a crooked branch while two cows sauntered past on the sand, as if headed in for a swim.

For the next fifteen minutes at the peak of my buzz, I listened as Vinnie offered his intensely pessimistic philosophy of life. I worked hard to let it go in my left ear and as quickly as possible out my right. Vinnie was a real downer.

A definite seediness had been woven into Vinnie's smug personal tapestry. His acerbic tirade was based around his impression life had dealt him a shittier hand than most. He also offered negative vibes about Puerto Escondido, saying the town, renowned for its awesome waves, was also full of Surf Nazis.

"The little pricks come from all over, though most hail from Texas. For many of them, it's the end of their road. Out of money, they call home, looking for an instant infusion from Mommy and Daddy who inform them their gravy train has come to an end; it's time to come home. Instead, they opt to start ripping off other Americans whom they casually befriend in order to feed their addiction to the waves. The moral of this story is when in Escondido, be careful who ya chum up to."

He also says Puerto Escondido is home to the mother of all rip tides, averaging two lives sucked out to sea each year. Heading there does not exactly sound like a vacation upgrade to me.

Vinnie headed back down to El Taco for beer and fresh oysters. Paco was out back talking in French to a tree lizard and Enrique lay motionless, crapped out in his hammock. It was time to head back and get organized for Puerto Escondido.

Back at ***LARRY LAND,*** it was celebration time. It was Larry's birthday. He was now officially thirty-two. His goal was to drink thirty-two Coronas before day's end to mark this special occasion.

When I had left at 11 a.m. he was working on brew number three, swinging about in his hammock, a half case an arm's length away.

I made my way back to Casa Del Playa to toast a couple of brown bottles with the birthday boy, yet when I arrived, the hammock was no longer swinging; Larry was DOA. No, not Dead On Arrival, our Canadian buddy was Drunk Off his Ass.

Below him, the half case held eight empties; twenty-four more liquid candles remained to blow out before his goal could be met. His snoring had succeeded in chasing away all occupants of Casa del Playa, who ditched to find more peaceful surroundings to pass what remained of the day.

Ted and Doris were off indulging in one last dose of beach time at Playa Madera and Kid had found the gumption to take a solo trek across town to the market in order to replenish his dwindling supply of seeds. Only Dangerous was back in old Numero Uno and he was sporting the foulest of moods as he paced from one side of the room to the other. Que pasa, amigo?

"That effin' Kid-- He's bailing on us! Check this out." He handed me a piece of notebook paper that looked like a chicken had dipped its claws in ink before doing the Poultry Boogaloo across its surface. No doubt about it, this was Kid's handiwork:

> *bus to acapulco 1st class 1955 2nd class*
> *taxi or bus to airport what bus, when, where*
> *one night please*
> *baggage below*
> *receipt*
> *get ticket (all the way to Pertland)*
> *check out baggage get receipt*
> *in case screw up Long Distance telefonos.*
> *Larga Distancia*
> *where's the Larga Distancia Telefonos*
> *please help me porfavor*
> *plane to Los Angeles California USA*
> *leaves or at 4:00 16:00*
> *please help me find where I board Mexicana to Los Angeles at 4:00 PM*

It took more than one attempt to successfully translate this gibberish, yet, in the end, it was undeniable, I was holding Kid's blueprint for departure in my hands.

We had underestimated our amigo. In the manner of a well-conceived prison break, Señor Kid had hatched a well-conceived *plot* to bail out, right under our unassuming noses.

I admired his craftiness, yet this decision may turn out to be best for all involved. Kid was having an entirely different experience than Dave and myself. It was as if we were dialed into a nice FM radio station while he was working the AM side of the dial. While Dave agreed, his feelings had been seriously stung.

"I can't believe he didn't have the gumption to tell me until this morning." He shook his head and continued, "That hurts more than anything."

According to Dave, Kid had called home and whined to Mom about how dismal this trip had been going. She arranged to have a ticket, destination Portland, Oregon, USA, waiting for him at the airport in Acapulco which, we conveniently would be passing through on the way to Puerto Escondido.

Sometime in the early evening, following his daily ingestion of sunflower seeds, two oranges, banana, and a handful of raisins, Kid quietly started packing his gear for the last time.

He began by dumping the entire contents on the floor before reorganizing them.

First, he stuffed two plaid wool shirts (quite handy in Mexico) in the side pocket. Next, he began filling the main compartment with his REI hiking/rain poncho, a large first aid kit (still sealed in plastic), his Swiss army knife (capable of killing a large mountain lion), and his two canteen-sized mountaineering water bottles which required the caps be screwed on by someone with the strength of Superman.

Next came his lone reading material, How Things Work.

He stuffed four pair of silk bikini underwear, lotions, medicines, and elixirs inside, carefully leaving room for his drum pad and drumsticks to top it off. He abandoned his collapsible toothbrush--instructions in French--there by the sink, in case our casa's next occupant accidentally left their own gum-scrubber back home.

It's a shame Kid's phobias and homesickness have stunted any potential of experiencing the same groove Dave and I thrive on.

While our compadre geared up to head stateside, Dave and I both agree our health, physical conditioning, and mental attitude here on the road are hitting a substantially nice peak. Our continually active existence has replaced the inactive existence I would be living back in my Bellingham comfy chair, remote in hand, and a minit mart burrito in the microwave for two minutes. Although I miss the many hours I spend listening to music, I seem to be surviving just fine.

Kid's bag was officially packed. He could now sit around considering just how he was going to pull this off without having Dave's coattails to cling to.

He'd had enough trouble wiping his tushie (and throwing it in the bucket) without needing to have someone confirm which hand he should use, let alone catch a flight in a foreign airport by himself. That was now his cross to bear.

As he whacked away at his practice pad, Dave and I snuck off into Centro, in search of the perfect going away present for our departing amigo.

We wandered the side streets looking for unconventional fare, yet the best we could come up with were those tacky Day-Glo ZIHUATANEJO souvenir T-shirts. Dave had already helped him buy one.

We considered going to the market and getting him a duffle bag- worth of sunflower seeds, overripe bananas or perhaps some niño-painted ceramic craftwork.

An hour spent impulse-shopping worked up considerable thirst, so we stopped by a corner groceria to purchase two sodas.

We waited patiently for the little old man wearing half-glasses behind the counter to count our change. With hands stained orange from years of chain-smoking Mexican cigarettes, he calculated, then re-calculated the three pesos worth of change he was going to hand back. He did this at least four times before finally dropping them into Dave's palm

While waiting for him to finish, I followed the hypnotic wisp of exhaled overhead rise above the gum and cigarette rack. It was there I spied the perfect gift for Kid.

A medium-sized bat--long dead and thoroughly dried out—which dangled from a six-inch piece of twine. Dave also spotted the mummified former creature of the night and agreed our search had come to the appropriate end. Here was Kid's door prize for wimping out.

Was it for sale? The Señor raised a suspicious eyebrow. Were these boys messing with him? What purpose could they have for his mummified mascot?

He reached up, unhooked the critter and laid it on the counter. An army of microscopic black bugs scurried from the underside of the brittle carcass, only to be whisked ever-so-casually off the counter by his tar-stained phalanges.

"*Trente* pesos." Negotiations had begun. Dave offered twenty.

Tar Fingers shrugged. Proper bartering procedure normally would require a counter offer of twenty-five, yet twenty pesos was more than reasonable for a mummified bat. He blew off the remaining black dots still clinging to the fur and pocketed Dave's twenty-peso note.

On our way back to Casa Del Playa, we concocted a plan which would allow me to sneak the bat into the recesses of Kid's backpack without his knowing. The plan worked flawlessly and the bat was packed with nary a hitch for its stateside journey.

I struggled to fall asleep that night. Pre-road downs once again took hold. I tossed and turned as my subconscious worked overtime, sorting through a wicked combination of anxiety, apprehension, and trepidation. These emotions were based primarily on Vinnie's negative pontifications regarding Puerto Escondido. I pictured surf nazis digging through my bag without an invitation and huge waves capable of sucking us out to sea. Damn...
Did I want to go? Hell yes--and hell no.
Hell no: Along with the just-mentioned surf nazis I've grown extremely comfortable with my daily beach routine and friendly frequented establishments. I am more than content gobbling down those peso-friendly dog brain taquitos, relishing ice cold eskimos, and perfecting the art of the siesta. A large part of me is struggling with abandoning that comfort zone.
Hell yes: I'm in Dangerous' hands and he hasn't let me down yet. So far ur game plan has been spot on. Time to take a deep breath and suck 'em up...
I need to replace these uninvited shreds of insecurity and doubt with confidence and anticipation; positives not negatives. If he tells me more adventures await, I'll do my damnedest to go with the flow. I REFUSE TO BECOME THE NEW KID!
It's now well past 1 a.m. The music from the discotheque is still competing with the waves in Zihuatanejo Bay. On and on they go; music I will miss, for at least a week or longer, as we travel inland to Oaxaca and hopefully beyond.
Seven days on the road chock full of insecurity along with the unknown is coming our way, riding a Mexican back beat.
Time to suck 'em up, strap on Elvin Bishop's Travelin' Shoes and tap into my Mañana Method cerebral savings account stored up for times such as these.
If the bus breaks down, I can handle it. If we're stuck overnight somewhere for God knows whatever the reason, I'll revert to the 'Shit Happens' bumper sticker mantra; riding out the magnitude of this grand experience like I am a psycho bitch Surf Nazi myself.
Let's roll...

16. Practice Pad Man's Final Rudiments

Friday Feb.10th

6:15 a.m. Zihuatanejo has no heartbeat; no bells ringing to drag you from your slumber. Only darkness and silent empty streets are there to greet us as we close the door to Casa Del Playa one final time. Our long trek to the far side of Z-Wat and the bus station was underway.

These pre-dawn streets belong to the mutant local perros. This is their prime time, aggressively prowling through tipped-over trash barrels, survival reliant on last night's scraps and discarded comidas.

These mutts growl upon approach, all the while backpedaling in fear. When in that mode, we will treat them as the locals do-- chucking rocks with velocity, hoping to land a blow to their emaciated ribcages and send them scooting.

In the United States dogs are considered by many to be man's best friend. They provide comfort, are loyal, naturally affectionate, learn tricks, perform acts of valor, and often serve as the best security alarm money can buy.

Here in Mexico, almost all perros are mongrels or feral beasts; coats tattered and covered with scars inflicted by rocks or from battle with fellow curs. Willy once said if there truly is an afterlife, Hitler's karma would be to return as a *perro*.

Our bus rolls at 7:45 a.m., yet after our previous early departure we were on our toes anticipating another possible premature roll out. We purchased our tickets promptly at seven as the booth's window open, then climbed aboard planning to snooze our way through blast off. Four or five others took a seat, our driver was the last to aboard.

Once behind the wheel, he combed his hair, adjusted the side mirrors, and fired up the engine. We departed at 7:15, a good thirty minutes earlier than posted on the reader board, still visible from our seats.

Kid sat directly behind us, pack by his side. As the wheels took to the asphalt, he pulled out his drumsticks and pad for one last session. Our friend and soon to be departed amigo, gave it all he had left.

Even with the dawn a good half hour away, Kid was sporting his reflective shades, hoping, I assume, to mask the anxiety flowing through his stressed-out corpuscles. His plane leaves at 4 p.m., giving him a four-hour cushion to locate the airport and get his prepaid ticket, yet his nervous mannerisms lead one to believe he has, at best, an extremely short window to work with.

Our bus driver did his best to push Kid over the edge and into anxiety gulch.

Compared to previous drivers, this gentleman was junior varsity at best. He handled the narrow, occasionally washed-out winding roadway haphazardly, drifting lazily across the ghost of a center line each time we negotiated a bend. Angry oncoming horns blared at us frequently on our way to Acapulco.

When he wasn't straying into the oncoming lane, he kept spitting gravel and white clouds of dust in our wake, continually trimming crumbling roadside shoulders. Usually composed, Dangerous and I remained constantly on edge whenever our bus leaned dangerously close to the guardrail-less edges where radically steep embankments appeared life-threatening. Strangely enough, none of the other passengers seemed concerned with his lack of precision. The closer we came to peril, the faster Kid worked his pad, sticks clicking together, louder and louder.

Twenty minutes out of Zihuatanejo our driver pulled over and killed the motor. Without a word, he opened the door, stepped off the bus, and headed straight inside a small roadside diner.

We watched as he plopped down in a chair by the window and dove into a whopping slice of pie, topped with a mini mountain of vanilla ice cream. All the while, early morning hunger pangs gnawed at the pit of our unfed tummies. Fifteen minutes later he was done, climbed behind the wheel, belched loudly and ground gears. We were on our way again.

For at least five miles.

Next, he got out and began negotiations with a farmer selling milk at a small roadside stand. After five minutes of bartering, a handful of pesos were exchanged for two gallons of leche, which he stashed beneath his seat. More gears were ground, then, tally ho, off once more.

As we crawled along, seemingly in no hurry to reach Acapulco by its scheduled arrival time, Kid's anxiety heightened. Dave and I went for the jugular, one last dose of Kid torture, for amusement purposes only.

At each stop, Dave and I would get off, only to hop back on with some concocted crisis that could potentially delay our scheduled arrival in Acapulco. The first time we hinted at a faulty brake line problem, the next, potential steering column failure. By the time we fabricated a cracked timing belt, we had Kid fully on the ropes.

He began pounding on his pad with a ferocity equal to Ginger Baker after a methamphetamine cocktail or Keith Moon, flying high on a double helping of animal tranquilizer. Something had to give.

"Kid, stop that incessant pounding or I'm gonna break those drumsticks over your head and shove them up your ass!" Doris had cracked.

The show was over. The one-man rockin' rhythm machine humbly stuffed his sticks into his backpack. Several passengers broke into cheers. Kid waved appreciatively, thinking they were applauding his skills, but we wise Americanos were certain the applause was directed towards Doris for putting an end to his incessant distraction.

Shortly before noon, and still on schedule, we began our approach to Acapulco, playground of the rich and famous. Vinnie had summed up this renowned resort capital as such: "Pay much more, get much less."

From the right side of our bus, the picturesque bay came into view; magnificently romantic postcard beauty. For decades, world travelers have designated Acapulco as a prime vacation destination for its pristine white sandy beaches. Today, that idyllic allure has been shat upon by development, development, development, spreading like malaria the entire four-mile length of coastline.

On our left, hundreds of primitive shacks consume the hillside. These are modern day Pueblo-like slums, stacked atop each other, row after row. Hastily patched together with ragged odds and ends of multi-colored lumber, they appear as little more than shaky-looking afterthoughts.

Most seem in need of immediate repair before they collapse and come tumbling down the steep banks they are stacked upon. One can only assume we are looking at the low-income district of this incredibly large metropolitan city.

From here we passed through suburbia; mile after mile of impressive modern-day examples of Mexican affluence, exquisite mansion after mansion. Each of them appears to be expensive as one may assume, The majority of these villas go on row after row, featuring architectural design nothing more than large tacky cookie cutter rectangular boxes, caked in stucco and enclosed by wrought iron gates.

Deep inside the heart of this crowded city we arrive at the bus terminal. Six hundred thousand people inhabit Acapulco and, for the first time since Guadalajara, the air we breathe is once again dominated by carbon monoxide. Once again big city hustle and bustle is back in our face.

We stepped down into hordes of lower-class poor, garbed in rags the Salvation Army would deem unsuitable for resale. Tattered, torn and smelly, they were gathered around the bus waiting for us; hands out, begging, weakly pleading for pesos. I suddenly felt very uncomfortable.

Eyes to the ground, we hustled past kids wearing mismatched shoes, and aged toothless beggar ladies with disfigured faces. We passed paraplegics, quadriplegics, everything but people with two heads. Many of the limbless poor, vying for strategic begging space on each street corner, sought our attention as we hurried past. They extended hats, tattered woven baskets and trembling palms, groaning for alms, summoning up the most pitiful of tones as they bemoaned their existence.

We continued as if they did not exist. I felt guilty, yet sensed that if I had given in and doled out a single peso, I would be swarmed upon nonstop until I boarded our next bus out of town.

Par for the course, the next bus to Puerto Escondido was scheduled to leave at three p.m. Oh boy--we had nearly three hours to look forward to. First matters first. We headed to the street and hailed a farewell cab for Kid.

Ted negotiated Kid's fee with the driver, who stood outside his cab shaking his head while we watched him trying and failing, then trying again to stuff Kid's oversized backpack into the cab's minute trunk.

My last memory of Kid had him standing there, nervous as hell, feigning to have the situation under control. Dangerous gave him one last soul handshake for the road, repeating over and over, "Air Puerto, Air Puerto...You got it?" Kid nodded weakly, trying to grasp onto one single strand of confidence with an extremely slippery grip.

He climbed into the cab, repeating that million-dollar phrase, several times to himself.

The big moment finally arrived. The driver asked him "Where to?"

We all held our breath, then through his open window we heard his reply. *"Air Puerta, por favoro"*, followed by an "Oh shit!" as he buried his head in his hands. The driver peeled away from the curb laughing his ass off. The Kid--life's subservient whipping boy-- was no mas. Just like that, our adventurous quintet had become a quartet.

Three hours to kill. Ted and Doris chose to hang out at the bus depot while Dave convinced me we should investigate the back streets of inner- city Acapulco. "If you're gonna tell the folks back home you've been to Acapulco, you should have a tale or two to tell, don't you agree?"

The side street congestion rekindled memories of urban Guadalajara, with bumper-to-bumper well-worn 70s style American economy sedans, most in immediate need of ring and/or valve jobs.

Traffic sat motionless, spewing exhaust, and honking horns for no purpose other than the fact the car sitting next to them was honking theirs. Hungry cabbies scanned every corner but there were few takers. Now several blocks removed from the bus station, Dave ducked into an entry to a low-lit unassuming cantina, yours truly close behind.

How he chose this particular location, I cannot say. There was no signage; nothing to suggest a restaurant even existed inside these dull plaster walls. Yet here we were, surrounded by pedestrian décor. Four tables, no silverware, menus, or napkins; only an uncapped bottle of salsa, a salt shaker and the smell of good things cooking suggested we had entered a potential eatery. Tinny Mariachi ballads blared from a juke box playing to an empty room.

I asked what drew him to choose this establishment and he went all Charley Chan on me with the type of fortune cookie-like answer the wily detective would have tossed back at Number One Son's inquisitions: "Sometimes a chance taken yields surprises which surpass one's expectations, so shut the hell up, stop your whining and read the menu, if and when it arrives."

Stop my whining! Oh my God, was I turning into Kid, Volume II, already? I immediately regrouped. Hang loose. Attribute this to road fever. Take things as they come. Positive vibes only, gringo…

Never mind I'm several thousand miles from home, attempting to steer my boggled senses through each new scenario which blows me away on a regular daily basis. So what—there is no waitress, menu, or fellow customers partaking in delectable Latino cuisine. Go with the flow, Señor Tunes.

Our waitress popped out from behind closed curtains with neither pencil nor paper to take our order. No smile or greeting to let us know we were welcome. Instead, she simply asked us what we would like. We requested traditional choice after traditional choice of entrees. Each time she nullified our request. *"No Más de tortas-Posible Mañana... No Más de Hamburguesas--Posible Mañana...No Más de Tamales-Mañana para sure...* After a patient deep breath Dangerous inquired as to what they *did* have.

"*Quesadillas.*"

Starvation was not a suitable option, quesadillas certainly were. We settled for two each. Twenty minutes later she arrived back at our table with two sizzling hot plates with three each (I thought we ordered two??) and I must say they were a first class treat.

We left, stuffed, satisfied, and with less than an hour to departure. While I unsuccessfully scanned a local newsstand for any newspaper printed in English, Dave popped into a Pharmacia, then returned with a small brown bottle he stuffed into his shirt pocket. *Que pasa*, Dangerous one?

"Azapaum-Valium: guaranteed to come in handy during the long bus rides ahead." I suddenly got the feeling this next leg of our journey was to be all about endurance.

Once again, the boys scored the death seat. Once again, the boys, and Doris, suffered the milk train route. One Azapaum each and it didn't really matter if our driver stopped for pie every fifteen minutes on this 230-mile trek, along a winding breathtaking coastline highway.

When we weren't doing the Poke Along Shuffle, we were making frequent military inspection stops. Each time, two or three baby-faced soldiers would board our bus, carbines swinging haphazardly from their shoulders. No smiles allowed, or at least offered, as they slowly made their way the length of the bus in silence, pausing occasionally to make the locals open their bags to show them what lurked inside.

Dangerous assured me that they were on the lookout for drugs, firearms, or shady-looking hombres, and since we qualified for only two of the three criteria mentioned, they would most likely leave us alone. We kept our heads down, trying to become invisible; out of sight, out of mind.

Not once did they look our way or towards Dangerous' backpack where Enrique's mind-bending shrubbery had been casually stashed in an easily accessible side pouch. Today they were looking for bigger fish to fry. Once their inspection was complete, we were off again, on the road to Puerto Escondido.

17. A Bump in the Road

"Puerto Escondido. Puerto Escondido."

Our driver's monotone proclamation stirred me from the veil of benzodiazepine fog I had been pleasantly enveloped in since leaving Acapulco; deep and dark as the bottom of the Pacific.

The relaxant had served its purpose well, perhaps too much so. I struggled to jump start my groggy senses from their vegetative state. Arriving after nightfall further enhanced my disorientation.

After wiping a thin trail of sleep drool from my shirt sleeve, I attempted to focus on my watch through snooze-caked peepers. 10:05 p.m. The last time I had looked, it had been daylight. 7:15 to be exact. Nice cat nap, Dr. Azapaum.

We were somewhere, oh yeah, Puerto Escondido, now just the four of us; four lone passengers, rummy from Dave's meds, arriving at the end of the road, rising abruptly to gather our backpacks as well as our wits.

On rubbery legs I rose from my seat, clutching the rail as I stepped slowly down the steps of the bus. I found comfort in noting my compadres were searching for their equilibrium as well.

Our driver nodded farewell, closed the bus door tightly behind him and headed down the road (for home?), one hand digging into his lunch bag, the other holding his two gallons of milk as he walked off into the night.

Where the hell were we? We stood there, dazed and confused, underneath the glow of a lone streetlight, silently and still unsuccessfully trying to collect our wits.

We were obviously on the outskirts of town, standing in front of a bus station the size of a porta potty, which had long since closed for the night. No landmarks, no eskimo stands or signs of civilization to help point us in the right direction. Only a dirt road to follow. And darkness.

Where was Puerto Escondido? The familiar sounds of the surf pounding in the distance suggested perhaps this was the correct direction our feet should move.

"Taxi, amigos?" We were saved. A chubby middle-aged cab driver materialized from the darkness, perhaps twenty yards behind us.

Still slightly stupefied, we threw our packs into the open trunk, then jumped in, each of us trying to be the first to regain the ability to participate in a translatable verbal exchange.

"Where to?"

"Uh, wwwe need a hhhotel, please."

"No problemo, amigos. I know a very special one. Cheap too!" Good fortune still walked beside us.

We paid the driver a hundred pesos and sped down the road. For the whole of two minutes.

The cab stopped and we got out. Off to the left stood a modest dwelling appeared to be hotel-like stood, its lights out, set back in the dark from the streetlight.

Our driver swiftly removed our backpacks from the trunk, set them on the gravel, jumped back into his cab and headed quickly off into the night. Only after his tail lights faded in the distance, did we realize we had been royally snookered. Taken for a ride, literally. Our ever so brief hundred-peso cab ride had taken us less than fifty yards.

Even though we had been delivered, as promised, to our requested destination, this ride worked out to cost damn near two pesos per yard. A profitable jaunt for our driver, yet an omen of things to come for your weary and disoriented crew. Welcome to Puerto Escondido.

It wasn't extremely late, yet Doris chose to knock gently on the office door. All indications suggested those inside had already turned in for the night. All lights were out, not a sign of anyone shuffling about. Without a clue of where else to go, she kept knocking, more aggressively. Desperation beginning to creep in. Still no response. Finally, a groggy-eyed Señora, her Mel Brooks look-alike husband close behind, popped open the door an inch or two, eyeing us suspiciously.

We inquired about a room for the night for four. She shook her head while her husband nodded yes. For the next few minutes, a heated argument between the two ensued. We stood by, rooting for the husband. Finally, things cooled down between them and she gestured for us to follow.

They led us to a well-worn green door adjacent to a power generator humming at higher than desirable decibels. The *Señor* grumbled, then cursed in Spanish as he tried over a dozen keys before finding one to fit the lock. He forced the door open with a grunt and a firm nudge of his shoulder, brushed away a small smattering of cobwebs which had accumulated face level in the doorway, then gestured for us to follow.

A flick of the light switch revealed a room no larger than an empty storage shed. He nodded to us, seeking our approval. No way would four cots fit in this little cracker box, yet we were much too tired, fried and frazzled to launch a sustainable argument of any sort. Let's see them make this work.

The wife wheeled in one folded roll-away cot, then another, placing them up against the far wall. Next, she squeezed in a wafer-thin cot the size and length of a Red Cross stretcher she placed adjacent to the roll-aways, forming a U. If the other cot could be made to fit, we would be one big vacuum-packed family, ultimately testing the hygienic limits of our friendship. God help us all should Dangerous launch one of his farting spells.

It appeared Doris was in for a 3 Dude Night, and, judging by the look on her face, close quarter intimacy was not high on her list of priorities, nor was it Dave and myself first choice.

We thanked them for their noble gesture in trying to provide us with shelter and were backing out the door when Señor gestured for us to wait while he wrestled to make bed four fit.

He arranged, rearranged, then rearranged his rearrangement, all to no avail. All the while, his wife tongue lashed him in Español for foolishly taking on this endeavor. I asked Dave for a translation. He told me I didn't want to know, as it was language more closely associated with sailors than with members of the feminine gender.

Between her harsh bursts of acerbic Spanish, she did pause long enough to tell Doris yes, there was a first-class hotel a short walk away, but expect to pay top dollar for any room they still may have available.

We climbed across the jumble of cots and offered one last gracias for their noble efforts. Closing the door behind us, we left the groggy landlords to their heated discussion, with some doubt it would conclude before the first rooster warms up his pipes to greet tomorrow's sunrise.

We regrouped under the light of that lone street lamp, batting away a hungry cloud of mosquitoes as we plotted our next move. Inner group tension could be felt brewing due to our current circumstance.

Doris made the first move, heading off in the direction of the pricy accommodations the Señora had suggested. "I don't care what you three jokers are planning to do with the rest of your evening but *I'm* going to get me a good night's sleep!"

Ted gave us the helpless 'she's my wife, what the hell am I supposed to do?' shrug, as he hustled to catch up with his road-weary as well as frustrated mate, already fading from sight.

Dave and I hung tight. The luxury of a warm bed in a comfortable hotel room was not an option. Ted and Doris' travel would extend no further than Oaxaca while our journey potentially had much longer legs. Cash was the most precious of commodities. Cash controlled our ultimate destiny.

We were on our own, reduced to dos amigos. We walked down the narrow, paved road to lord knows where in silence, confusion and darkness; our intuition our only compass leading us towards the sound of the ocean and, hopefully, the town of Puerto Escondido.

Along the way we encountered a local, smoking a cigarette while pissing in the roadside brush. We struck up a conversation in regards to potential lodging. He suggested we follow him back to his casa/Restaurante and, if we weren't picky, we could sleep on hammocks for only twenty pesos each. In our current position, one step this side of desperation, this offer sounded as good as a night in the Presidential Suite of the Holiday Inn.

We followed him down a short yet steep grassy trail in pitch black conditions into a cluster of bushes. Suddenly the smell of home cooking filled the air, a more than subtle reminder we hadn't eaten since Acapulco many hours earlier.

Just ahead, an illuminated clearing came into sight. A very tired-looking mamasita shooed her children off to bed as she and an apparent teen age daughter gathered dishes from the large outdoor dining table where a meal had recently taken place. Blessed sanctuary was at hand.

As we watched, feeling much like the hungry beggars we had scorned back in Acapulco, our host convinced her to whip us up plates of Huevos Rancheros, with brown eggs, fresh peppers, onions, cilantro, and salsa, served with a mound of freshly-made tortillas. Two generous platefuls were placed before us and devoured in an embarrassingly short amount of time.

Gracious thanks, along with a handful of pesos brought an end to the meal. It was now time for bed. Blankets were offered but we declined; our sleeping bags would do just fine tonight. We bid our hosts goodnight and headed off to Hammock Land for a good night's sleep. That was, at least until the simple act of slumber turned upside down. It seems the mosquitoes we had met beneath the streetlight had passed the word two Type A gringos were ripe for the taking.

Let the feast begin.

The first wave of blood guzzlers was a medium-sized battalion of aggressive agitators buzzing loudly about our ears. While we fended them off, a second wave feasted upon our backsides, choosing to draw their calculated targets safely out of swatting range; targets impossible to land a successful 'squito-squishing backhand swat upon.

Dangerous battled futilely until his arms grew weary from fruitless attempts to either discourage or destroy these incessant blood mongers.

Unleashing a tirade of verbal malevolence second only to the Señora back at the hotel, he leapt up from his hammock, grabbed his sleeping bag and grumbled off into the darkness.

"Hey, where are you going?" It was now one man against a million.

"I'll be down somewhere along the shoreline if you care to join me." No matter how effective the Valium may have been at successfully shaving off travel time, it had turned us into groggy, disoriented frumps.

Determined to stand my ground and get my twenty pesos-worth, I held steady in my hammock bunker. I was determined to win this battle, after all, my brain was bigger than a mosquito's, wasn't I?

I pulled my sleeping bag up until it completely covered my head.

With forearms across forehead to avoid smothering beneath my down shield, I relaxed as the buzzing around my ears ceased.

Things were fine for a half hour until I realized my mite-sized adversaries had one upped me. While my feet, front side and head had been taken off tonight's menu, those sneaky little bloodsuckers back-door-played me, floating underneath the hammock where a wealth of beefy epidermal lay exposed, pressed into bite-sized squares by the hammock strings' checkered grid. My backside had become open game. Gringo plasma cocktails were now being served up, free of charge.

I too decided to throw in the towel. Screw that twenty pesos, this battle was lost. I gathered my belongings and sauntered off, hoping to find sanctuary as well as Dangerous Dave's lair, somewhere down by the sea and sand.

Led along solely by the lone sand path, I stumbled through the tall grasses, playing a hunch this was the same route my friend had chosen. The grass ended some forty yards from shoreline, where, by the glow of the moon, I came upon a six-foot-two chunk of sleeping bag, safely out of reach of the tide's shifting touch.

"Dave?" I inquired meekly.

An unintelligible grumble followed by a series of rip roaring flatulent *fraps* officially identified my traveling mate. I staked out my own space nearby. With only my arms to serve as a pillow, I laid on my side and closed my eyes as the waves rocked me to sleep.

My eyes popped open just as sunrise had begun to paint the horizon a light shade of orange. My body felt chilled, aching, and disoriented. What am I doing here less than twenty yards from the incoming tide? To enhance this already strange situation, something large and warm was lying on the back of my legs; something which had not been there last night.

Rolling over slowly brought me face to face, inches away, from a large unidentifiable species of mutt. Sometime during the night, it had burrowed into the gap there between the back of my calves, taking advantage of my body's natural warmth.

As soon as I began to stir, the pup, its eyes--one blue, one gray--stared intently at what had been the source of his warmth and comfort, and a soft warning growl suddenly became audible.

Slowly it rose, backpedaling until there was a considerably safe distance between us. At first the pup seemed reluctant to leave, as if it could not choose its next move. It looked at me in a caring, domesticated manner rarely associated with Mexican perros. Then with a bark lacking any semblance of authority, my bed mate hit the road, tail between its legs, all the while looking over its shoulder, just to make sure I wasn't firing any projectiles in its direction.

Dangerous woke up during this commotion, in serious need of a shave, shower, and three stiff cups of roadhouse coffee.

He pulled his watch out from deep inside his down bag and took a groggy reading. "Seven fifteen. In a half hour let's head into town and see if we can find Ted and Doris."

Shortly thereafter we rolled our bags up and attached them to our backpacks in silence. No more Azapaum, unless absolutely necessary. We wobbled off in what we considered the general direction of Puerto Escondido. Our bodies longed for hot water, a deep tissue massage, and at least three more hours of uninterrupted shut eye.

Ted and Doris have always been early risers and there they were, sitting at a prime seat by the window, inside Escondido's lone coffee house, looking relaxed and refreshed.

They both claimed to have had a great night's sleep. We plopped into two seats they had saved for us and quickly ordered coffee and a roll. As we waited for our caffeine to arrive and revive, we took in our setting and the strange vibes being emitted all around us.

Shifty eyes scrutinized us from every direction; territorial, unwelcome glances, scoping out these new cats in town. I pulled my backpack a bit closer towards our table. Vinnie's negative La Ropa ramblings were quickly gaining credibility.

We were sitting dead center, amidst a room full of Vinnie's Surf Nazis. Most patrons/characters sitting here, fit the Vin Man's description to a T.

"Beware. Those drugged out little bitches love to wear those one-way wraparound shades so ya can't tell when they're looking at ya. They aren't natural blondes either. Ninety per cent of them have peroxided their tops and either wear it in a Mohawk, or in unkempt bangs; the traditional surfin' Beach Boys, via 1964' style doo. No in-between.

"Ninety percent of them are fueled exclusively by surf punk bands like Black Flag, Fear and the Circle Jerks. They've all got tattoos, some of them self-inflicted, bearing macho slogans like 'Ride 'em or die.' Their standard mode of clothing is tank tops, or t shirts pimping their favorite surf shops, surfboards, or hip gear. Some endorse beer shacks on beaches back home with names like The Howling Pig or Kahuna's Hideaway." Looking around me, Vinnie had nailed this observation perfectly.

"The most important thing to remember is this: Approach anyone giving you the red-carpet treatment for no apparent reason with extreme caution. More often than not, they will befriend you, show you the ropes, maybe even set you up with a room in town or at the hostel. Sometimes they'll even take you down to where the best waves are caught then get you stoned on cheap local weed.

"But when the time is right--when you least expect it, they'll give you a screwin' better than the best top-dollar piece of tail money can buy out at Mustang Ranch. Wallets backpacks, Travelers

Cheques--anything they can nab swiftly and turn into cash for a ticket out of town or a bag full of weed-- maybe both. That's their game."

When I asked if this was fact or just urban legend, Vinnie stared me down hard. "Been there, done that."

Vinnie's Surf Nazis were up and running, live and in color, as well as traveling in heavy numbers. Apparent cliques wandered in and out of the coffee shop door; pasty zombies in Night of the Living Dead Heads, moving about in slow motion; driven by the need for a handful or two of fresh brain cells. Or perhaps just your wallet.

We finished the last swigs of our hair-of-the-dog: extremely hot and effective black java, then headed back to Ted and Doris' room for a shower and summit conference to plot our next move.

They had paid five hundred pesos for a room a third the size of our two-hundred-peso Playa del Casa habitat. But in the middle of the night one best take what one can get. We quickly used up what remained of the hot water which successfully brought us back into socially acceptable appearance.

Puerto Escondido is a modest village, larger than Barra, but not nearly as large or modern as Zihuatanejo.

The beach, nearly a mile's worth of sand, palm groves, and crashing shore break is the town's focal point.

It is only ten in the morning and already dozens of surfer heads can be seen bobbing up and down in the bay like zany dots as they wait patiently to catch the next big one. Enticing as it seems, the lethal riptides discourage novice riders and body surfers from overzealous participation.

Having recently become a fledgling (and somewhat cowardly) body surfer, I have no clue or even the merest stitch of interest as far as the sport of surfing is concerned, so Escondido offered little to get my juices flowing.

There is no farmer's market in town, and only two modest eateries to choose from. Avenue Perez Gasga is one half-mile of unpaved main-street featuring a drugstore, and a handful of small shops manned by straight-faced locals who seem to be waiting for something of interest to inspire their day.

We have traveled two hundred and thirty miles to get here from Acapulco and I really can't tell you why, other than this is the only length of highway one can travel to reach Oaxaca from Zihuatanejo. Oh, yes, and there is the possibility of running into Alison and her friends.

Walking towards town, away from the beach, we encountered a group of friendly young Americans, none of them surfers, who told us they were staying at a youth hostel/campground down by the surfing beach and that there was plenty of room available, if we were interested. We recounted our evening spent on the beach and they seemed blown away by our bravado, or was it stupidity?

"You two are quite the lucky muchachos." Ernie, a caterpillar-mustached lad, informed us, "We were told when we first hooked up in town never to camp on the beaches because several people, as of late, have ended up severely beaten in the dead, pardon that expression, of night." He smiled, then gave me an unexpected high-five.

"Looks like you two dudes may have a guardian angel looking over your shoulder." I recalled the mutt there at the base of my bag and wondered how soon after we crashed he had shown up, serving as a potential deterrent to any deeds of a nefarious nature. Mexico Magic at work, I would say.

Ernie's freshly-mohawked friend, Aaron, showed up halfway through our conversation. We suddenly smelt Surf Nazi infiltration in our midst.

Ernie continued, "We have been here a week and have seen a lot of gringos ripped off. Not by the locals as much as shifty elements working the campground. Keep your eyes on your valuables at all time. Don't smoke any dope with anyone you don't know. Rumor has it there's a lot of Angel Dust-tainted boo being sold to new arrivals. That's some real evil shit. Trust no one. Except us. Wanna buy some dope?" They both laughed, then bid farewell.

A decision was needed. Should we stay or keep on moving to Oaxaca? Meeting friendly characters such as Ernie and Aaron made our decision easy.

Between last evening's shifty cab driver, blood-sucking mosquitoes, gut-rotting coffee, and a preponderance of skinhead-types, the vote was unanimous. Time to keep rolling, check out some ruins, perhaps even buy a blanket or two. Oaxaca here we come.

Travel options were simple--by bus, or air, as Ted noted an airport was located a short distance away. Bus travel was pesos, but, Dangerous assured me, a flight of this distance (one hundred fifty miles) would cause a slight dip into our budgetary red zone.

Inquiries revealed a second-class bus left from Escondido twice daily, yet Doris told of a brief conversation she had had with their next-door neighbors earlier that morning, who offered first hand testimony that Oaxaca by bus was a rather treacherous endeavor.

These folks had arrived here yesterday, overland from Oaxaca, and were still getting over a nasty case of jitters induced by their bumpy, perilous ride over dusty, rutted, and at times even unpaved and one-lane roadways that wound trepidaciously through steep, mountain passes.

Maneuvering along at snail's pace, they had gazed over embankments lacking guardrails, only to notice more than a few skeletons of rusted-out cars, trucks and even unfortunate busses who failed to successfully navigate the dicey hairpin curves. The entire trek took them almost ten hours to complete. Time for us to check out the friendly sky's alternative.

We found the office of Aero Mexico on the main street of the downtown among the many surrounding idle shops and vacant buildings prominent. Even though it was noon, they had not yet open.

Just then a cab driver hailed Dave and told him a flight from Puerto Escondido to Oaxaca cost 440 pesos; twenty-five dollars. Now the stickler: This being Saturday plane tickets could only be purchased at the airport.

None of us favored another grinding overland bus marathon, especially after the horror story we had just heard, so Ted and Dave volunteered to check on the availability of tickets while Doris and I passed the time watching Surf Nazis hang ten.

Suddenly I heard my name called out, and there was Suzy, Alison's giggly girlfriend. She threw her arms around me like I was an old friend she had not seen in years.

"God it's so good to see an American we can trust!" The fact they had been running the bad vibes gauntlet as well since arrival reinforced our need to vacate the premises as quickly as our huarache-covered feet could move.

"Yesterday we met some nice, really clean-cut guys from Austin who bought us cervezas, then offered to take us surfing." I could smell trouble brewing. "We were on our way back to our room to change into our bathing suits when I noticed that my backpack was missing. So were the nice guys. We checked the hostel, both hotels, anywhere we thought they might pop up but we have not seen them since."

My good friend Alison? Seems she was back in her room, reeling from a debilitating bout of Tourista and was not up for a visit by anyone other than, perhaps, a priest or mortician. As badly as I wished to see her, I could relate to her dire circumstance and told Suzy to pass on my very best. So much for destiny, dammit.

It was also time to cash in more of my dwindling Travelers Cheques to pay for the flight and whatever else may come our way over the duration of the weekend ahead.

Since it was Saturday and the bancos were closed, I had to take my chances with the local Pharmacia. I bid farewell to Suzy and stepped inside, where I waited patiently for the better of ten minutes while the sour-faced middle-aged Señora behind the counter treated me as if I was invisible whilst she continued conversing with a friend.

Cold-shouldered and out of patience, I interrupted their conversation to ask for assistance utilizing my weak Spanish. She shook her head and pointed in the direction of a young girl cleaning the shelves with a dust mop who graciously took time from her chores to come to the cash register and help me out.

Amidst all the bad shit we had experienced the past twelve hours, the scales of fortune suddenly tipped in my favor.

I handed over my signed Travelers Cheques, worth the equivalent of five hundred pesos. In return, she placed fifteen hundred pesos in my hand with a very warm smile.

I glanced at the wad of bills in shock, then back to my still beaming clerk while trying to sort this transaction out in my mind. I tried to point out her mistake, but she did not want to hear it. Instead, she closed my hand around the wad of sudden wealth, gestured towards the front door and said "Adios." My plane trip to Oaxaca was on the house with enough left over to take care of several days lodging and meals as well.

Ted and Dave returned, stepping out of the cab in an obvious uptight manner. Dave called the driver a bandito and refused to pay him. It seems they got to the airport only to be told that all tickets had to be purchased *in town, No Exceptions!!!* What is with the cab drivers in this town anyway? Chalk up experience number two in the Scam-o-rama category.

By now, the Aero Mexico office had opened and Ted purchased four one-way tickets for our short jaunt aboard a twenty-eight passenger DC-3. The lone daily flight lifts off at noon, less than an hour away.

With a stitch of reluctance, we hailed the next passing cab, thankful to see a different driver. We surely couldn't go three for three, could we?

We asked his price. "Thirty pesos."

For all passengers, together?

"Si." With a set price agreed upon, we were off to the airport. Adios Puerto Escondido...

Within minutes we arrived at the airport--A landing strip built on what I assume to be the town's only flat parcel of land. There was a wind sock, a control tower, what I assumed was our plane, as well as four or five smaller aircraft sitting about.

We all hopped out of the cab and flew into action, Ted hustling off to check us in, Doris, Dave, and I in charge of our gear. Our driver opened the trunk for us to unload our bags and Doris handed him the thirty pesos. He stopped, looked at the pesos and informed us that, no, the deal was thirty pesos *per* person. Another cab ride in Puerto Escondido gone sour--Three for three!!!

We disagreed. Whatever was in the air that turns this town's cabbies into banditos was not going to succeed this time around. He closed the trunk with two thirds of our gear still inside, folded his arms and sat on the rear with a stubborn scowl. No money, no backpacks.

A crowd of locals, gathered nearby waiting for a bus edged closer to watch how this plays out, chuckling under their breath at the plight of the well-played gringos. Dave, Doris, and the cabbie began a heated dialogue, yet the driver remained steadfast. Ninety more pesos, *por favor*. In Spanish, Dave and Doris accused our guy of being a low-life money-grubbing piss head. Still no luggage. The time of our departure grew closer.

Suddenly our normally calm Doris went ballistic, poking her finger aggressively in his chest while cutting loose with an impressive array of words I'd never heard; words which stirred the crowd into a hearty round of chuckles. Suddenly it seemed we had the hometown fans rooting for the underdog Americans.

Doris paused, took a breath, then let out a long sigh. Her battle was over. "Okay, Señor, you win. Thirty per person."

He grinned, then reopened the trunk. Doris got out her wallet. What was going on? Why did she cave so quickly? As I pondered these questions Dave and I removed the remaining belongings from the trunk.

The smirking driver held out his hand and Doris, seeing all bags now in our possession, pulled the deal off the table and offered thirty total. "Screw you, chucklehead-- --TAKE IT OR LEAVE IT!!!"

The crowd roared at her superb display of one-upmanship. Our cabbie, embarrassed because he hadn't demanded the money before opening the trunk, snapped the peso notes from her hand, climbed quickly back into his cab without a word and peeled out, leaving an impressive ten-foot patch of rubber for us all to remember him by. No doubt he would find more Americanos to screw before the day was through.

The locals cheered again and gave Doris a unanimous thumbs up as they climbed aboard their bus.

Our adrenaline spiked, we found Ted, checked in our gear and retold the saga as we watched our flight fuel up. Dangerous produced a celebratory joint from his pack and motioned for me to follow him over to the bushes where we burned the red-haired good luck doob, to help get us on our way. After tossing the roach, we arrived back in the waiting area just as the door opened for boarding.

We took our seats and Ted tapped me on the shoulder, offering to share a pint of rum. The herb had been successful at taking the edge off and I was feeling just fine, thank you.

We sat for at least twenty minutes before the hatch finally closed and liftoff appeared imminent. My seat looked directly out at the left wing where I could not help but notice a puff of dark smoke emanating from the engine housing as the pilot fired up the motor.

There was only one dark cloud, no others followed, but my psyche had been rattled. I asked Ted if his offer of Bacardi was still on the table and the bottle was passed my way. I finished a full cup, minus mixer or chaser, just as we lifted off from the ever-so-short runway, rising towards a landscape of endless prominent barren mountain ranges. From the air, they looked a lot like the NASA photographs I have seen of Mars, only with a dark brown terrain replacing that planet's red texture.

Brushing aside visions of Jim Croce, Buddy Holly and Lynyrd Skynyrd, I forced myself to conjure up highlights of our short time in town.

Like the beautiful Alison, all pale and hunched over a toilet, shaking from dysentery's Devil fever; no one nice like yours truly there to comfort her.

Like two muscle-headed surf punks sliding aboard a bus leaving Escondido with a brimful of other people's scammed belongings.

Like a bloodthirsty gaggle of goons, walking the beaches after midnight; looking for anyone stupid enough to spend the night by the sea, only to come upon an unidentifiable species of dual-eyed mongrel, causing them to move on and seek out other knuckleheads in similar scenarios.

I even visualized two off-duty cabbies, sitting in a grimy Puerto Escondido cantina, playing poker, a coffee can brimming with pesos accumulated from a day's worth of weaseling unsuspecting gringo customers beside them, all the while wondering why their third partner had yet to show up.

Dave nudged me from my pleasant stony-boy daydreams. "Auzapaum?" Hadn't I just recovered from that Valium stupor that left us goo-goo under a streetlamp in the middle of bum-fuck Puerto Escondido with nary a clue as to which way was up? Hadn't I just vowed not to partake ever again in those powerful mother's little helpers while rolling deep into my sleeping bag there on the beach?

I looked out towards the left wing with a silent prayer that there would be no more puffs of smoke coming from that engine. Hey "Peggy Sue", please have "Bad Bad Leroy Brown" pass that little blue "Freebird" of a Valium my way. Just to take the edge off; just to make it through this flight... Like The Big Bopper himself would say, 'Oh baby that's a what I like.'

As the warm little fuzzies crept in, I glanced out my window to the treacherous-looking earth below. We had most certainly made the right choice.

Mile after mile of highway ribbon wound up and over pass after pass after ever-loving' pass. A lone bus was visible, crawling up a long hill with at least ten antsy cars and trucks closely in tow. Down below the steep guardrail-less embankments, the framework of many unfortunate vehicles could be seen, validating the claim of the couple Doris had met that morning.

I switched my attention to the magazine rack on the back of the seat before me. There a remarkable coincidence occurred. I peered inside, hoping to find suitable reading material to divert my attention from the road of death below and came upon quite a surprise. Fate, destiny, or just plain goose pimple-making weirdness?

A copy of Carlos Castenada's The Teachings of Don Juan occupied the space. The same copy I had come across back on my roof hangout, many days ago in Barra--that is, unless, each printed copy comes with the bottom right-hand corner ripped off and the same bookmark tucked inside. Now that's some damn freaky coincidental happenstance.

On my way to becoming more than a bit anesthetized by the various substances cruising through my bloodstream, I took the novel out, and put it in my pack. Destiny dictated that this was the next book I would be reading.

Shortly after my discovery I drifted off, soothed by the vibrations provided by our well-chosen mode of transportation. We flew towards Oaxaca; the hum of the engines a happy, happy song.

18. Oaxaca

Monday, February 12

As our plane touched down in Oaxaca, our Mexican experience changed lanes. Six weeks of beach bum living was yesterday's news. Toss out the old play book, bring in the new.

First, no more Kid for comic relief. Now alongside three well-traveled veterans, I vowed to avoid falling into the same self-imposed state of oblivion Kid had descended into.

We were back in urban-oriented inland Mexico, yet in Oaxaca, automotive pollution or bumper to bumper traffic was minimal. The citizens are different as well; folks lean more towards Indian descent, and who do not approach you with persistent capitalistic intent. My biggest transition involved trading crashing shores, sandy beaches, and intense sun for this cooler, arid mountain terrain.

According to Ted's Peoples Guide to Mexico, my huaraches were now treading along at a lofty 5070-foot altitude, snuggled amidst a rugged rolling mountain backdrop which goes on far as the eye can see.

As stated on page twelve, the locals are descendants of the Zapotec Indian, people who lived in these hills 800 years before the birth of Christ.

Over time, the inhabitants have built a charming city with a flourishing culture centered on the pyramids Monte Albán, six miles from the downtown area. Centuries later, the ruins still stand, a stunning glimpse into the past. Hopefully we will find the time to make a brief trip there while we are here, but first, a tad more history.

The Mixtecs built a rival community at Mitla, thirty-six miles away on the other side of Oaxaca. These two tribes struggled for control of the valley for decades, until they were united in their attempts to fend off a common enemy--those savage warriors, the Aztecs.

Some of the very finest rugs in the world are still made in Mitla, but unfortunately time, as well as financial restrictions, eliminates that visit on this trip.

Oaxaca is a major cultural hub of central Mexico, with its abundance of ruins, cloth makers and rug weavers. Twenty-seven churches with skyward-shooting cathedrals are distinguishable features one observes on a city walkabout.

Two highly-touted museums present a detailed history of central Mexico as well as diverse samples of cultural handiwork. Oaxaca also is home to magnificent Spanish colonial-style mansions worthy of viewing. Unfortunately, time spent here will be short, a pit stop on our marathon trek, as Dave and I have decided to push on from here to our ultimate destination, Palenque.

Our first night in town was spent at the Hotel Del Valle, located in the heart of Centro. One hundred and fifty pesos bought us tile floors, warm baths, a central terrace with oversized wicker furniture which provide a great view of central Oaxaca.

In the heart of Centro, a large gazebo bandstand presents live music every evening. At 7 p.m., we ate at one of the many sidewalk cafes along the square. There we enjoyed tasty Snapper Veracruz and fine Mexican coffee as a fifty-piece brass band performed from the stage for nearly an hour.

After dinner, we took a mile-long jaunt through the Calles surrounding our hotel, then early to bed; no celebratory cantina-hopping tonight, as we focused on saving cash as well as brain cells.

The highlight of our second day in town was an afternoon spent exploring the marketplace. Not nearly as grandiose as Guadalajara's, still our visit kept us moving for well over three hours. Hundreds of craftsmen were in action, eager to sell their goods at "very special prices--today only!"

Once again, the smells rising from an amazing array of spices provided olfactory delight. Chilies powdered as well as fresh, seemed to be the most abundant spice on hand. Wheelbarrows brimming over with exotic colorful fruits and unfamiliar vegetables, filled row after row after row.

Turn a corner and you are greeted by ripe meats spoiling in the heat as they lack refrigeration. Rows of chopped off cow hooves destined for pots of Pozole hang like laundry on a clothesline. Disembodied pig heads dance on hooks, while halos of flies buzz in and out of their grinning mouths. Our thoughts turned to Kid and the many variations of horror his face was capable of bearing as he passed through this specific area weeks ago, back in Guadalajara.

The greatest percentage of Oaxaca's marketplace is artesian-based. Rugs, rugs and more rugs; tapestries and carpets of every size, style, and price imaginable are here for the taking. Their many different designs represent a different culture or tribe that inhabits the vast hills surrounding Oaxaca. It is in this area of the market we spent most of our time. There, Ted and Doris bartered for blankets as well as some of the beautiful pottery.

Harboring an affinity for pro wrestling, I was tempted to further deplete my remaining funds as I came upon six incredible wrestling masks hanging from one of the booths, each featuring a different colorful and creative design.

Fiscal reality was such that in order to own a mascara, or wrestling masks, I would have to pass up two days of meals, yet they were soooo cool.

I had to try on the one with jagged bolts of lightning running down both sides. Fortunately, it did not fit, *"para los niños solamente"* (only for kids), the vendor regretfully informed me. He continued to lobby for purchase--for the day I do have children. I passed.

Dave admired my willpower, reminding me if we run low on funds and end up on the verge of starvation, a wrestling mask is not an easily digestible item.

Another of Ted's travel guides recommended a hotel called The Scalpel. Located a healthy cab ride into the hills, away from the heart of Oaxaca it caught our interest and even though it was a financial cut above our usual choice of accommodations.

According to this publication, The Scalpel offered a tennis court, Jacuzzi, sauna, along with a swimming pool--creature comforts for the rich and famous--available at a price even the average Jose could afford.

Since this was the furthest south Ted and Doris would be going and since Dave and I would only be staying in Oaxaca a day or two longer, at most, we decided to splurge. In an admirable gesture of true friendship, Ted offered to foot the bill for us all.

Twenty minutes later our cab dropped us off at The Scalpel. As we checked in, Dave inquired if the tennis courts were available this afternoon. Marcello, the desk attendant, stifled a smirk and pointed out beyond the west side of the office. "Check them out yourself, amigo." he offered in Spanish.

Dangerous and Ted headed off in the direction Marcello had pointed while I hung around the front desk.

After our recent experience with Enrique, I decided to brazenly play a hunch. "So, Marcello, are these hillsides full of mota?" I inquired, a friendly and innocent smile pasted across my mug.

He looked around to make sure we were alone. "Si. It is fair to say that there is an abundance here in Oaxaca. Sinsemilla, red hairs, very good and, how you say, *sticky*" Marcello smiled and began rubbing his index and middle finger together.

"If I may ask, what are one's chances of actually acquiring some of this very sticky herb?"

"That my friend depends on the amount one might be interested in. One kilo? Two kilos? Perhaps more…?" A business-like gleam suddenly shone in Marcello's eyes; one I wasn't expecting. I had gotten myself in deeper than intended, and quite quickly so.

"Uh, I was thinking more like an ounce, maybe."

"*Una onza*? I am sorry my friend, I must get back to folding these towels before my manager returns from town." I took my room key, grabbed my backpack, and headed off towards our room. Dipshit-itis can truly be a humbling phenomenon.

Before I even had time to dig into the dresser drawers, checking for a copy of Gideon's Bible, *en Español*, Dave came in, shaking his head, and gestured for me to follow him back outside. "Follow me. Ya gotta look at this."

We scurried past the office, around the side of the building to where Marcello had informed the potential tennis buffs they would find the tennis courts. Former tennis courts, that is.

There before us stood a large, chain link concrete enclosure, which at a previous time in history, had been two regulation length tennis courts. Running vertically down the center of court one was a long large crack, the result of a recent earthquake. Knee-high grass and thorny weeds sprouted ran the full length of the gash.

Court two housed a pair of scrawny yet mean-ass looking Rottweilers, tied up haphazardly to a five-foot length of thin half-gnawed rope. They saw us approaching and struck an aggressive pose that meant one of two things: I haven't eaten for a week now and here comes some fresh-looking Carne Asada or I haven't eaten for a week now and here comes some fresh-looking Gringo Burritos. Fortunately, the formidable midday sun convinced them to remain in the shade of their doghouse.

Further investigation led us to The Scalpel's pool. It too was not as advertised. Apparently empty for a lengthy period of time, perhaps even years, the pool bore long gaping crevasses along the bottom. A six-inch layer of stagnant green water, source of the strong swampy smell we had noticed earlier, was all that remained. A rusted-out pump sat in the middle of the pool, its hoses about two feet too short to extract the pungent agua from the recesses of the concrete shell. Impressed by all we had seen so far, we eagerly sought out The Scalpel's Jacuzzi.

It was more difficult to find, basically because it had been partially dug up and filled with sod. Overcome by embarrassment and frustration, Ted chucked his handy book of popular resort choices far down a nearby embankment. We laughed as we watched it tumble, end over end, until it disappeared into the brambles far below.

Our flight on Buddy Holly Airlines, sandwiched in between two butt-numbing bus journeys can tend to heat up the tension meter, yesiree, so when situations such as this arise, you have two choices: You can crumble, blow up, and will yourself right into a deep morass of bad karma or you can laugh, give yourself a slap on the head and move on. The latter was the most prudent choice.

Since he was footing the bill, we let Ted make the call, which was spend our last night in Oaxaca right where we were. In the morning, we would find the bus station, say our good-byes, and head off to San Cristobal.

A sudden kink in our game plan lie just ahead.

The next morning, we high-tailed it to the bus station around 9:30 a.m. to discover only one bus per day travels between Oaxaca and San Cristobal. Unfortunately, it left here an hour ago, at 8:30.

Dangerous was extremely frustrated at his lack of foresight in checking schedules, going as far as to say if we miss tomorrow's departure we may have to turn back to Z-Wat, due to our ever-decreasing fragile budget.

We headed back to Centro, walking distance from the bus station. To compensate for this oversight, we partook in a self-imposed twenty-four hour fast. Hardcore, yet doable.

To help make the most of the day, Ted treated us to an eighteen-peso bus tour, off into the mountains, up to the ruins of Monte Albán.

The road to Monte Albán was a rolling coil of pavement besieged by endless chuckholes. We wound our way up, up, up, through lush kelly-green countryside, in a never-ending series of Ss before rolling to a stop, six miles from town on the top of a mountain.

Stretching there before us lay the ruins of Monte Albán, roughly forty square acres of brown grassy flatland.

The city of the gods, as it was known to its inhabitants, was once the center of civilization from 1500 BC to 1400 AD; almost 3000 years ago. Humbling stuff for those of us who consider one hundred years an eternity. In the distance, rolling hills give way to lush green Oaxacan valleys that stretch out far as the eye can see.

Excited to explore the ruins, we stepped off the bus. Immediately hordes of pint-sized child vendors came at us as aggressively as the swarms of mosquitoes we had battled back in Puerto Escondido.

From the moment we arrived until the moment we left, they were in our faces, thrusting a variety of replicated artifacts our way, pleading for us to purchase these treasures in squeaky pre-pubescent voices. *"Authentica!! Authentica!!"* That was the extent of their pitch; two words, pummeling all prospective customers with incessant tenacity until you open your wallet and buy them off.

We did our best to ignore them. This only intensified their efforts to close the deal. They followed us everywhere; temples, pyramids, ceremonial platforms, even into the tombs. You would stoop over to examine a hieroglyphic, turn back around and there they were, smiling as they waved their wares in your face. *"Authentica! Authentica!"*

We kept walking, they kept following.

When we were sitting there at the Up & Up, way back when, I had no clue whatsoever regarding the significance of Monte Albán. I knew nothing about its history, cultural significance, or the purpose of everything I was busily exploring.

My favorite site was a ceremonial temple, massive in size, full of courtyards and secret passages. I was busy debating with myself whether this was the coolest thing I had ever experienced when I overheard two fellow tourists chatting nearby.

Tourist One was expounding on the architectural wonder of a well-preserved temple standing before them when Tourist Two cut him off in mid revelation, "No matter what I see here, Benny, these ruins ain't squat. If you don't do anything else while here on this trip, you've got to get over to the eastern seaboard and check out Palenque. Now _those_ are ruins!!"

Hmm. This intercepted snippet of conversation had me fired up for tomorrow's 8:30 departure. I'm ready to hop on board and hunker down in San Cristobal de la Casas, our next destination. Then on to Palenque, to check out some real *ruinas* before we boomerang back to the west coast.

19: KARMA, THE MYSTIC & THE DIVINE CACTUS

"A man of knowledge is one who had followed truthfully the hardships of learning." Don Juan

Valentine's day, yet for Dangerous and myself, no roses, no romance. The only word beginning with RO in my ever-expanding vocabulary is ROAD. Once again, that is where we find ourselves.

Doris' recommendation we buy our tickets the night before turned out to be a wise move indeed.

Dangerous and I arrived at the station at 7 a.m., tickets already in hand, to learn today's bus was already sold out. Many people who had lined up to purchase their boletos were agitated and groaning, having to spend another day in Oaxaca.

San Cristobal was twelve hours away; time to find a happy zone to make it through another marathon haul. We both agreed to tuck the *Azapaum* away and handle the challenge *au natural,* as the residual hangover experienced on our previous extended road grinds had not exactly worked in our favor once we arrived at our destination.

With hours to kill, I pulled out the Castaneda book, *The Teachings of Don Juan,* and fell deeply into the story. For those unfamiliar with the journeys of Don Juan, it's difficult to describe the scope of what our protagonist achieves in this first of many volumes. Consider the following as little more than notes on a subject one can spend an evening or two dissecting and discussing.

During the summer of 1960, Carlos Castaneda, an anthropology student involved in researching and obtaining information about medicinal plants of the Southwest, met Don Juan, a Yaqui medicine man, considered by many to be a sorcerer or brujo-- "holder of sacred knowledge"-in a border town of Arizona.

It takes a year for Castaneda to convince Don Juan that he is sincere in his desire to learn these ways. Thus begins the long, somewhat convoluted process of introducing Castaneda to a world, not merely different from that of our own, but of an entirely different order of reality.

Don Juan believes that what one sees lies within the beholder, that not only do people have different customs, we worship different gods with different fates awaiting our demise, and that the worlds of different people have different shapes.

With these concepts only a slight part of the picture, Castaneda embarks upon bridging the world of the Yaqui sorcerer with that of his own; the world of non-ordinary reality with the world of ordinary reality.

Don Juan says that by experiencing other worlds we see ours for what it's truly worth. So, they begin opening doors to Don Juan's world by the use of three hallucinogenic plants: peyote, Datura (or jimsonweed), and mushrooms--used primarily for pleasure, curing, witchcraft, and for attaining a state of ecstasy. While their most common use is for getting high, Don Juan treats them with the utmost reverence, using them solely for the acquisition of wisdom, or the knowledge of the right way to live.

Along the pathway to shamanic enlightenment, Don Juan learned how to fly, talked to a bilingual coyote, and encountered amazing columns of singing light.

Over the next few years Don Juan takes Castaneda into states of non-ordinary reality using each of these plants in order to teach him the secrets or insights which make up the foundation of a man of knowledge.

Often, these introductions are unpleasant, often confusing; one minute bordering on intense ecstasy, the next, full of fear and disorientation. This is fascinating stuff but I think I'll stick with mere libations and shrubberies as I have no desire to be crawling around naked on the desert, suffering mass hallucinations, smoking jimsonweed, regurgitating peyote bile, all the while howling like a dog. Leave that to the true seekers of knowledge, thank you. I think I'll just stick to trying to be the best person possible, calling on basic common sense to be my recourse, at least this time around.

This accumulation of knowledge is introduced in *The Teachings of Don Juan*. There are several volumes that follow which I may or may not get to, but this first introduction has most certainly served as food for thought.

There is only the slightest thread of correlation between Castaneda's journey and that of my own, yet I understand why Dave suggested I read this literature in order to enhance my trip.

Don Juan believes that knowledge is power and power rests on the kind of knowledge one holds. I've come to this country basically ignorant of what to expect and have had to adapt to what goes on around me many times already in order to make my experience as enjoyable as possible. His statement "Nothing in the world is a gift. Whatever there is to learn must be learned the hard way." certainly resonates with this leg of our journey.

So far, this leg of our journey has been dominated by lengthy hours spent on the road, confronted by a whole array of obstacles: bus delays, mosquito wars, rat attacks nefarious Surf Nazis, and lack of hotel vacancies, Lets us add more than a handful of miscreant cab drivers to that list.

A month ago, this level of adversity would have thrown me into a mood so foul, negative, and pessimistic I'd have earned a ticket on the next plane home without even a wave goodbye. But I feel my demeanor has delivered mostly positive responses whenever any crisis has come before us.

For one who embraces his American life of leisure, I have begun to thrive on this steady stream of adversity and adventure. Much like a long-distance runner feels once they pass the midway point, I'm feeling my second wind in this race. Bring on that next bus trip. Six hours--is that all? Haven't showered for two days, but I did brush my teeth last night. Three-hour delay? No problem, I'll just kick back and people watch until it is time to move along.

As Castaneda's Don Juan says: "For me there is only the traveling on the paths that have heart, on any path that may have heart. There I travel and the only worthwhile challenge for me is to traverse its full length. And there I travel-looking, looking, breathlessly." Sounds like where we are going; right here, right now.

Many Americans who experience Mexico opt to choose the easy route to attain their vision of leisure, Mexican style; staying in four-star hotels, eating meals prepared solely by four-star chefs, never straying too far from the comfort zone these hotels provide.

Most of these folks choose resort-provided pools over the warm salt-water magic the Pacific, or Caribbean Oceans offer. For them, the playgrounds of Mazatlán, Puerto Vallarta, Acapulco, and Cabo San Lucas are the perfect destination.

I would like to think we have enjoyed ourselves equally as much by experiencing this country via the grittier hard-core route. Let this be our interpretation of *Mexico Magic*.

Don Juan also believes the limits of one's learning are determined by one's own nature. How far do you want to go and what do you want to see? I read that line to Dangerous, somewhere about the eighth hour of today's ride, and his eyes lit up.

"You have stumbled onto something mighty heady for a lad of your sorts. Keep going and we will re-evaluate what level of resilience you've actually accomplished, three or four days from now when we're winging our way back to Z-Wat, ok?"

It was eight thirty, twilight time, when we finally staggered, stiff and exhausted, off the bus in San Cristobal, in the state of Chiapas. This city sits 7000 feet above sea level, therefore the chill which has greeted us upon our arrival. While at the market yesterday in Oaxaca, Dave suggested I should sacrifice a few hundred pesos for a colorful wool serape. It was a wise investment.

One hundred pesos bought us a room at Hotel San Francisco. Here we kicked back on our verandah hoping to catch our breath and to finalize the last leg of the road to Palenque.

Across the landscape, several impressive church spires dominate San Cristobal's mountainous skyline. Once again, I stand in awe of the many geographical contrasts Mexico exhibits from one coast to the other.

Palenque is the last 'to do' dot on the map on our southeastward journey to the land of the mummified Mayans, or whatever wonders of immeasurable magnitude we were heading off to partake in. Guatemala, lies less than one hour to the south.

We have made a radical transition-from sun to mountain chill, from tourist-friendly terrain to an area where you most certainly are among very few gringos, and non-natives. An eerie feeling of isolation has begun to add a slight edge to my weariness, making me irritable and more than a slight bit manic. Dave's resilience test has begun…

As we began this morning's trek to San Cristobal, I was ready to take on the world—Andy Clark, king of long-distance endurance.

Now, as the very same day comes to a close, anxiety starts to manifest within, yet I am too committed to the miles we had already put in to start whimpering like you-remember-who.

I'll battle the uneasiness building inside, although if Dangerous suddenly had a change of heart, opting to abort Project Palenque here and now, I doubt I would object.

Edginess, irritability, and exhaustion, as well as the enormity this marathon has demanded keep trying to edge their way into my psyche, yet a special sense of purpose continue to remind me to hang loose, keep cool; don't start treading water in the shallow end of the pool.

Around nine, we decided to seek out well-deserved subsistence; nothing like a hearty meal of regional cuisine to snap a guy out of a funk.

As we walked single file down the narrow streets, cars and busses whizzed by, mere inches away. Oblivious to any or all danger, I move on, eyes scanning each calle we pass for the right source of nourishment--one where I will find the perfect meal to bring comfort to my carbohydrate-deprived constitution.

20. Dangerous Wields the Pen...

       2/15   9:30 am
Dear Sis:
   Happy Valentine's Day!!! Please give my best to all those worthy of it, as well as those who are not, and tell them that we are trucking along just fine, thank you.
   As I write, I am sitting in a second-story room in a cheap but adequate hotel in San Cristobal. Look on the map-- towards the southeastern seaboard, east of Oaxaca yet west of Palenque, our final destination on this whopper of a marathon. That is where you will find us.
   Outside our window, I spy an archaic temple on a high-pointed hill in the distance. If we had more time, I would be there checking it out, but tomorrow, at noon, we're outta here. A floor below, a monkey in a cage gives off an occasional shrill bird-like whistle.
   This morning I was standing in the line at the banco and I met this guy with a cool set of bow and arrows he had just purchased from some native Indians in the town square. He said that they only come out of the hills once every few years to sell their wares. A dandy price--only five dollars.
   You know me, I now have a bow and six different tipped arrows shaped to kill anything from a tree squirrel to a rabid panther. There was even a tip guaranteed to stop a two-ton rampaging elephant. I'll be sure to bring them by for show and tell when I see you, sometime in March.

I'm unusually loaded down with souvenirs at this point. I have four or five pieces of pottery, a bevy of miniature clay tequila shot glasses, some hand-made dolls, an obligatory picture of Jesus, a hand-made purse and some huaraches which have proven to be very functional for the journey at hand.

By now Kid is probably bagging groceries back at Thriftway, but the Tunester has risen to the occasion and shows a fine nose for the road. We are trying to pump up for the long leg ahead but are showing signs of fatigue and altitude sickness from the radical changes every day brings.

After immersing ourselves in the archeological wonders awaiting us in Palenque, we will have to dash back to Zihuatanejo by bus where we will wind down on the last of our Travelers Cheques before heading home.

Last night we found a casual little pizza palace off the beaten path where we had a great cheesy pie that reminded me of home, and even made a new friend, a beautiful lady named Elaine from Eugene, of all places.

She invited us back to her abode where she pulled out a bit of the old green herb she graciously shared with the two of us.

For a while I thought Tunes might score, romantically so to speak, but either he misread his opportunity or (like myself) was totally scrambled from our pace or perhaps his molecules had been a little too modified to pick up on Elaine's apparent interest in him. What we did score though could enhance our Palenque experience beyond wildest expectations.

Seems like Elaine has made good friends with some of the more prominent people here in town who have provided her with very nice little stash of peyote buttons. She asked me if I was interested, then gave me a handful, five to six buttons~a sufficient quantity to make howling monkeys of us both (for an appropriate duration of time).

This fits in perfectly with the fact that Tunes now has his nose buried in The Teachings of Don Juan. What could be more apropos than cavorting through the mighty jungles of Palenque, totally out of control on THE DIVINE CACTUS? Do not worry, I guarantee we will both come home in one piece!

I could scribble on for hours but it's time to pack up, ride a rickety second~class bus full of Indians, chickens and pigs, for almost a dozen hours through the thick, laborious jungle which boasts one of the heaviest annual rainfalls on the face of Mother Earth. Sounds like a gas. Love U All, Dangerous...

21. JUNGLE BOOGIE

Highway 199, the road to Palenque; off to an adventure beyond the wildest limits of my imagination.

Sitting back there at the Up & Up, all I envisioned our trip would consist of was surf and sun. Oh, and I must add alcohol.

Not once did I consider finding myself riding along, here in the southern region, watching the terrain swallowed up completely by endless miles of tangled jungle vegetation sharing the land with forests as we moved deeper into the heart of the region.

I'd never ridden a bus before January, let alone patiently queued up for train tickets. I had no idea how to speak a lick of Spanish, yet now I can barter with the street vendors, negotiate competently, and even end up getting a deal.

Before Mexico, I had never heard of a no-see-um. Now I have perfected the technique of thoroughly wiping my legs free of any sand before crawling into bed, in order to get a decent night's sleep without suffering the wrath of their tenacious microscopic mandibles. It surely has been quite the enlightening experience.

Yours truly is just a mere hop, skip, and one sideways jump away from Belize. That's Latin frickin' America for those at home keeping score.

Just yesterday I stood sporting my new serape, freezing my cojones off while admiring the snow-capped mountains surrounding San Cristobal. By daylight, no serape is necessary, but when the sun disappears, it best be close at hand. Just the other side of those mountains,

Dangerous promised the landscape would soon again transform, this time into a far-reaching wonder-world of dense jungle, full of waterfalls, deep canyons, and gorges. So far this morning as we close in on Palenque, that has been coming true.

The farther we have traveled the more primitive the roads become. Our bus crawls along at a pace which makes the milk run we experienced seem like the Indy 500. We approach the Gulf of Mexico, cautiously, on uneven and crudely paved one and a half-lane road; currently winding slowly through pine forests reminiscent of the Pacific Northwest. As San Cristobal faded away behind us, the pines continued to grow thicker and the asphalt gave way to red clay terrafirma.

From San Cristobal, the road to Palenque is roughly 112 miles. Dangerous says to get in a zone, as this trip will most likely take us between six and eight hours, based on crude road conditions.

As hour after hour passed, we watched the pines grow scarce and the panorama morph totally into dense dark green jungle. Our bus proceeded at ten kilometers per hour as the driver negotiated crater-sized ruts with prudence and care. A broken axle while in this remote unpopulated wilderness would most certainly result in a very unhappy day for all involved.

Throughout this stretch of road, civilization was close to nonexistent. Occasionally, we would come upon a village consisting of, at most, a row or two of haphazardly constructed thatched huts. No stores nor electricity, no marketplace, no automobiles--as primitive as can be.

The few villagers we came across were of true Indian descent. They wore brightly colored clothing like the natives of Guatemala, I recalled from my National Geographic reading days. The majority carried baskets of unidentifiable goods on their shoulders; many on their heads. They were quick to wave and offer friendly smiles as we passed by.

And then, a truly mind-boggling moment to be taken in.

There, deep as one may ever find themselves in this jungle, stood a single-level abode, pasted together with mud, sticks, and odd-sized 2x4 scraps, topped off by a tin roof which, in another time and place, had been a jumbo-sized weather-worn Coca Cola sign. How it had managed to make its way to bum-fuck nowhere was certainly food for thought. What a score for its inhabitants!

We moved on, ever so slowly, deeper into the wilderness. At one point, it became impossible to tell if we were getting farther away from civilization or actually getting closer to it.

At times, our pace on this leg of the journey reminded me of the classic French movie *Wages of Fear*, in which desperate low-life truckers drove a truckload of highly combustible nitroglycerin across the jungle roads of darkest Africa at a white-knuckle crawl.

Our driver, obviously valuing his bus and its shocks, axle, oil pan and all other critical elements of operation, patiently edged forward, his semi-bald tires dipping down cautiously into each crater's recess, then back out again, only to repeat this process another hundred yards or so down the road. Then again. And again…

One rut resulted in the 'bang our heads in unison on the luggage racks above' routine. Most passengers laughed, only a few cursed. To me it was just part of the package.

Eight hours after boarding in San Cristobal de la Casas, we arrived at our ultimate destination: Palenque.

"Double sixes again-you're toast bucko!" Dangerous moved his pair of blue backgammon pieces past my death-defying blockade of white warriors, down the homestretch to the end of the board, bringing another game to a quick and frustrating ending.

Arriving in Palenque, Dave had pulled a major boner afternoon by absent-mindedly leaving his new set of authentic bow and arrows behind on the bus. He never even noticed their absence until a few hours after we had checked into Hotel Avenida, a cockroach-infested cousin of Barra's Scorpion Heights.

Dave paid for our rooms and signed us in as Charles Bronson and Clint Eastwood, USA. In the space marked occupation, he scribbled Liquidators. We laughed and hauled our backpacks upstairs to our quarters where we began what was intended to be nothing more than a friendly, tension-releasing session of backgammon. Unfortunately for me the tension-breaking aspect failed to materialize.

"Once again, victory is snatched from the jaws of defeat." Dangerous yapped. This type of banter is common between us, yet today his taunts hit home--a sharp jab to my tender mental psyche.

I had just lost my fifth consecutive 'best two out of three' series to my gammon soul mate with whom I have rolled these bones hundreds of times over many years.

During this early evening stretch of stench, I had been unable to even manage to force a third game, losing all ten in a row, most times quite handily. Whenever he needed doubles, he got em; whether they were threes, fours, monster sixes or just modest twos, there they were--conjured up and delivered on demand. My own shitty dice, bad luck (karma?), and mental blunders combined with my inability to come up with a clutch roll whenever needed contributing to subliminally mounting frustration.

I perceived his smile as gloating while he spoke the obvious, "your dice are shit." Hence, I chose the ultimate low road of sportsmanship etiquette. Instead of internalizing my frustration, I reacted in a reprehensible manner by grabbing the folding backgammon case at each end, then slamming it shut with an unearthly he-man growl.

Dice flew in opposite directions and the round blue and white game pieces scattered across the floor. This whole journey was supposed to be exciting, invigorating, the thrill of a lifetime, right?

You would think that after absorbing the three hundred-plus conscious-expanding pages of Castaneda I had just completed I would have proceeded in a much calmer state of mind. Not tonight. I was overpowered, overwhelmed by a massive dose of anxiety; more than a wee bit over the edge.

Dangerous rose silently, grabbed a paperback and an apple, then headed off to the courtyard below to allow me the space necessary to gather my disheveled constitution back together again.

Suddenly alone with the realization of what a hot-headed jackass I had just been, I went introspective, analyzing this self-inflicted condition of high-strung stress I had just demonstrated. After an hour or so of chilling out, I came to this conclusion:

Ever since leaving Z-Wat I have felt like the rubber band man; stretching and stretching--getting tighter instead of looser with each mile traveled. The further removed from those simple beach-side comforts I'd come to enjoy/rely on, the more uptight I've become.

Ironically, the limited amount of Spanish I now comfortably comprehend has become my greatest frustration. I feel as if I'm clinging too much to Dave's coat tails.

I can order foods, count and clearly enunciate the necessary basic greetings, but I crumble when the person I am conversing with takes conversation further and at a more rapid pace. Whenever that occurs, I immediately turn to turd. Dangerous barters for our rooms, he buys our bus tickets and provides any necessary dialogue needed whenever we get into crucial situations-i.e., the airport in Escondido, bartering in San Cristobal, or when I stumble with the correct verbs needed to correctly complete a cohesive thought.

Unable to control these circumstances, I am beginning to feel as if I'm morphing into The Kid Part II. That is the last thing I can conceive ever taking place. I'm fully aware of this, do not like it one damn bit and will do my darndest to avoid letting that metamorphosis take place.

At one of the infrequent bus stops on the way to Palenque my tummy urgently demanded food. I nudged my sleeping cohort, hoping his stomach was singing the same tune. He grumbled; said something I assume meant hunger was not a priority before going back to sleep. Time for a rare solo journey. I told myself I was ready. I could handle this one.

Cautiously I stepped down from the bus, one eye locked on the driver seated at a nearby card table enjoying his lunch break. I needed to make sure he wasn't suddenly going to drop his ham and cheese torta, jump up, close the door and speed off without me. With a full torta, unopened bottle of Coke and a plate of half-eaten frijoles still before him, it was safe to assume our departure was not imminent.

I lined up at the sandwich stand. When my turn came, I smiled confidently at the young girl behind the counter, then gave it my best shot.

"*Una torta con queso, por favor.*"

She reached behind her and grabbed a delicious-looking cheese sandwich wrapped in plastic and laid it before me. "*Viente pesos, por favor.*"

As I handed her my hundred-peso note my solo venture suddenly encountered turbulence. She handed me my change and, just before I could make a smooth getaway, threw me a curve. "*Como te llamas?*"

My shit falleth apart.

Feverishly I dug into my mental Spanish phrase book, fending off any significant sign of panic, only to come up empty-handed. I smiled, then shrugged. She turned to her little sister, exchanged a comment, then both burst into laughter. Demoralized, I swiftly boarded the bus.

Cheeks still afire, I sat down and nudged Sleeping Beauty.

"Hey Dave?" Puffy red eyeballs sized up my sandwich. "What the hell does *Como te llamas* mean?"

"Why?"

"The girl at the *torta* stand--she handed me my change and said '*Como te llamas.*' What's that all about?"

He did his best to stifle a chuckle. "That's a tough one. She just asked you what your name was."

Full essence of *Kidness* swept over me.

I wanted to get back off the bus, step to the front of the line and pronounce my name proudly. Instead, humbled as well as grandly embarrassed I remained seated, inhaling my sandwich in silence.

I longed for Playa La Ropa, far from this stinkin' inland scene. The magnitude of our quest suddenly seemed to start swallowing me alive, yet we were too close to Palenque to bail out now.

So, there I was, soul searching in our room as I retrieved, then returned, each game piece to its rightful place inside the backgammon case. An hour or so had passed. Guilt therapy successfully behind me, I ventured forth to track down my partner.

I apologized, he accepted. High fives exchanged, we were readjusted and ready to conquer the ruins, Time to do a lap around the old town.

22. Deep Breath, Dark Dream

Palenque is closer in size and population to Barra than Z-Wat. Once again, the people were of Indian descent, and once again, dressed in brilliantly colored regionally traditional clothing. They speak a variation of Spanish that differs at times from the traditional Spanish I was learning. Dave occasionally found it difficult to communicate with the same phrases we had been using on the western seaboard.

Due to its proximity to South America and the distance one must traverse in order to reach this wonderland, Palenque is not a true tourist destination. A predominate third world vibe is in the air; a vibe not reliant on tourism or the capitalistic hustle necessary to bolster their economy.

Centro consists of many modest restaurants and shops, grocerias and a town square, yet something seemed different compared to other towns we had frequented. Many of the people we meet seemed friendly more out of necessity/tolerance of tourists than of a sincere desire to make you feel welcome

Most of the gringos we encountered came off as aloof, almost unfriendly as they traveled about. Everyone seemed to be concerned with their own agenda. You could pass them on the street and try to make eye contact yet they tend to look right through you as if you were not there. Dave pointed out that most were Europeans who did not speak English either, eliminating the potential for small talk.

After taking a lap from one end of town to the other, we chose a small family-style restaurant for dinner, then hit the sack much earlier than usual.

But, before bedtime, a pre-Palenque pow wow was in order. Peyote or not peyote--that was tonight's topic. I have never experienced this Divine Cactus, but have heard tales of its potency and extraordinary powers, from experienced friends as well as what the Castaneda book presented. Although volume one only briefly mentions Don Juan's experience with Mescalito, through the volumes that followed, Castaneda continually turned to peyote for enlightenment.

Dangerous had that gleam in his eye which I know quite well as the source of his nickname. "Enlightenment—these little buttons are going to provide the proper insight needed to experience these pyramids in THE perfect state of mind."

He emptied the small paper sack Elaine had given him. Six dried-out round and rather unappealing-looking peyote buttons tumbled onto the table. "See there, before you, the gateway to unchartered pathways of knowledge."

No way Dangerous was to be denied. *If he takes it, we take it* is the motto of the royal brotherhood of eternal stoners of which we were both card carrying members.

The major negative aspect of experiencing peyote lies in its truly bitter taste. What would be the best way to process these buttons--to choke them down without gagging?

We decided chewing them was off the table. To drink them would require the tedious process of pulverizing the buttons to powder, locating fresh leche and then...ah to hell with that one.

So, it came down to chopping them up as fine as possible, into equal portions, throwing our dose down the hatch, then quickly chasing it with swigs from our water bottle. Good golly miss Molly! The buttons were chopped efficiently and divided into two equal packets. Early morning fun awaits.

Often, the standard aftereffect of ingesting peyote is a serious session spent retching until one begins to ascend. Dave looks at that reality matter-of-factly. "We can only react in the manner the Peyote Gods choose us to." Not really the inspirational oration I was hoping for. Short and to the point worked just fine.

That night I had the most unusual dream.

I was lying on my back, at nightfall, staring up at a sky of bright, brilliant celestial 3-D stars, fully illuminated against a jet-black universe, behind. A special lady friend from home, Rebecca, was straddling me, far from sexual, instead as if I was a lawn chair and this was the appropriate way to converse.

The world revolved swiftly; stars and constellations whizzing past, anxious and intent on reaching other destinations.

As this dizzying rotation went on, an intimate one-sided stream of consciousness conversation ensued, me doing all the talking. Enthusiastically I was attempted to explain all I have experienced and absorbed this past month; how Mexico was *this*, how Mexico was *that* and...

Suddenly, she lay a finger upon my lips and laughed; soft, sultry and amused. Over her shoulder, the stars continued to crackle and dance--a thousand points of light shooting towards a red shimmering dot far off in infinite space.

She bent over, coming closer, yes closer, as if we were about to kiss. Her eyes opened, one gray, the other blue. Rebecca spoke with a dark raspy voice she did not own. "**ALL THAT YOU OFFER HAS NO RELEVANCE. IN FACT, YOU ARE NOT EVEN HERE RIGHT NOW**"

Her words were ice. I could no longer breathe. Unable to respond, I watched as she transformed into a crow. Her claws dug sharply at my sternum, yet did not break skin. Then with a shrill caw, shot off towards the cosmos, a bright orange comet trail of star-shaped sparks left behind as she quickly disappeared into the dark of night.

I awoke with a start, thoroughly drenched in sweat. I wanted to wake Dave up and describe in detail this Fellini-esque mind bomb just experienced. Unfortunately, as with most dreams, its bizarre symbolism and intense nature would be little more than meaningless gibberish when processed. Instead, I opted to lay there, eyes wide and heart pumping full throttle. I waited for dawn to come.

23. Liftoff

6:30 a.m. Time once again for the pre-sunrise ritual of hopping out of bed, dressing silently, and getting out the door with great haste. This time both of us are aware a very special day lie ahead.

Groggy and with less than half a dozen syllables uttered between us, we made our way to the small neighborhood groceria, the location the Avenida's manager had assured us the bus to the ruins left from at 7 a.m. each morning

A small contingency was already on hand; two gringo males in their mid to late twenties standing alongside seven locals, in work clothes, hard hats and toting lunch pails, who had already formed a que where we were told our ride to the pyramids would arrive.

Ten minutes before seven, a well-worn second-class bus with a squealing fan belt rumbled up. The driver hopped off, his rig still running, and ambled into the store. The workers hustled aboard. Could this be our ride? Signage on the passenger side of the bus read '*Ruinas Arqueologicas*' suggesting we were on the right track.

The driver reemerged, chowing down the Mexican equivalent of a Hostess Pie and hopped back aboard, barely giving Dave enough time to inquire if this was the correct bus to the ruins. He shook his head, apparently not understanding the question--or was he telling us no?

"*Palenque de Arqueologicas?*" Dangerous repeated, slower this time. Again, the driver shook his head then shrugged his shoulders. Dangerous patiently sought the right phrase.

He motioned the driver to step down from the bus for a moment. Once he stood beside my amigo, Dave pointed to the sign on the side of the bus and spoke slowly, emphasizing each syllable "*Ar-que-o-log-i-cas Ru-i-nas.*"

The driver studied the words intently, as if he had never noticed them before. Finally, his light bulb turned on and he nodded and smiled. "Ah…Si, si-*Ruinas!*"

The seven seated workers, looked at each other, held a hasty conversation, then grabbed their lunch pails and hustled off the bus to stand in front of the groceria once again. Our day was off to a very unusual beginning.

Four to five other passengers joined us on board, then we were gone, speeding with reckless abandon down the narrow dirt streets away from Palenque.

As we headed off into the countryside Dave confided that he too had experienced a peculiar dream as well. His lacked symbolism, 3D galaxies or mystical crows. He conjured up Kid.

In his vision Kid, back home in Longview, sat in his room, unpacking his belongings, perhaps even reliving a moment or two of the journey he had craftily bailed on.

He dumped the books, clothing and other articles out onto his bed then suddenly stopped dead in his tracks as he noticed something unusual he did not recall having packed. A long string dangled from the bottom; one he had no recollection of being there before. A foul unpleasant odor suddenly filled his nostrils.

Kid began tugging on the line, pulling it from the recesses of the near-empty pack until the mummified bat was fully exposed, spinning clockwise like an unwound yo-yo in his trembling hand.

Dave's vision concluded with Kid sitting in the corner, as far away from the pack as possible, staring at the devil bat upon his bedspread, knees pulled up to his chin, a trail of urine slowly making its way across the floor.

His mouth opened, as if to scream, as an endless flow of black microscopic bugs poured forth from the mummy bat. They quickly started filling Kid's pie hole until his face was no longer visible-only his hair, which had had turned completely white.

What a night of dreams! We both laughed and wondered what would occur at his moment of discovery. It would be a few more weeks until we would have our answer.

Dangerous tapped me on the shoulder and I felt something drop into my lap. It was the finely chopped peyote. "Show time." was all he said. I hedged.

"Should we be partaking this early in the day, and on an empty stomach?"

He gave me that look--the one he gave back at the Up & Up while convincing me why I should come along. "Do you want me to start calling you Kid Junior?"

I opened my packet and downed the bitter tasting cacti, chasing it with a large volume of water, followed by another. Oh my, the stuff tasted super bad nasty! The peyote's psychoactive properties were officially introduced to my bloodstream. Oh Don Juan, please bless this novice on his inaugural voyage, or, *awakening*...

Our bus bounced along. Dave banked a bit more shuteye and I watched the countryside pass by. I made eye contact with the person sitting directly in front of me. Funny, but I didn't really remember him taking that seat. He smiled and turned my way, obviously intent on striking up an early morning conversation. He spoke in English, a thick yet quite understandable German accent detected.

"Food morning, fellow traveler, my name is Kaspar. I take it you are American?"

He had slicked back curly reddish-orange hair and an unkempt handlebar mustache; both in serious need of a trim. He wore dark wrap around shades--Girlwatchers, they were called back home--which fit off-center upon his long, pointed nose. A huge gray backpack loaded with several cameras rocked from side to side beside him as we moved along.

My first reaction was to ask him if he was a friendly ghost, you know, just to get a chuckle, but if that quip didn't fly, I would have come off looking like vintage Ugly American. I nodded.

He informed me this was his fifth visit to Palenque in as many years. I complemented him on his mastery of English, which he informed me, had been shaped nicely by two years of college abroad at Cambridge. I inquired if he was an archeologist to which Kaspar shook his head.

"I am what is known as a perceiver of energy--a seeker of the many mysteries this world offers. Did you know all human beings have the capacity to see energy directly as it flows in the universe?"

Oh boy. I shook my head. Dialogue regarding metaphysics was well beyond my grasp, coming my way at 7:15 a.m., and made even more difficult as the peyote had already begun sending a subtle yet perceptible tingle up my spine, working its way up between my shoulder blades.

Kaspar continued. "Everything we perceive and feel, as well as act upon, is determined by the position of our individual *assemblage point*. Most humans can only move or shift their assemblage points in dreams; by way of drug use, love, hunger, fever, exhaustion or, as is preferred, through intentional awareness. Remember that, as it may come in handy with what you see and partake in here today."

Sounded like solid advice to me. So far I have partaken in hunger, fever, exhaustion, and drugs, along with last night's extremely peculiar dream. Now if I could only latch onto a little of that love part mentioned, I'd be right on schedule to be grasp Kaspar's plane of existence. I nodded, offering up a polite smile. This all sounded so familiar. Castaneda talk?

He queried on. "Are you a scientist, tourist, or, like myself, here to experience these incredible energies of Palenque firsthand?"

I resisted the temptation to come up with a typical Andy Clark smart ass retort, instead I stated that, in all honesty, I wasn't certain why I was here. Kaspar grew excited, "This is a good sign!"

My willingness to indulge in this conversation left the door open for Kaspar to give me a mini-course on the history of Palenque. At first, I thought, why me? and wished he would just turn around and shut the hell up; Go some rest like everyone else around us, pal.

Instead, I found myself listening with increasing interest to his informative narration, even feeling quite fortunate to be the recipient of his introduction to Mayan civilization. This is what I remember, as close as I can possibly come to verbatim:

"You are now deep in the land of the Mayans, who ruled these hills and valleys two thousand years ago. A highly-civilized society-- very violent yet capable of creating exquisite works of beauty. They were known for their complex writing and mathematical systems, practicing astronomy and building majestic pyramids with little more than primitive stone tools.

"Throughout the time the Mayans civilization thrived, Palenque was one of the most prominent Mayan cultures. At its peak, ten to twenty thousand people lived right here. That is an enormous group of people existing in one place, my friend.

"They developed a sophisticated system of mathematics that helped them calculate the movements of the night sky thousands of years into the past and well into the future. Scientists believe that the tower at the center of the palace was most likely an astronomical observatory.

"The Mayans relied on their astronomers or priests to predict the best days to plant their corn, marry, and perhaps even the best day to die." He paused, took a long swallow off a water bottle, then continued.

"I bet you didn't know that these astronomers and priests predicted December 23, 2012 as the day the earth will end, did you?" He bet-eth correctly.

"Their relationship with the gods made them bloody, brutal people. The Mayans thought the gods had made them out of corn, or maize, combined with blood so they held sacrifices to reciprocate. The

Mayans felt that if they continually gave their gods these offerings, their civilization would per...per...per."

"Perpetuate."

"Yes, perpetuate." (Hey, now I actually felt that I was contributing to this lesson).

"The kings played a major role in this bloodletting, appeasing the immortals by perforating their own penises, and letting the blood drip onto paper strips which were then burned to awaken the gods.

"Palenque was once ruled by Pachall, one of the most important rulers of Mayan legacy. Pachall's rule was an extremely bloody period. Sacrifices were quite common, performed to demonstrate to the gods the power and prowess necessary to be a king.

"Here in the courtyards you will find a gallery of carved stone tablets, each of these representing a king or people that had been attacked and conquered by Pachall and his soldiers. Do you like basketball?"

The answer to this was easy. "Hell yes, I'm an American male." My reply coaxed a smirk from Kaspar.

"1300 years ago, a primitive form of basketball was played just north of the courtyard. Unlike basketball played today, in which remarkable passes and accurate shots are necessary, Mayan basketball was played by keeping the ball in motion without using hands or feet. This game had high stakes. The losers would be slaughtered--for the gods, of course--in brutal sacrificial decapitations. Are you all right my friend?"

The talk of penis perforations and decapitations along with the bouncy bus ride this early in the day, began inducing a hint of queasiness to the proceedings. This feeling passed without drastic results, yet internally strange feelings continued to manifest.

"At the height of Mayan rule, their entire civilization disappeared. They did not destroy their kingdoms. They left behind exquisite remnants of their culture, their handiwork as well as their history. It's as if they just walked away from it all, never to be seen again! Where did they go? They couldn't just walk off the face of the earth. It is here this mystery begins.

"Were they called home to the skies? Was this what they lived their lives for? Did they die of a mysterious disease or were they wiped out by their rivals? Not likely, as millions of bones would have been left behind to be discovered later." He leaned closer, speaking slowly, dramatically. "This, American friend, is mystery personified."

"Jungle vegetation took over and Palenque became a lost civilization until the 18th century when it was rediscovered by surprised Spanish priests. To date, archeologists have unearthed only a small area, one-half mile of ruins--a palace, a ceremonial center, and a series of magnificent stone temples--amazing clues to an amazing civilization.

"Then, in 1952, Alberto Ruiz made a significant discovery. Deep within the belly of The Temple of Inscriptions, he came upon a stairway that led seventy-three steps down into the tomb of Pachall. This discovery asked more questions than it gave answers. When removed, the large limestone slab which lay atop his casket revealed stone-etched artwork which lends to the interpretation that Pachall is seated at a spaceship, hand on the control.

"UFO people say that this etching, 'The Ascension,' verifies the Mayans had a connection with life on other planets or worlds, and adds to their theory Palenque was a landing site for alien spacecraft. A more moderate school of thought suggests 'The Ascension,' based on their high beliefs in astrology, symbolizes a flight to the next life--reincarnation."

As if on cue, our bus rolled onto pavement, through a gate and came to a halt. Palenque, our ultimate destination was at hand.

Three quarters of the way through Kaspar's historical tour, my stomach began to rumble, much like it had during Scorpion Night back in Barra. His words began to resonate with a hollow ring, and the sweat began to bead beneath the brim of my hat. *Señor Peyote* had arrived, pounding uncomfortably on my door.

Kaspar offered his hand. "Thank you for listening to me. I have such passion for these ruins, when I find someone who will listen, I just begin and find it hard to stop. Palenque is a very magical place. Do you believe in magic?"

The first thing that came to mind was the stray perro burrowed at the base of my sleeping bag back in Puerto Escondido and how he may have potentially saved me from a first-class ass-whooping that night on the beach. "I think I can answer yes to that."

"Keep your eyes open. There is a good chance more is coming your way. Remember, a man of knowledge is one who has followed truthfully the hardships of learning."

There it was, Don Juan, live and in color. I was caught off guard by his use of that quote, ever so subtly woven into his rap. He leaned closer. "Have you come with the proper catalysts to open your mind fully? Peyote? Mushrooms, perhaps?" I assured him we are fully prepared.

He smiled, and removed his sunglasses. "Seek and absorb. Embrace that which you shall experience."

Holy freaking Déjà vu--I had been here before-staring at one gray eye and one blue eye both twinkling mischievously as he added, "Connect with that which others take for granted. It is, as you young Americans would say, 'The Shit.'"

Kaspar flashed a peace sign, grabbed his backpack of cameras and turned back one last time as he walked off towards the bushes, "Have a happy day, and be sure and enjoy Morelia. It is my second favorite city in this country." With that, he was gone.

Suddenly my head felt lighter than a skyward-bound balloon. My stomach rumbled and lurched. Only a sleeping Dave, myself, and the bus driver remained on board. He continued to check his rear-view mirror, as if trying to coax us off his vessel. Gazing towards the front, my visual perception took on that of a fish-eye lens. Maybe he would just let us sit here an hour or so more until…

Dangerous woke, his eyes rolling wildly as he spoke. "Grab your gear; let's go, before it's too late."

I started to ask "for what?" yet I already knew. We were on our way to becoming dueling puke boys.

Wobbly legs navigated an even wobblier path towards the bus steps. My backpack felt as if I were toting a baby elephant.

Once outside, we managed to make it as far as the back of the bus before all hell broke loose. I fell to my knees vowing if fortunate to survive what comes next, I would never, ever partake in this peyote madness again.

Two Park attendants watching nearby hooted wholeheartedly at our plight: *Mas Tequila, eh? The big guy, he is down on his knees. Looks like a drunken puppy. Check out the color of the other one's face, the one in the white hat. He bears a resemblance to the walking dead. When they are through, which of us will be the unfortunate one to have to clean up their messes before the next busload arrives?*

And just like that, it ended.

We sought refuge on a bench just outside the park's main gate. Relieved. Exhausted. Severely stoned. Intense yet insightful clarity held sway. In just a few short moments an amazing surge of energy, revival, and rejuvenation replaced our nauseous condition. I was going to survive. I still had one question to ask before we could move on.

"Where the hell is Morelia?" I asked Dangerous out of the side of my mouth. He didn't answer; bigger fish to fry just ahead...

We had reached our destination in one piece. We surveyed the entranceway and contemplated our next move We both took a deep breath and rose.No time like the present. Let's make this a day to remember.

24. Ruinas

7:45 a.m. The Park opened at eight.

I asked Dangerous if he had caught any of Kaspar's oration. He shook his head, adamant that the seat in front of me had been empty the entire time. I shrugged that one off. Perhaps Kaspar had slid in after he had fallen asleep. Perhaps the hallucinogens had been working their wonders. No matter the case, I sure had received one comprehensive history lesson. Metaphysics tossed in as well!

A badge-bearing attendant in a tan uniform was busy sweeping the sidewalk before us. An unusual creature, armadillo-like in appearance, scurried into his path and the ranger/maintenance man swatted at it with his broom. The animal rolled into a ball and lay motionless in his path. With a shrug, the broom pusher whisked the critter harshly back into the bushes as if he was merely sweeping away a hockey puck, then continued without missing a beat.

"Mexican curling," Dave quipped as he pulled out his shades and slipped them on to mask his dilated pupils. He had begun entering the Psychedelic Grin phase of the journey; facial muscles involuntarily pulled back into a full-moon grin bigger than a smiley face button.

Near impossible to describe accurately, I spent the next half hour adjusting to the peculiarities or perhaps characteristics, of my inaugural peyote ceremony.

Like most psychedelics there is a great deal of awareness and introspection going on. At times you feel as if you are taking in the experience in third person, senses working overtime as the journey unfolds: acutely cerebral, very personal.

It will be some time from now before I'll be able to sort out all which will take place. Today I will try to relate this experience as is. I am sure after a post-trip debriefing takes place between Dave and I, what all occurred will be fully comprehended in an a more accurate light. But right now, buckle up and let er rip...

Palenque offers a unique and accordingly ideal locale to investigate via mind-altering substances. Exploring ancient and incredible ruins here in the tropical warmness of the jungle while cavorting on the edge of insanity, was just too tempting a concept to let slip by. Perhaps even the Mayans participated in one form or the other of other-worldly state of being.

I feel it necessary to state this whole plane of psychedelic adventure/monkeyshines was not truly planned. Fate could have led us to a different restaurant back in San Cristobal and our path would never have been blessed by a visit from Elaine from Eugene. Chance did its dance and all fate had to do was whisper in my ear to come along. I think the drugs have taken hold full throttle…

Time to open the park gates. As if on cue, a roar of impressive magnitude came from afar. Our animal-sweeping custodian put down his broom, as his job requires, he doubles as head ticket taker.

Even though our bus mates had patiently lined up five minutes before the gates were to open, early admission was not a consideration. The smug satisfaction of power etched upon his mug, our guardian of the main gate glanced down at his watch, making sure we didn't gain entrance one second before exactly eight o'clock high. He checked, rechecked it once more, then, beckoned for us to proceed.

One price was posted, fifteen pesos, but the gatekeeper, told us that it was incorrect, now demanding twenty pesos before we could enter.

Dave was eight pesos short because Mr. Gatekeeper refused to make change for his hundred-peso note. We pleaded our case. He would not budge. Finally, a mid-twenties Californian behind us stepped up and handed us eight pesos. "I hope this makes him happy!" It did. He smiled as he gestured for us to enter the magical kingdom of Palenque.

We headed down the gravely road towards the ruins. An early morning mist lay heavy as Bay Area fog. Only a handful of others-- the Californian, his wife, and a pudgy photographer, already snapping away as if there was no tomorrow--followed. Kaspar was nowhere to be seen.

Ahead, off to our immediate right, a huge pyramid suddenly came into view; a magnificent work of ancient stone standing tall amidst this massive jungle; the hot morning sun just beginning its path across the sky

. Monte Albán was child's play compared to these ruins before us. We approached without a single souvenir hawker clinging to our heels!

We spent our first half hour shooting pictures, hoping to get as many shots in as possible before the hordes of tourists arrived, and before the ever-increasing rush from the mescal buttons transformed us into raving lunatics.

Today was well on its way to being a first-class scorcher. Dangerous had already stripped down to his trunks and huaraches. Beads of sweat were flowing, as we spent our morning climbing and exploring the variety of pyramids, temples, and other stone structures which dominate this half acre of Mayan wonderment.

The peyote enhanced the many unfamiliar microscopic insects buzzing by, resulting in a unique audio commotion unlike any I had ever experienced.

Busy caretakers sharpened their sickles, then swung them in rhythm as they performed the daily task of chopping back prolific foliage which threatened to claim back the ruins if proper maintenance ever ceased.

We wandered about the dew-soaked grounds continually in awe of the majestic landmarks there before us. I shot over two rolls of film, explored many secret passages, and sat on various grassy knolls, contemplating the scene before me.

Kaspar had nailed it when he said there was an unusual amount of energy taking place here, with or without psychedelic enhancement. I am certain we would have picked up on its intensity in a conventional state of mind just as well. Many theories abound as to what the source of this energy is, but whatever it may be, it has contributed significantly to what was the most awe-inspiring day of my life.

With only a half dozen others wandering about, today felt as if Palenque was ours and ours alone. What impressed me most was the fact that, even though these pyramids and temples rose hundreds of feet towards the heavens, they were dwarfed by the amazing thick green jungle backdrop, looming above and behind.

Around 10 a.m. the next busload of tourists pulled into the lot; a whole gaggle of them, dressed uniformly in baggy shorts, black knee-high socks and gaudy over-sized Gaucho-style cowboy hats, tilted cock-eyed on their heads. Germans, Dave suspected. We watched from atop a corner of the Temple of the Inscriptions, as they comically serpentine from ruin to ruin clicking their cameras in a frenzy as they moved along their way.

As the sightseers continued to arrive, that feeling of solitude we enjoyed quickly began to evaporate. We truly had been spoiled those first two hours. Time for a change of scenery.

We made our way into the woods, back behind the museum, seeking to maintain our state of cerebral enlightenment. With nary a clue or care as to where we were headed, we followed the music of a jungle tributary as it trickled downstream, away from civilization; down to a series of small, yet splendid domestic waterfalls.

The fourth and final fall emptied into a round, deep blue waist high pool big enough for two, encased in cool, smooth aqua-gray rock. Stoned silly and uninhibited, we peeled off our clothes and indulged in the chilly refreshing pool we found out later to be The Queen's Bath. Here we stayed, immersed to our shoulders, well over an hour, listening to and experiencing the jungle coming to life around us.

There in the serenity of The Queen's Bath, boosted by the Cactus Magic, I experienced a personal epiphany of relative significance. Never in the nearly thirty years of my existence had I felt as close to total peace within myself; absolute serenity

Was this to be my ultimate reward for the hundreds of miles traveled? Or, perhaps, the perfect counterbalance to the unsolicited bout of anxiety I confronted last evening? Most important, how could I make this moment of serenity last, and, if possible, for how long?

Yeah, Kaspar, my assemblage point is certainly in focus this afternoon. But still, question unanswered, where the hell is Morelia? In the back of my mind, I seemed to recall having a dream sometime I left the Northwest about the jungle; a pool of water involved as well. Wow…

"Hey, check out your shirt." Dave was pointing at my pile of clothing at the edge of the pool. We had a guest. Hunkered down on my pullover, a tarantula, approximately the size of a small crab, was checking out the two odd creatures intruding upon its domain. Slowly, and oblivious to caution, I edged closer. As I came within two feet, the furry-legged spider had seen enough, and scrambled back into the safety of the nearby vegetation.

Shortly thereafter, we headed back for ruinas exploration, round two. Before slipping back into our clothing, we shook the smithereens out of them, checking down each sleeve twice, in case any of the tarantula's friends or relatives considered these items a comfortable place to rest. Our buddy the Kid would never have survived what had just taken place.

The park was now crawling with a mass of inquisitive humanity. We ducked inside the museum to regroup.

Casually, we blended into a tour group consisting of fat, pale, and wrinkly Instamatic snappers listening intently to a tour guide who appeared as if he might fall asleep at any given moment during his own dissertation. The incessant flashing of cameras wreaked havoc with our metaphysical state of well-being.

Chronological charts of Mayan history covered the walls. Glass cases housed fragments of statuary, stones with calendar glyphs, and hundreds of handmade figurines, many of which suggested a Mayan connection to the stars.

Odd fact: While observing these figurines, we came across a row of hand-carved oddities that looked remarkably like the Saturday Night Live Coneheads. This discovery triggered an uncontrollable bout of giggles which left us looking like madmen. Time to ditch and explore further.

Next up was another trip to the Temple of Inscriptions--the tallest of the ruins and by far Palenque's most majestic masterpiece.

A steep hike almost straight up was required, then, once inside, it was time to visit King Pachall. Slowly we made our way down the steep, dark, slick, dank-smelling seventy-three steps. There at the bottom, behind a set of bars installed to deter vandals as well as the overly-curious, lay the tomb of Pachall and the sepulchral slab, ten feet long and seven feet wide.

The hairs rose on my arms as I viewed the inscription. Sure enough, there was the king himself, seated in some sort of device that looked like a time machine. 'The Ascension.' Didn't that have something to do with space travel from that Erich Van Daniken movie, *Chariots of the Gods*? I told myself that when I got back home I would research this incredible temple along with any other Mayan connection to UFOs.

From here we made our way back into the woods; back into the Queen's Bath to immerse ourselves in the sights and smells of the jungle one last time. Far off in the distance another loud roar came our way. Later, we found out those roars emanated from an area outside the park called the Temple of the Jaguars. Hmmm... I wonder how it got its name?

Sometime around 3:30, still lounging in The Queen's Bath, while holding steady to the righteous buzz of the bitter button, reality smacked us right between the eyes. Dangerous realized we had committed an inexcusable oversight potentially capable of imploding our impeccable game plan.
Here we were; middle of the jungle on a Friday afternoon, and oops!

During our focus on our day spent in the ruins, we had overlooked the necessity to stop by Palenque's banco and cash enough

Travelers Cheques to sustain our needs throughout the weekend. As small a town as Palenque was, we were bound to be out of luck trying to cash them elsewhere this late in the day.

A quick financial evaluation resulted in realizing we were down to five hundred pesos between us--Enough, Dangerous estimated, to get us to Mexico City, where we could be certain to find a banco at either the airport or bus station. Time to say a hasty and unexpected adios to the land of Mayan culture and boomerang back to the west coast.

Another slight problem. The availability of a bus returning to town had been overlooked. Off we went, traveling on foot, riding the energy provided us by the peyote. We began retracing the route we had traveled--an estimated twenty minutes by bus.

A mile or so down a winding backroad leading away from the ruins, we encountered two totally bewildered English speaking backpackers, engaged in heated debate as to what day of the week this was. One was adamant today was Friday; the other damn certain it was Wednesday. We let them hash this out for about five minutes until Dangerous remembered his ticket stub which verified today's date officially as Friday. They thanked us, then gave a rave review of the youth hostel/camp less than a half mile ahead.

"They've got mushrooms there" mumbled the wild-eyed gringo who had been certain today was Wednesday, "Magic mushrooms!!" Oh boy, just what we needed…

"Yeah," chimed in backpacker Two, "this guy made shroom omelets for us and twelve other campers at breakfast this morning. Quite tasty. Shit man, I'm still seriously seeing tracers!"

Magic mushrooms were a subject we both were well-acquainted with. Each fall, Bellingham and the surrounding Whatcom County farmlands are home to prolific psilocybin mushroom fields, attracting hippie vans full of jolly pickers, armed with empty bread sacks, from various locations throughout the United States.

Heck ya, I've indulged in them--at least three or four times each season. I'm fortunate to say I've never experienced a bad trip.

More often than not, negative experiences result primarily take place when an individual ingests one more handful of shrooms than advised. *Piggies Pay*, has always been the psychedelic mushroom veteran's credo.

As with peyote, shrooms are most appropriately enjoyed when taken outdoors; where the incredible flow of energy and insight they produce can be appreciated as they are meant to be.

A half mile or so later we arrived at the campgrounds. A variety of polka-dotted tents and canopies were staked out upon a large, flat, dirt field ideally suited for that purpose.

Twenty yards inside the dusty confines we were greeted by a Canadian who introduced himself as Luke, garbed in an awesome tie-dyed well-worn Grateful Dead baseball jersey.

This self-described mushroom magnate had arrived here two weeks ago and had yet to find the desire or motivation to move on. He inquired if we wished a tent site or if we had just come to indulge in the wisdom Palenque's magic fungi could deliver. Dave inquired about the latter.

I stood by nervously as Dangerous negotiated a deal--six stones worth for one hundred and fifty pesos. We were now down to three hundred and fifty pesos. Looks like we just downgraded to a second-class bus to Mexico City.

Luke handed over three plastic bags full of ugly flattened shrooms, then invited us to dinner, "mushroom soup at eight o'clock." I recalled the loco backpackers; the breakfast they had indulged in, as well as the wasted state of mind which had resulted. Thank you, but no thank you we already have a dandy buzz well underway.

Dave handed me the tightly sealed plastic bags and helped stuff them deep in the recesses of my day pack, "These will make for one bodacious homecoming party back in Z-Wat, eh?" His gaze turned to a makeshift circus tent cantina from which rock music drifted our way. "One beer for the road?" What the hell. At this rate, we might be headed to our destination riding in the luggage rack.

We walked into a true den of iniquity--Star Wars meets Twilight Zone. Futuristic new wave classics pounded through two very impressive Bose speakers. Elvis Costello, The Cars, followed by the Talking Heads; bands I had yet to embrace, but sounded quite fine in our current condition. Elvis' spaghetti-meets-surf guitar solo in "Watching the Detectives" lured me into the cantina.

We treated our cottonmouth condition to lukewarm Superiors while taking in the freak show unfolding there before us: Welcome to Zombieland.

A short-haired Kraut bearing a self-inflicted swastika tattoo on his left forearm staggered past. His bone-white hairless appendages, skinny as clothes pins, stood out obscenely from his lazily tied calf-high army boots.

His skin-tight tan trunks/underpants called unnecessary attention to the fact he was a male. A European thing, definitely.

He joined a French speaking woman with two large safety pins poked through her nostrils and her adolescent daughter, both drinking beers in the far corner.

Across from them, amid a row of four hammocks, a precocious pre-pubescent girl in pigtails playfully fought with a squirrel monkey while a semi-obese, yet cute auburn-haired lil' queenie chain-smoked filter-less butts all by her lonesome in the tent's shadows. She swung back and forth, with a look vacillating between bored spit-less and wasted. One could easily assume she too was under the spell of Luke's mushroom cuisine.

At the table across the way, a trio of stereotypically-garbed hippies huddled closely, throwing shifty paranoid glances in our direction as they proceeded with a not so subtle drug deal. Various packets of substance were exchanged with a whisper and a nod. A pile of pesos slid from one side of the table to the other. Another satisfied customer, here at the *Casa de la Whacko*.

A bird-like French writer with a bony shaved skull sat scribbling furiously in his journal. Hunched low, deep in concentration, he would pause for a moment while holding his massive head in his hands, then begin scribbling manically once more.

More nefarious looking low lives continued to float in and out of the tent. We decided it was time for us to move along. This show was over. Three hundred pesos now remained.

Still smoothly tripping, mushrooms in my pack, and a mouth still suffering from cottonmouth one lone beer failed to eradicate, we resumed our long trek back to civilization. One of my huaraches had broken a strap, slowing our pace a bit, all the while the afternoon sun continuing its formidable assault.

Our goal was to hitch a ride back to town, well over five miles away, along a seemingly desolate stretch of roadway. To add to our dilemma, it was already 3:45. The weekend was almost officially upon us.

We had all but given up hope of a motorized savior coming our way
when a '57 Chevy pickup appeared over the ridge.

Thankfully the driver stopped in response to our frantic waves. The back end was already loaded down with construction rebar, pallets and huge coils of wire, so the driver motioned for us to hop onto the truck's side rails and hang on tight as he shot off down the road. Traveling forty miles an hour, brain full of psychedelics while holding onto a rusted door handle, our fate was now in the hands of the gods. I kicked back. I enjoyed the ride.

Good fortune continued as our driver was kind enough to drop us off at the local bus station where we immediately checked the status of a possible departure. More good news--we could still catch the next bus bound for Villahermosa, which in turn would take us on to Mexico City, but we had best not dally. We had less than an hour.

We sprinted back to Hotel Avenida where a lightning-quick Grab-Your-Shit-and-Run maneuver was executed to perfection. Dangerous hustled up the steps, grabbed both backpacks and came back down the steps, two at a time, until he was out the front door.

The startled manager tried to garner his attention; to ask for the money due for another day, but Dave never looked back. We were now on the move, double, make that triple, time.

25. Running on Empty

We were at the bus station, 42.80-peso bus tickets in hand with twenty minutes to spare. Time for a celebratory licuado. As we drank, we assessed our finances. Two hundred fifty-four pesos remain.

While discussing how best to disperse this meager amount, fate introduced us to two beautiful young ladies, Marlice, and her luscious dark-haired friend Antonionice.

They had come to Palenque via Switzerland. Marlice spoke English and eerily reminded me a lot of Rebecca. Antonionice, spoke Spanish, yet no English. We could work this out…

They were off to the Yucatan for adventure and had to make their next connection in Villahermosa. We had between now and then to hang out, perhaps even convince them to pass on those crummy old ruins and instead chase the sunshine of Zihuatanejo with two great guys like ourselves.

Our peyote high was still working its magic. It had hit its peak but still provided me with enough energy to keep my motor running, alert and ready for the long road ahead.

The ride to Villahermosa, by our typical travel standards was small potatoes; only three hours.

We arrived close to 8 p.m. The ladies were scheduled to leave at approximately 5 a.m. while our bus was scheduled for a 7:30 a.m. departure. With all that downtime at hand, we decided to make the best of our time as a quartet instead of a duo.

After circumnavigating the heart of downtown Villahermosa, we chose an inexpensive place to dine. The lingering effects of the peyote rendered our food tasteless, yet, not having eaten for nearly twenty-four hours, ingesting nutrients had become imperative.

I sat nervously calculating the cost of this feast until Dave surprised us all by picking up the bill. Our waiter informed us the restaurant did not take Travelers Cheques so Dave dug deep into the recesses of his pack and produced a crisp green American twenty-dollar bill. This was his emergency fund, he later told me, and since this predicament was as close to an emergency as hoped could occur, it was as good a time as ever to spend his last Jackson. Then it was back to the bus station to patiently wait for our buses to depart.

Sometime around midnight, Dangerous faded to black, going horizontal on the concrete, using his sleeping bag for a pillow.

Antonionice was next, nodding off around twelve-thirty. Marlice and I sat up talking until1 a.m. when she too ran out of gas after giving me a warm hug goodnight.

I'm not sure if I got the larger dose, was riding high on adrenaline or paranoia, but I was nowhere close to nodding off. My legs had gone numb from sitting on the concrete and I needed a nice warm bath and a couple of breath mints. Other than that, life was just dandy.

At 3:40 the window on booth four slid open and the early birds milling close by hastily queued up. I woke the girls, helped them over to the line with their packs, for which I received an appreciative hug and a peck on the cheek from both, then watched as they climbed aboard Tres Estrellas number 17. I could only sigh and thing about what might've been.

Shortly after our friends departed, two gringos, Charley and Mark dropped their bags down beside us and kept me going, exchanging tales of the road. We bonded quickly, each taking a turn sharing our rip-off experiences. They too were on their way to Mexico City having just spent a week in Belize.

Traveling two steps in their shadow was a long-haired Coloradoan with a dark karmic storm cloud hanging over his head. He drifted into our circle of conversation and became part of our Mexico City-bound entourage.

Mark introduced him as Mike, but before parting ways in Mexico City we had officially anointed him Bad Vibes Mike. Only in Mexico three weeks, his passport, backpack, and cooking stove had all been stolen. I did my best to avoid interaction, yet he carried on, bringing us down with negative comment after negative comment.

"This bus trip is only supposed to be twelve to fifteen hours long but I ran into this cat who told me to expect twenty. The roads are totally messed up from here to Mexico City" he sniveled.

Other choice Mikeisms before our bus arrived: "Man, it's just not safe anywhere around here. You *always* gotta watch your ass," and "I've yet to meet a beaner I can trust--They're always eyeing your wallet for a piece of the pie." was another.

When he got to "If *they* aren't trying to rob you, *they* were trying to kill you on their roadways, or make you late on purpose." was worthy of a punch to the solar plexus, as was "They average at least one bus crash per week, but nobody'll tell you that or the bus services would go out of business (he snaps his fingers, dramatically) --just like that."

Around 5:30, I managed a blissful half hour of sleep before being stirred from my short-lived dream state. Dangerous was awake, revitalized and looking fit as a fiddle. "The booth just opened. Let's get those tickets."

I staggered into line behind him. After six people had purchased their tickets, the line bogged down. From somewhere close behind, Bad Vibes Mike reinforced his nickname. "These bastards better not tell us the bus is full or I'm gonna raise holy hell!"

Seconds later we started moving again. At the window, we laid down the last of our pesos for tickets, receiving one measly peso in return. Better put it somewhere safe as it may come in handy to buy a pack of Chicklets on the long journey ahead.

Packs stored in the compartment below the bus, we milled about waiting to board. Those around us appeared mutually groggy and mellow as hell. Only Bad Vibes Mike responded when the driver hopped aboard, closed the doors and pulled away, leaving us where we stood. "Hey, he's stealing our stuff!!" He ran alongside the bus, banging on the doors." Open up, bandito!"

The driver glanced at him quizzically then picked up speed until he had disappeared around the other side of the depot. Maybe Bad Vibes Mike was right; our bus was nowhere to be seen.

What the hell was going on? Stinking banditos? His negative energy had the masses grumbling in unison.

Mike started ranting about how seedy *this country* was, pointing out that we were already a half hour late and nobody even apologized to us. Anarchy bloomed among the pack. Even the Mexicans, who did not know why all these gringos were getting uptight, were feeding off the tension.

Suddenly our bus reappeared around the corner. Pulling up in front of where he had left us, the driver swung the doors opened and beckoned us to climb aboard. He had been restoring adequate air to a low tire as well as filling the tank with gas. The revolution was over.

Everyone except Bad Vibes chuckled with relief. He was busy demanding our driver hop down and open the baggage compartment to verify our baggage had not been taken around the corner and sold. Someone suggested he shut the hell up and get on board. With a scowl, Bad Vibes consented. The bus rolled out.

For the first time this entire trip, we passed on the Death Seats, opting instead for the long row at the back of the bus. Here we could stretch out for an entire day's worth of rest and recuperation. Unfortunately, the seat in front of us remained unoccupied until Bad Vibes Mike laid claim to it.

As the miles passed by, the energetic rush of the peyote subsided. We would make intermittent stops in small towns, exchanging passengers, then rolling again. I spent most of the day deep in sleep, recharging my constitution. When not asleep, I pretended to be, as every time my eyes popped open Bad Vibes was staring my way, eager for an audience to torture with negative yip yap.

Once, as we were exchanging passengers in a remote Indian village, I awoke to life in Mexico, playing out before me, full of contrasts you don't experience back home. These are the memories I hope to recall years from now, when our excursion becomes little more than memory dust:

Three shoeless niños kick a soccer ball down the street without a care in the world as, yards away, a pig snorts around the ankles of a woman in a black dress busy washing clothes in a trickling stream. An old man sits motionless in his chair, staring at our bus as if he were watching television. Just across the street two middle-aged men in stained T-shirts with pomade-slick duck-ass hairdos and bellies gravity has let fall far below their respective belt lines stood over an opened hood, intently discuss the finer points of replacing a carburetor.

Two beautiful women stand side by side in a dark hazy doorway. One smiles at us; front teeth missing. Two loaded well-worn donkeys crossed their path and the women wave at a short mustachioed *campesino* dressed from head to toe in white. He waves his rusted machete in greeting, slaps one donkey on its flanks and keeps moving, on past the scurrying soccer players.

A naked and crying niño waddles past. Once across the street he uses the back of his hand for Kleenex to wipe his runny nose before heading into a hut held together by nothing more than sticks and mud. Deep inside, the ghostly glow of a television lends irony to this primitive habitat. Someday they may have cable. In the grassless yard, a mongrel with a hard-on chews furiously at a well-gnawed bone.

A solemn funeral procession emerges from around the corner. Casket on high and smothered in flowers, this large ensemble comes our way. An old man walks behind, tears down his cheeks. A younger man walks beside him, arm wrapped around the old man's shoulder, steadying his gait as the procession moves past. New arrivals on board and seated, our bus departs, but those moments have been filed away.

We pass by small town after small town; stopping to pick up, stopping to let off. With a full load, we began to climb up into the mountains, heading west, off to Mexico City, the largest city in the world.

Foggy conditions slowed our progress but as we neared the top, rising above the clouds, the stars pop out, glimmering fine diamonds.

At the summit a magnificent view of Mexico City comes into sight, there in the crater below, still many miles away. A halo of gray haze serves as a reminder we were about to enter one of the most polluted cities in the world. Twelve and a half hours later, 8:30 p.m. Mexico City Time, to be exact, we arrived.

Flat-ass broke, and with nary a Chicklet in our tummies it was desperation time.

Our plan--take a taxi out to the airport where, we have been assured, Travelers Cheques can be cashed twenty-four hours a day. Once there we will cash forty of my remaining sixty dollars, then attempt to catch the earliest possible bus back to Zihuatanejo.

These sixty dollars were not the last of our money. We had sent two hundred dollars back with Ted and Doris, who by now had regrouped for a few final days in Z-Wat, just in case one of Bad Vibes Mike's experiences of dread actually came to pass. Still, our cash flow had dwindled into the red zone. Waaaay too close for comfort.

Even though our view towards cabs and their drivers soured in Escondido, we decided there was strength in numbers. Five of us, all in need of cash, took part in *Operation Pesos*, piling into the first available cab.

Unfortunately, Bad Vibes was one of the five in need. By virtue of that necessity and that only, did the dark one manage to weasel his way into this expedition.

While gathering our belongings, Mike immediately caused a ruckus, negotiating for a cab by telling the cabby two hundred pesos was too high and that he would give him twenty pesos for the ride. The cabby just laughed and continued negotiations with the rest of us.

To remove him from potential further trouble, we appointed Bad Vibes the group watchdog. His job would be to hang in the cab and make sure our driver didn't run off with our belongings while we were in the airport cashing out. He rose to that role, assured us he wouldn't let us down, even if he had to club the now nervous looking cabby with a roll of quarters he kept in his shirt pocket. We convinced him to remain calm at all costs. Do not bludgeon the driver, do not put him in a sleeper hold or tie him up with any loose cords available. Just make sure the cab does not leave.

When we returned from using the exchange, the cabby was still free of knots, abrasions, or flesh wounds. With pockets replenished with pesos, we were once again on our way.

At 10:30 p.m. we purchased tickets for the midnight bus to Z-Wat.

Good fortune rewarded us with a first-class meal at an uncharacteristically elegant bus-station restaurant; only my second meal in forty-eight hours.

Recharged and well-rested, we kicked back, waiting for midnight to arrive. I felt a strong surge of accomplishment. Our mission was almost complete. We would be back in Z-Wat by noon, totally burnt out, yet still in one piece.

There were many tales to tell, some still needing to be processed, as well as sorted out, such as the bizarre hour spent at Mushroom Hostel and its handful of comic book characters.

On schedule, we hopped aboard, occupying the coveted Death Seats once again on this, the last leg of our marathon run. Next stop, Acapulco, 7 a.m., then Zihuatanejo--to spend one last glorious week tanning, like gods, there upon the sands of Playa La Ropa.

I couldn't wait for the sun to bake these half-dozen frenzied bus rides right out of my system. Sleep, beautiful sleep, promenaded me home.

26: Paradise Revisited

We're baaaack...

After ten mystifying days on the road, Z-Wat sure looked fine.

Our first task was to find suitable living quarters, upgrade our personal hygiene with a blissful lukewarm shower and perhaps even a shave, then make tracks to the Eskimo stand to get back in the swing of things.

As expected, we found Ted and Doris, kicked back in the courtyard of Casa del Playa anticipating our arrival. One problem-- there were no rooms left. All rooms were booked for the next two weeks.

Our friends had been fortunate to score their two-bed unit on return from Oaxaca, arriving just as Ray and friends were checking out. Larry abandoned Larry Land shortly thereafter, completing the turnover of our good times crew. Nirvana's Playground would not be the same without him.

We made plans to meet for dinner and a Yucatan surprise, got our remaining funds and headed off in search of affordable alternative lodging.

Our search ended two blocks away at a modest no-frills inn behind the torta stand, where we negotiated a reasonable one-night-only rate. This would give us the rest of the day and tomorrow morning to find the right location for the duration of our stay.

Even though the shower's flow trickled weakly over my body, it was pleasantly refreshing. Ten minutes later, I emerged, cleaner than a range-wrangling cowpoke getting ready for Saturday night. Dangerous took his turn, then we were off for Eskimo Time.

As we rounded the corner, Dave panicked, fearing the worst-- that they may be closed for siesta--but there, standing steady behind the blenders, rinsing out already clean glasses just to pass the time, stood our trusty Eskimo Goddess. For the first time, she actually acknowledged us as we sat down, asking where we had been.

Dangerous told her we had come all the way from Palenque to get one of her fabulous *Eskimos con Rompope*. She blushed as she delivered the bad news: Once again they had run out of Rompope.

Dave's passion for our favorite mind-chilling concoction was not to be denied. He was a blur, disappearing off his stool, only to return in near record time from the corner market.

He set the Rompope on the counter and gestured to the girl that it was now hers.

"*Con mucho hielo, por favor.*"

In the weeks we had spent loyally patronizing her shop we had seen the quality of her work progress significantly from mediocre to satisfyingly outrageous. The two frothy glasses she set before us was no exception.

We took long near-desperate swigs, savoring that moment when the chill started numbing the brain stem. When our straws could be heard slurping the bottom, two more were in place before us. In unison, we consumed them as if this was our last day on earth. Perfecto.

Back at Casa La Playa a major feast was in the works. Doris had gone solo to the market and returned with a half dozen ripe avocados, one large sweet onion, two dozen brown eggs, a slab of cheddar cheese, green and red bell peppers, three bags of chips and a bottle of habanero hot sauce. Homemade guacamole and omelets (mushrooms optional, of course) sounded exquisite, yet something was missing from tonight's menu. Leave it to Dave to add the dessert as well as the appetizer. Anyone for Dirty Mothers?

A subtle head nod from the dangerous one suggested we meet round the back. Once there he removed the mushrooms from the depths of my daypack, then held them up for inspection. "Whoa, check this out."

Something was wiggling within the bag. Something microscopic and white. And, it appeared, there was more than one. "Well I'll be a scorpion's uncle; roundworms!" Wiggly little marvels of science had hatched; born right there in a baggie, on our journey back to Z-Wat.

I examined them, confirmed his findings, and headed off to dump them in the trash. Only a day removed from a first-class peyote experience, I was reluctant to jump right back into the psychedelic saddle for yet another spin, and the moldy worm-infested shrooms totally dampened any enthusiasm I could possibly have mustered.

"And where do you think you're going with those mushrooms? I paid good money for those fungi. I can still use them for tea."

Two hours from dinner, Dave and I wandered over to La Ropa for an early evening dip. A skinny mellow-looking stranger came our way and asked if I would watch his daypack while he went in. No problem, park it right here.

He was Mike, from Edmonton. Coincidentally, he too was staying behind the torta shop, a few doors down from ours. Dangerous immediately coined him Cheesehead—a moniker Bellingham folks have anointed British Columbian our neighbors north of the border good-naturedly with.

Cheesehead was a master of good-natured verbal assaults, which made him fit in well with our crew. He was more than capable of rapid-fire witticisms fired back when any barbs were tossed his way. If he was a Cheesehead, then we were Pussheads. Fair enough. We bonded quickly. As our good-natured ribbing proceeded, he produced, then fired up, a reefer of substantial strength which rendered us immediately stupid.

Inviting him to tonight's dinner/Dirty Mother/mushroom tea party feast was a no-brainer--perhaps even as the guest of honor, whom Dave almost always guaranteed would leave the party crawling on all fours. He accepted our invitation.

We arrived around 6:45, still a bit goofy and befuddled from our afternoon *shrubnanigans* to find Ted and Doris whirling about the kitchen. The veggies were diced, and the large bowl of eggs thoroughly scrambled. A mountain of cheese stood grated and five paper cups were lined up and filled with ice.

All signals were go.

The next hour and a half were a whirlwind of *Welcome Back* mirth, adventure, hyperbole and hijinks, as we shared the highs and lows of our expedition with our friends who listened patiently. Graciously, good friend Dave omitted the backgammon incident.

Cheesehead had finished off his third Dirty Mother by the time Dave brought out the tea, strained and ready for consumption. It was nasty, brown in color, and bore a funky-smelling essence which should have raised red flags to those considering participation. Neither of us mentioned anything about the worms. My four friends threw caution to the wind as they raised their paper cups in a toast.

Still exhausted, as well as experiencing an occasional psychedelic aftershock or two, I declined. They were on their own tonight.

By sunset my friends had a good glow going, so we headed off into Centro to catch 'The Pom-Pom Girls' at the outdoor cinema.

Standing in line with what seemed the entire population of Z-Wat, the tea drinkers experienced Liftoff Grin, which signified their buzz was officially underway.

An intense bout of uncontrollable giggles commenced, forcing the shroomsters to quickly abandon the movie line. Sitting still on wobbly benches while attempting to focus on this slice of Cinema Americana, projected on a cracked concrete wall was no longer a consideration.

All but yours truly headed back to Casa La Playa to destroy what remained of the alcohol, tea, and leftover food.

Having somehow managed to miss this cinematic masterpiece during those golden years of my adolescence, I felt the need to stay put; to be a part of this whole Saturday night scene. One hour twenty-nine minutes later, the credits were rolling and the pleased masses rose to file out.

The flow of humanity bottlenecked by the front door as many stopped to excitedly point at the coming attractions placard on the wall by the entranceway. Jaws II was the main feature next week, all but guaranteeing a packed house.

Behind me, a loud voice rocked the airwaves. "Hey Bellingham!" It was my fishermen friends, Daryl and Richard. I gave them the mini-version of our Palenque trip as we walked along, but their minds were elsewhere.

"Hey, man, we're going down to the whorehouse. Wanna come along?" I told them I would have to pass, due to lack of finances. This late in the trip I was too poor to be a player, so to speak.

"Hell man, we aren't going there to get laid. They got the best damn drinks in town! Stiffer than a porn star's pecker."

I dug for excuses but came up empty.

Daryl put his massive arm around me. "Don't be a wuss, Bellingham; we'll take care of you." They both laughed. "I'll even buy your first round--if you're lucky, maybe the second and third too."

So far I have stared down dangerous hairy-legged tarantulas and survived the negative karma of Bad Vibes Mike. I've conquered cloud-touching pyramids and helped send Ugly Americans packing in the dark hours of the night. Being a whorehouse virgin, I was honestly a bit nervous, but being with these two dudes I was in good hands. What the hell, I'm down for a drink in Z-Wat's den of ill repute.

Off we went, heading away from the heart of Centro, out past where the streetlights end; where tourists had little reason to venture;

places my momma would certainly not approve of. May Mexico Magic come along for the ride.

Daryl was having a little trouble getting his bearings. "I swear the son of a bitch was right here last night." He stopped, wiped the sweat off his brow, then kept moving. "We gotta be getting really close."

Richard just rolled his eyes, lit another Camel, and spoke from the corner of his mouth. "Just humor him. He is bound to find it sooner or later. A good rat always remembers where the garbage can is located."

Two blocks later, we came upon a large group of working-class males, milling about outside a long, well-illuminated one-story, rambler-like structure. Richard recognized our destination first. "Boys, I think we've hit pay dirt."

Daryl led the way to the lone entrance. There he was greeted like an old buddy by the toothless yet official-looking doorman. They exchanged pleasantries and a subtle handful of pesos. The doorman flashed his gums, and gestured us to enter. He nodded and winked as I walked past.

"I think Patricio is rooting for you to get laid." Richard put his hand on my shoulder. "Maybe for an extra hundred pesos you can even have his daughter. She even has a few teeth left."

A scrumptious long-haired jezebel with gorgeous baby blues walked past and smiled at Richard. Their eyes met as she kept on walking, Richard turned and followed. Just like that, one amigo down for the rest of the evening.

I had no concept of what a Mexican whorehouse would be like, but the world I stepped into was as surreal as any I have ever encountered. Even the pyramids of Palenque paled in a weird kind of way.

The fragrance of stale, cheap perfume competed with dense clouds of expelled nicotine for the rights to any remaining oxygen.

It's not even 9 p.m. and already the dance floor is damp with sweat as a 1950s mothership of a jukebox drops 45 after 45 of traditional Mexican dance music onto its turntable. This flow keeps the clientele on their feet in a constant shuffle. A continuous and varied blend from mariachi to cumbia, corridas to mambos, sambas and even traditional reggae blare forth. Song after song, style after style, without a pause the music plays on, late late late into the wee hours.

The building's layout is reminiscent of a miniature-sized airplane hangar; made of concrete, long, expansive, and perfectly rectangular.

Twenty-seven (yeah, I counted) rooms line its perimeter, each room approximately fifteen feet apart. Every unoccupied love nest kept its door open and, under the low glow of candlelight, a modest-sized bed is visible, neatly made up and ready for action.

Thirty or so card tables fill the main floor. Each table had four chairs, four cocktail napkins and four coasters. Every half hour a no nonsense, hard-working waitress comes by to take your order. Be ready, if not, you will have another half hour to wait before she stops by again.

The bar is up front, right beside the jukebox.

The ladies of the house can be found here, between the bar and the dance floor, milling about. Tonight, eleven ladies are available for action. Some spend their time chatting up potential customers, others are laughing and smoking in clusters of two or three.

For me, tonight is solely about watching the locals interact.

They enter in groups of three or four, never solo, then quickly set up camp in prime locations. Once seated they fraternize with their amigos, drinking in order to summon up courage, playfully goading each other as to who they are going to poke, if they manage to remain sober enough to participate.

Time goes on. Once the booze begins to boost their confidence level, they get serious about choosing their particular lady of the night.

Once their libido finally shifts into overdrive, small talk commences, until it is time to seal the deal on tonight's price and availability. She then chooses a song from the jukebox with his peso and the mating dance begins.

As the song concludes, she whispers in his ear and he returns to his table where his buddies razz him in animated, excited conversation. While he's busy deflecting their barbs, she heads off into her designated room and lights a candle in preparation for what is to come, pardon the pun.

As we slugged down a never-ending string of very potent rum and Cokes, ten gallant lads performed the dirty deed. Each emerged approximately twenty minutes after entering, each wearing a grandiose grin while their compadres provide raucous ovations. It was now time for the finished to deliver the catcalls while their chums take their turns behind closed doors.

Daryl was having a jolly good evening, a regular non-stop consumption machine, chugging down Cuba Libre after Cuba Libre. As soon as he finished one round, another was there. I worked hard to keep pace but seemed always to lag about a Libre and a half behind.

He was a most gracious host; one mean-looking sucker with a million and one stories to tell. Still, not once since we've met have I seen him use his muscle for leverage.

Many of the locals on hand recognize him, many even dropped by to say hello or shake hands. Even though I harbored a Kid-like paranoia that made me feel we were being scrutinized the entire time, nary a hostile vibe was cast our way.

I have partaken in some seriously strong alcoholic concoctions over the years, especially those mixed by my comrade, Dangerous, but the drinks set before us tonight rated second to none. My initial Cuba Libra consisted of a tall glass full of ice, a healthy double shot of rum and a bottle of Coke. I poured the entire Coke into the glass, the fizz ending a quarter inch shy of the rim.

The amount of alcohol increased with each ensuing round until, five rounds later, less than a third of a bottle of Coke was needed to fill the glass to the top. They were obviously applying the 'the drunker I get, the better she be lookin'' approach. Still, I had neither desire nor money to yield to the temptations on hand.

Three hours passed swiftly. We sat and bullshitted, immersed in smoke and numbed by the Bacardi's pleasurable kick. Since this was Saturday night, the dance floor continually remained buzzing with customers, who strut like peacocks in heat as they summoned forth their masculinity.

A fossilized old timer moseyed through the entrance in slow motion, over-sized Gaucho hat wavering on his head and a holstered pistol riding high on his right hip. Daryl watched me eyeballing Pappy as he slowly sauntered up to the bar. "That is the boss. Some say he's in his late seventies, others swear he is not a day older than ninety-five." Daryl held up his drink and swirled the cubes. "The booze you are drinking is *his* booze. Those girls out there working are *his* girls. He be de man."

The old man made his way over to our table where he hugged Daryl, wiped the slightest string of slobber from his unshaven cheek, then bent down and whispered in his ear. They both looked at me, then belly laughed. The old man shook his head then creaked along to the next group of regulars. "Francisco says he can always pick out a whorehouse virgin when he sees them, right Bellingham?" Busted.

Sometime around midnight, the energy level reached its peak. Not enough action here for Daryl, so we finished the drinks in front of us, and headed to the exit, a stumble here, a wobble there as we made our way back out onto the cobblestones. We parted ways as the road veered left to LaRopa and I emphatically thanked him for the drinks as well as tonight's never-to-be-forgotten sociological experience.

He asked where we were staying and I told him that we were looking for new digs.

"Come on over to the Toussaint Toilet Monday or Tuesday. Early! Don't go sleeping in all day. The Norwegians are checking out so we'll see if we can get you into that room." No problemo.

Back at Casa La Playa, Dirty Mother mania was starting to wind down.

Propelled by mushroom madness, Ted, Doris, Dangerous and Cheesehead had successfully finished all bottles before them. All remaining ice cubes were less than a quarter of their original size. Four empty fifths of Cuervo lay strewn across the table; two upright, the others not as lucky. Two flies danced in a pool of syrupy delight around the base of an empty Kahlua half gallon. A lone pint of cream sat by, unopened.

Three or four new faces, also residents at La Playa, had joined the festivities, chatting with enthusiasm, but the Cheesehead was not in the thick of things.

"He's resting in our room." offered Doris, who had resorted to sunglasses, to cut down the glare from the bright quarter-moon. I opened the door.

There was the Cheeser, snuggled tight, in fetal position on the concrete, his face ivory in color. I assumed the worst, that he was dead, until one eye suddenly popped open "Ready to party, eh?" then closed back up again.

27: **Cheesehead's Demise**

Dangerous' mission, to initiate Cheesehead into DM infamy had been achieved. Not even bothering to suppress the smirk of success, he led me away from the babbling masses, down to the beach chairs where he could spin the longer version of the priceless events I had missed out on. Dave spun a good one:

"You know, Tunes, I hadn't planned to roast him until he got cocky. When that happened, I just could not let this golden opportunity pass.

After aborting the movie, we came back and Doris appointed herself bartender so I could concentrate on brewing the Shroom tea appropriately.

"She whipped Cheeser up a medium-grade Mother which he pooh-poohed. Mere Mother's Milk, he claimed—innocuous pussy drinks.

He was on his way out the door to pick up a six pack of Molson's 'to get a real buzz going' until I convinced him to hold tight; to let me whip him up a real Dirty Mother." Having watched Dangerous in action, earning his nickname over the years, I surmised the inevitable.

"I quickly tossed aside Doris' lightweight version and grabbed the largest glass in sight. Next, I poured in seventy percent Cuervo, thirty percent Kahlua, then, ever so lightly, touched it with an afterthought of paint thinner (cream). The ice crackled and churned as the ingredients began to coagulate into highly toxic molecular properties.

"I stirred it with my Camp King army knife and its blade immediately rusted. I knew we were getting close to the real thing. It took two of these Filthy Mothers to drop Clem the Limey down in Arizona a couple years back, so Ted started timing Cheeser to see how long exactly it would take before his face started melting.

"He downed the first in near record time, yet his eyes revealed a slight tinge of panic when I jumped up and started making him another. We then proceeded to blow a couple of reefers with two gay caballeros and a mean-spirited trash-talking sow with a blouse which conveniently kept coming unbuttoned. Her name was Freedom or something equally celestial. When the dope disappeared so did she, thank God."

"The Cheesehead began to exhibit early signs of turbulence halfway through Mother *Numero Dos*. His head bobbed and weaved from side to side in the manner of a ceramic dashboard bobblehead doll. He became extremely vociferous, even though half his words were slurred and unintelligible, the other half in French-Canadian, which he swears he doesn't even speak.

Next, he entered the introspective withdrawal stage, becoming exceptionally quiet after flopping down into a wicker chair. Shortly thereafter, a well-deserved form of partial paralysis took hold.

"He shut his system down, for perhaps twenty minutes, and we all grew wary, watching for early warning signs of imminent projectile vomiting. Just when it looked like he was down for the count, he leapt to his feet, and staggered out of the room. Apparent cookie-tossing time was at hand, still Cheesehead rallied gallantly and announced he was going swimming.

"We all watched from the courtyard as he staggered through the sand, down to the dimly illuminated Playa Principal where, before God and all else within sight, he discarded his trunks."

"Several couples were walking along the beach, enjoying a touch of romance under the moon above, when suddenly, a maniac, testicles swinging freely as he screamed obscure NHL hockey chants, shot past them into the surf. His pasty white Cheesehead ass was the last thing I saw dip below the surface."

I had seen Dave assist in the *transformation* of several Dirty Mother rookies over the years and, often, I have proudly served as his accomplice. This Mother tale, as had many others, was bound to only get weirder.

"Fueled by impulses which, more likely than not, result when Mothers collide with Shrooms, I could not resist the child-like temptation to abscond with his discarded clothing. After long moments of soul searching, I altered my cruel plan, leaving them instead forty yards or so from shoreline. Unfortunately for Cheesehead, they landed under the glow of a street lamp less than thirty feet in front of a young Mexican woman relaxing in one of the beach chairs.

"She joined in the revelry, egging him on in broken English, 'Come out boy, come out for your shorts!'

"A few minutes later as a flustered Cheeser remained put, she started feeling sorry for him and ended up walking his clothes down to the dimly lit waterline where he wouldn't have to embarrass himself whenever he finally got the gumption to hop out and retrieve them."

"I figured that the show was over and turned to go back to the party when two shadows became visible, moving quickly in his direction as he hustled into his trunks. Federales! Within seconds they had their rifles trained on him, asking him questions in loud authoritative Español."

"One problem, well actually two: One, Cheesehead was thoroughly shitfaced on a combo-dose of mushrooms and D.M.'s. Two, the sorry sun of a gun did not know a lick of Spanish. They continued their questioning, yet his efforts to communicate by pantomiming swimming wildly, made him come across more lunatic than moonlight swimmer.

"The youngest Federale was grinning at Cheezer's bizarre performance. Unfortunately, the elder Federale, who appeared to be in charge, lacked even the slightest sense of humor. Just when it truly appeared our man was knee-deep in dog doo and sinking fast, the girl in the chair came to his rescue."

"Cheesehead was destined to spend the night in Papillon's Den, until she stepped between the law and potential outlaw. In rapid-fire defense, she told them he was her brother--that his trunks had accidentally washed ashore. The federales looked at each other, equally confused and disappointed."

"Before they could say another word, she grabbed Cheeser by the ear and led him away from the gun-toting public servants and back to our party. We all cheered, then invited her for last call, but she declined.

I thought a possible spark may ignite between her and the Cheeser, but after he kept kissing her hand apologetically and flicking hot cigarette ashes onto those close by, she slipped off into the night, a modern-day heroine. And that, my traveling mate, is tonight's true story."

We sat laughing, satisfied to have inducted another member into the Dirty Mother Hall of Shame, then I offered an account of my night at the whorehouse.

As I recounted my experience, a certain glint of recognition shone in Dave's eye. As I assumed, he had patronized this particular establishment several times during his last visit. He relived one particularly wild Friday night, full of bar room brawls between federales and locals, when high energy collided with sexual tension and way too much tequila.

Somewhere around 1 a.m. we helped clean up and revive the Cheesehead, then headed back to our torta shop. We literally carried him back to his room. All the while he stuttered semi-intelligible syllables of gratitude, assuring us he could get home fine on his own, thank you, eh?

We watched him attempt to fit his key into the lock for well over five minutes. When this was finally accomplished, we bid him goodnight and added good luck. If Dirty Mother history was consistent, tonight would be far from over for the Cheeser. Once the cream starts to curdle in one's lower intestine a turbulent aftermath inevitably takes place. Speaking from experience, it is not a pleasant experience.

Dave casually inquired just how far away the whorehouse was. I knew what was coming, yet I declined the invitation to accompany him back there. I had had as much stimulus and alcohol as this guy can handle for one evening, thank you.

Instead, I lay in bed, eyes wide open, staring at the ceiling as the sugar and caffeine from five Cokes poured over rum overruled any attempt to sleep. Around 4 a.m. I was finally drifting off, right around the time Dangerous slithered ever so silently through the door. For a guy who'd had as much fun as he had tonight, he was unusually quiet while easing down onto his cot.

"Earth to Dave."
"Wassup?"
"Where's Morelia?"
"I dunno, up north a ways, why?"
"Are we going there?"
Only silence.
"Hey, roomie!"
"I'm here."
"Come on, I'm dying for an answer."
"Well... It's like this. Right now, I don't think there is much of a chance we're going anywhere."
"You now have my attention. Would you mind perhaps going into a little bit more detail? Something seems to be missing..."
"Her name was Carmelita. She had brilliant white teeth, a stunning red gown and was ugly by Mexican standards because she did not have a fat ass."
"And what about this Carmelita?"
"She cost me my last hundred dollars. I'm out of cash!"
From my end of the room, stone silence.

"I went in for a beer and *she* came to *me*. We started talking and one beer led to another. Next thing I knew she was sitting on my lap. There is a fellow working there with an instamatic that will take your photo with the lady of your choice for fifty pesos, so I asked if she would pose with me. 'Me no like pho-toe. Me like fucky-fucky.'

"Well, hell man, what am I gonna do? All I wanted was a photo—a casual remembrance of a night spent back at the Zihuatanejo whorehouse. What a treasured memory I could pull out and show my kids someday; a table full of empty Superiors, wasted locals in the background and the lovely lady in the red dress sitting innocently on their father's lap."

"So, you caved in." I was as jealous as I was pissed. I had not seen any beautiful woman in a red dress, dammit anyway…

"Like yourself, I haven't touched a woman going on two months. Suddenly this beautiful, sweet-smelling tomato is sitting on my crank, massaging my shoulders. What would you have done?"

Case closed; money gone.

28. Toussaint Toilet and the Western Union Blues

Monday, Feb. 19 Black Clouds and High Flying Rocks

Sunday, we lived like peasants. Beans, rice, dog brain tacos—limit: two each. Hung over from travel as well as excessive libations, we did little more than sleep and crawl out for less than a half day's-worth of rays. It was Monday morning when reality finally took hold.

Broke. What an exciting new subplot: How To Turn An Adventure Into A Nightmare, by Dangerous Dave and Andy Clark. **Sperm-drained Americanos Resort to Desperate Criminal Acts**, may soon be headlines in newspapers throughout Southern Mexico.

This is not my idea of an enviable predicament. So, what was Dangerous' master plan to save us?

"Western Union is our lifeline. There's one here in town. Remember the contingency plan we made back home?"

Oh yeah, *that* plan--the one where *I* would call home to my brother with whom we had stashed an emergency fund of two hundred dollars for this exact type of desperate situation. But the real contingency plan was to contact him when we realized funds were running low, not when we were flat-out broke.

Our only other option was to pack our bags and bust ass for the border, but quick arithmetic confirmed we would arrive in Guadalajara with less than a beggar's handful of pesos left tinkling in our pockets. Western Union here we come.

We found the office and made our *Larga Distancia* call back to Salem. As expected, no one was home, so I left a message with Sandra, his live-in girlfriend, who I hoped would convey the urgency of our predicament. We needed money wired, ASAP!!! Western Union man assured me that, if wired immediately, our money would be here by Wednesday, possibly Thursday.

The money left in my wallet was now our money. We could make it, yet constraint was of utmost importance. Prudence and discipline became our sole credo. No more Eskimos-wait, only one eskimo a day instead of three. No more barbecued shrimp slathered in mouth-whoopin' barbecue sauce. No more Snapper Veracruz.

We would survive on a diet consisting of five-peso dog brain taquitos each from the Taco Loco. No more breakfasts, no more ceviche, no alcohol, cigars, most of all, no more Carmelita for my adventuresome partner. Dangerous was already bumming because we had to pass on Lady Frankenstein, tonight's one-night-only feature showing at the outdoor cinema.

We were playing a longshot by taking Darryl at his word, still we climbed the vertically challenging hill of death that leads to Playa La Ropa with the hopes a room would be ours once the long haul had been completed.

Walk east, almost the entire length of La Ropa and you will find the Toussaint Toilets, a long concrete rambler someone divided into six equal-sized duplex/quadrants. Each square concrete unit consists of two mosquito net-covered beds and a bathroom: solar shower, a fan, toilet, and sink. Pretty basic package, made desirable by their proximity to primo beach, located less than fifty yards away from warm mild surf and only a moderate amount of foot traffic passing by. It is also about as far as any sane person would trek under the midday sun with a backpack bending your bones, yet there we were.

A sour official looking Señora busily washed laundry behind in the courtyard. Dave stepped up and inquired as to the availability of a room. Her reply, a quick, curt "no". We had come a long way to get kicked in the chops so swiftly. He asked if one may be free tomorrow. Again, her answer was the same.

Whipped pups, physically spent from the long jaunt from Centro, we prepared to retrace our steps. If nothing else we can always return to our room there in the shadows of the torta shop.

A familiar voice resonated from under the palapas. "Hey there Bellingham, where the hell you two been?" There sat Daryl, hair mussed, eyes bloodshot, at a card table, playing solitaire as two young women watched passively. "Did you get your room yet?"

I told him we had been rebuffed, refused, denied--no rooms for the taking. He stubbed out his cigarette and went around to the courtyard where he began a long one-sided conversation with the Señora. It was comforting to see that she was equally as grouchy to him before waving him away.

"Number four is yours. The best I could get you is three days; one hundred seventy-five pesos each, per day." Dangerous and I looked on, happy, yet in disbelief. Our trek ends here, after all!

Daryl relit his cigarette and reshuffled his cards. "Well, what the hell you looking at! Better pay her, quickly before the old battle-ax changes her mind." I felt like hugging him, yet I'm sure he would've squished my head like a grape. Instead, I offered my heartfelt thanks.

The rates were a bit stiff, three hundred and fifty pesos a day for us both, bringing us closer to poverty that much quicker. We paid up, got the key and tossed our packs inside. We were headed off to Majahua, but first back to town to see if the Cheesehead had survived Saturday night.

We pounded upon his door well over a minute before any distinguishable sound of life could be detected. The lock rattled and he cussed in frustration as the struggled trying to slide the pesky little chain aside. Finally, the door opened. The soul who greeted us was a sad sight indeed.

There stood the Cheeser, glasses cockeyed and bent on his pointy nose, flesh ghostly pale, and eyes crusted over, pitiful, and lifeless. Putrefied Mother cream was distinguishable, still thick and clinging to his mustache. It is impossible to begin describing his breath.

"So, tell me, did they taste the same way coming up as they did going down?" It was a question asked by the master maker of Mothers himself.

Cheeser's eyes rolled back in his head. Using the door for support, he pointed to the pile of sheets askew on his floor. "I don't know, they were just there when I awoke yesterday morning." *They* that were just *there* were yucky looking chunks of Saturday night's dinner regurgitated into his sheets.

A maid stuck her head in only to back off quickly, as the odor she met left her frozen in her tracks. She pointed to his sheets, Cheeser handed them over. She left with a disgusted scowl and an armful of funky linen, destined, more likely for the garbage can than the laundry line.

We waited while Cheeser struggled to slide into swim trunks. He rolled a joint (to take the edge off) with quivering hands, then quietly followed us out the door. We were off to Majahua. I had to admit, he was quite the trooper.

Dave had forgotten to warn Cheesehead about the marathon lung-bursting, thigh-killing, ball-buster of a hike necessary to get there, but we paused only once while he dry-heaved in the bushes. This came about after he'd gotten a nose full of the same roadside refuse which had gagged us as well while on our last visit. Today, even the flies gave Cheeser his space.

Everyone we met who had experienced Majahua seemed to have a wild tale about the place; tales of rip-offs, sagas of seedy looking knife-wielding banditos frequently bullying tourists. Each time we told them where we were bound the locals would offer a solemn reminder to be very careful. So far, our experiences had been one hundred percent positive.

We followed Dave's game plan to the letter; ever-cautious, never bringing anything of excessive value; only water, fruit, sunscreen and reading material in our backpacks. We always traveled in numbers, five or six strong every visit, and always made sure at least one person stayed back on our blankets to discourage any temptation our modest belongings may offer. Today was our turn to add to the legacy of Majahua.

The three of us arrived to thunderous waves, sending thick foam rolling towards the uninhabited shoreline. We laid out our blankets, accessed our location and prepared to take on some darn big whompers.

Ted and Doris straggled in shortly thereafter, having gotten a late start as they too were still trying to shake off last night's case of woozies.

Cheesehead whipped out one of the joints, fired it up and passed it clockwise. While more than moderate use of pot may result in lethargy and paranoia, herb is great for chasing away nausea-- quicker and more effective than any aspirin or painkiller I have ever used. We all gave the Cheeser thumbs up for his role as official attitude adjuster for the day. For that alone, Dangerous and yours truly vowed to lay off all post-barf humor.

After the last lip and/or fingertip had been burnt by the stubby roach, we all sat back to enjoy the magnitude of this real-life postcard doing its thing there before us. The huge waves crashed, each with its own distinct rhythm, breaking sharp as thunder. White beery foam crackled as it rolled toward shore before reversing its flow with the a crispy hiss and popping bubbles.

The palm trees began to sway like cartoon hula dancers and a trio of large gray gulls provided shrill cackles as they plunged towards, then away from the rocks. Brother, nature in action doesn't get any better than this.

Doris was the first one to notice the well-tanned shoeless local working his way towards us from the far end of the beach. Closer he came until he arrived where we were seated before coming to a stop. He then stood there, in silence, for well over a minute us. We did our best to ignore him.

The buzz from the herb added greatly to the uncomfortable feeling growing within the group. "Dave, what should we do?"

Dangerous looked straight ahead as if this intruder wasn't even there. Invisible. Nonexistent. "Just ignore him and he'll go away."

Instead, Smiler stayed put, then dropped down into our circle, sitting cross-legged, before glancing from person to person, silly grin still glued to his puss.

Finally, he spoke. "Mota."

Shit. He uttered the one word guaranteed to make our nerves tingle. We all grew immediately uncomfortable. Smiler just sat there.

He had been out of sight while we participated in our illegal deed, and the wind had been blowing out to sea, yet he was onto us. "Mary-Wanna." he squeaked in a mirthful and knowing tone. Oh great, Smiler knew two words.

Stoned out of our gourds, we continued giving him nothing but the coldest of shoulders. Undaunted, he continued beaming at us on for at least five minutes, perhaps even longer, until at last, I concocted a Hail Mary to deceive our intruder.

I bummed a cigarette from the Cheeser which I then lit. Holding it between thumb and middle finger, the way a toker holds a joint, I passed it around from person to person. When it was 'Smiler's' turn, he declined, laughing. "No no no--Mary-Wanna" he pointed first to his eye, then to his temple, letting me know he wasn't stupid. Nice try. Back to plan A, ignore his smiling ass.

Finally, he tired waiting for us to break out the big bud. He rose, waved adios, then headed back down the beach, all the while that eerie grin still etched upon his face.

We sighed collectively; weird uncomfortable energy left in his wake.

I tried to focus on the screaming gulls but my buzz was officially on edge, knowing most likely we were still under observation. My eyes scanned the direction he headed, but Smiler had already vanished, as quickly as he had appeared. Immediately I was extremely nervous, and was sure the others already felt the same vibe. Screw it, let's go swimming.

As we wave-whomped, trying to recapture the once righteous modified mood intended, a pair of gringos came down the hill, waving our way as they headed down the beach in the direction Smiler had sauntered off to.

They stopped at a convenient and very accommodating plywood lean-to built at the end of the beach. What a wonderful place to set up camp! Once they had placed their towels and belongings inside, they joined us in the splendiferous surf.

After about four sets of monster waves, they bailed, and were on their way back to the lean-to when suddenly they started yelling and waving frantically for us to come join them.

"Some scumbag just stole my backpack!!! Little prick just popped out of the brush headed this way and then he was gone! And so was our stuff. My frickin' Rolex and a hundred-dollar pair of sunglasses were in there too!!!!"

Dangerous asked if they could describe the rascal. They did. Sure enough, it was Smiler.

Dave, Cheeser and the gringos organized a short scouting trip into the undergrowth but obviously Smiler held home court advantage.

By now he was long gone, divvying up the goods with his pals or, perhaps, even setting up a trap with consequences possibly far outweighing the value of the lost belongings.

It was obvious the lean-to was a textbook come-on; a grand lure set there to entice those unaware enough to be fooled by the false convenience it suggested.

It reminded me of the trap Elmer Fudd always builds for Bugs in the cartoons--the kind where he puts the carrot with the string under the box and sits in the bushes for hours while nothing happens. Only difference was this time Elmer caught his bunny.

After an ever-so brief jaunt into the brush, the scouting party returned with nothing but cactus scratches on their legs. No Smiler, no backpack no frickin' Rolex.

Doris, Ted, and I decided we had had enough excitement and were ready for the hard, hot hike back to civilization. Cheeser and Dave decided to stick around as the best waves of the day had just begun.

"This place is like a Toussaint toilet," Richard looked up from what I had counted to be his third mid-day Bloody Mary, scrutinized his Cribbage hand, frowned, and laid his cards down.

Across the card table Daryl cackled as he moved his pegs closer to the finish line, "It attracts all of the flies around--right into the middle of the whole smelly mess." Richard gestured to the area around us. Six palapas, shade, and six card tables where the cast of characters, or, as Richard has designated them, flies, come and go.

I have only been under the palapas for less than two hours and already I see what Richard means. "My friend, you yourself are now floating in the murky sewage of humanity--the Toussaint Toilet itself. Enjoy your stay."

A glance at those seated under the palapas were hunkered down over a cribbage or backgammon board, gorging on ever-flowing baskets of chips and salsa, while a half-gallon of local dark rum sits within an arms-length of a pour. First impressions lead me to believe many of this crew has earned a degree in Party Science, most having gone on to earn their Master's.

The *flies* we have observed so far are an interesting lot indeed, Richard continued, willing to serve as my guide to '*Flycology 101*'. The lion's share of patrons consistently offers up positive energy along with the level of stamina necessary to elevate all potential good times into memorable events. Everyone is aware they have a good thing going."

As you will come to realize Killer sunsets, a consistently cool breeze, and sense of privacy come with the territory. Playa La Ropa beach is also a wonderful, as well as safe place to obtain, imbibe and enjoy high quality Mexican weed, or *Mota*--indigenous to the region--without paranoia."

He then points to a man and woman seated at the last table. She is counting silverware while the man cusses angrily as he tries in vain to tune in his static-blasting radio. "Those two are Steve and Adi. They run the restaurant. Damn good people making damn good food. You have got to try the Red Snapper before you leave.

Steve's from Brownsville and Adi's Mexican-American. Be really nice to her, she's a sweetheart. Whenever you need cold beer, a soda or something to eat Adi will take care of you. She's the boss."

He went on to say Steve and his missus have only been here at La Ropa since May; hired to give the diminishing restaurant business a well-needed shot in the arm. Since then, word around town has spread and things have started going gangbusters, especially on weekends when Daryl contributes about a hundred dollars a day for food/booze, Richard adds. "Keep Daryl smiling and everybody benefits."

The lion's share of patrons consistently offers up positive energy along with the correct level of stamina crucial for elevating all potential good times into memorable events. Killer sunsets, a consistently cool breeze, and sense of privacy come with the territory. Everyone is well aware they have a good thing going. Playa La Ropa beach is also a wonderful, as well as safe place to obtain, imbibe and enjoy high quality Mexican weed, or *Mota*--indigenous to the region--without paranoia.

"Toussaint Toilet is a community—crazy-ass dysfunctional, but a community, just the same. Most on hand drink hard, play hard, and don't wake up until noon. When we do, we are hungry and need immediate gratification. That is when Adi does her magic.

"Once we have rejuvenated enough brain cells to move about, we gather right where you are sitting, to regroup and fire up our proverbial engines, with a crisply executed hand or three of Cribbage, Poker, Go Fish--you name it, we'll play it, as long as there are at least fifty-two cards in the deck. Some of us even manage to get some sun before siesta." His last comment a direct shot at Daryl, who responded with a lengthy stream of profanity.

"We usually reemerge to get a bite to eat, before heading into town in the Mafia staff car for some a-c-t-i-o-n." Richard nods towards the carbon monoxide-spewing, muffler-deficient hunk of iron resting on four bald tires, backed up against the picket fence out behind the casa.

I remembered the violent way it snorted and shook when fired it up the first night we met back in Centro. Richard noticed my skepticism as I eyeballed his vehicle, so he added "Hey man, what can I say? It's functional--except most of the time the brakes are non-responsive."

Over the next two hours, most of Richard's flies land nearby for either a meal, a beer, a special guest appearance, or a quick hand of cards.

In Room One we've got Mike, Collette, and Kathy from Denver.

Mike's well-to-do parents are moored here in La Ropa bay in their sweet-looking yacht, the Mañana. Right now, they're two hundred yards away or so from shore, drinking wine, tanning on the deck, swimming, and whatever else people who own yachts do with their leisure time. Twice a day they come back ashore to load up on supplies, grab a bite to eat, then back aboard the Mañana for a first-class view of the setting sun.

David the Limey is grousing because he locked himself out of Room Two. Richard says this happens to him every other day.

He paces back and forth, as Choina, the grumpy caretaker we met earlier, won't be back from chores in town until early this evening and he's feeling a tinge of Tourista coming on. This curly blonde mop-topped cat from London is Richard and Daryl's running partner as the boys make their nightly rounds.

Daryl throws him the key to his room, then reminds him to be sure and light a match when he's through. Limey utters some form of verbal gratitude as he catches the key on the fly and quickly slams the door behind him.

The two bored Cribbage-watching ladies are from Belgium.

They are aloof and in their own world, traveling with a George Carlin look-alike Frenchman, Marcel, whom a jealous Richard assumes is enjoying the best of both worlds after the lights go out in Room Three. Richard has tried his best to give Marcel a breather but so far, all efforts have fallen short.

Dangerous and I occupy Room Four.

The only resident of Toussaint Toilet not here specifically to bask in the sun is Daryl, next door in Room Five. The tattooed giant is here to drink and to relax. This is his fifth straight winter spent on La Ropa.

Richard paints a profile of his friend. "His life consists of a double order of runny eggs around noon, Cribbage or Solitaire until the sun hits its peak. When he starts getting grouchy, we send him off for a siesta. Around five, we start waking his snoring derriere up. He comes to life about six fifteen and from that point on he is not to be denied."

Daryl is also an ex-boxer who, like Dangerous, is highly bummed that live boxing is no longer a Friday night fixture in Zihuatanejo. Richard says his pal often spends his Saturday nights off in the smaller towns, getting his boxing fix in seedy, smokey community halls.

Then there's Richard: good looking, smooth talking, woman-chasing, thirty-two-year-old, silver-haired fox, who's a cross between Jimmy Buffett and Clint Eastwood, if that's not too much of a paradox to imagine. Totally mellow, he does get a seriously-crazed look in his gray eyes when sufficiently-liquored.

He shows me his room, Room Six. On the wall, covering cracked plaster is a pinup girl with breasts huge as cantaloupes. Someone has signed it 'To Richard--Just wishin' we was fishin.' A gigantic handmade wooden pyramid hangs from the ceiling above his bed to ward off the mosquitoes. Richard swears he has not been bitten once since he has been here.

As he began elaborating upon the benefits of pyramid power, a mosquito the size of a small hummingbird lands on his shoulder and helps himself to two pints of plasma. Without missing a beat, Richard carries on about positive energy flows.

He was just about to go in depth on their various benefits when Dangerous and the Cheeser burst in, back from Majahua with a tale of their own.

The waves had been worth their time. After about an hour of riding and whompin' and getting tossed about, the Rolex-light gringo and his backpack-less partner were whomped out. Cheeser and Dave lasted about another twenty minutes before they too were spent by their workout.

Back on their blankets they spent time arguing the merits of four down football vs. the CFL's three down style when an unidentifiable thud was heard close by.

Dave began: "We thought very little of the first thud. Neither of us lost our stream of thought until the third rock landed a mere two feet away, not quite the size of a baseball, but bigger than a golf ball, that's for sure.

"Suddenly the cloudless sky was ablaze with projectiles headed our way. We quickly ruled out meteors and, after figuring out their path of trajectory, were certain they were launched from the underbrush, a short way back in the jungle. We were under attack!!! Someone armed with a slingshot had commenced taking target practice and we were the targets!

"Rocks continued thudding around us, many much too close for comfort. When one whizzed by within a foot of Cheesehead's skull, we hastily gathered our gear and pulled out of Dodge."

"As our retreat was underway, a potential rock launcher was spotted watching us from the bushes—someone who looked a lot like Smiler.

Unarmed and on foreign turf (literally) we were torn between wanting to go get the sucker, risking a rock suddenly and unfortunately imbedded in our foreheads, or doing the chicken dance and getting our tushes to safety as quickly as rock-dodging allowed. We chose the chicken dance."

Smiler reclaimed his beach. One bad episode in almost a half dozen visits stood as a sobering reminder that no matter how wonderful an isolated beach like Majahua could be, you must always be on your toes. Expect the unexpected.

It was inevitable. I have fallen in love with Zihuatanejo.

Its beaches, cast of characters, sunny climate, and orange sherbet sunsets we have come to take for granted made it hard for me to accept that our trip must come to an end.

Our 'biggest obstacle to achieving total bliss' award would have to go to the town's mosquitoes, who constantly force one to lather from head to foot in slick coats of repellent in order to enjoy Z-Wat after dark. The aggressive taxis navigating the narrow streets at breakneck speed finish a close second. For them, there is no repellent.

After dinner, a large black Brahma Bull lumbered through a nearby row of eight hammocks as it made its way down the beach at sunset. Twenty minutes later, a frustrated gaucho came by and Adi pointed in the direction our four-legged visitor was last seen headed.

Around nine Daryl, Richard, and the Limey, all freshly showered and lathered in musky cologne, are off to La Tortuga where its Ladies night. Half price drinks. Conga line at eleven. We pass, Dave's whorehouse extravaganza has eliminated us from all possible social endeavors until Western Union comes through.

Shortly thereafter, a half dozen American acquaintances of Steve and Adi drop in for ceviche, snapper, and freshly-caught lobster.

As their meal ended, two congenial Brits, Dexter and Finn, tuned acoustic guitars they'd brought along, then strummed their way for over an an hour of familiar pop classics ranging from Creedence to the Beatles, Neil Young to the Hollies, with even a touch of Steely Dan, all of them my favorite artists.

After they dispersed Dangerous and I decided to finish off the last of our well-rationed bag of reefer. The smoke put me in a proactive mood while Dangerous faded quickly, so I decided to take a solo moonlight munchie run to Centro and grab some form of junk food gratification.

After living almost two months-worth of travel and a leisurable lifestyle, I have managed to achieve a thoroughly sublime state of mellowness. The Mañana Method seems to be THE antidote to successfully chase away life's intense pace, yet comes with a price.

In order to attain and appreciate this groove, the formula requires one to spend a reasonable period of adjustment, as simply put, the more time put in, the more the return.

Most of those who come to Mexico seeking rest and relaxation are short termers; folks restricted by a limited amount of time their real world allows them to unwind. One week is nice, but doesn't cut the mustard.

The longer an individual can afford to unwind, the more casual your pace of life becomes. That, friends, is how best I can describe The Mañana Method.

Along this road we have met many folks dedicated to the pursuit of social activity whom we have enjoyed being around, yet it seems they're more structure instead of spontaneity.

I have come to learn and embrace a more extemporaneous path; one of waking up in the morning, putting on my t shirt and huaraches, and stepping outside to see which way the day will take me.

Dangerous has been a great mentor, offering insight that comes through the gist of accepting going with the flow. The rituals of the road and the mysteries revealed have played a major role in this enlightenment.

We have executed a solid game plan: Barra, to acclimatize; Z-Wat, the meat and potatoes of our trip; an intense, amazing and illuminating sojourn to the eastern seaboard, before heading back to Z-Wat for this final dose of rest and relaxation. All has been accomplished for less than a thousand dollars. Try and top that one.

The aftermath of the herb, warmth of the jungle at night, along with the contradictory sights and smells before me; all overwhelm this traveler as I started my trek from Centro back to the remote edge of La Ropa.

I'm walking along this paved lane-and-a-half's worth of road, yesteryear's jungle, munching on a bag of Sabritas, and toting a sixer of mineral water back to the Toilet.

Even though I've all but run out of pesos as well as time, tonight I have not a single care in the world, let alone the universe.

Five years ago, this road was a dirt path, maintained by men wielding razor-sharp machetes. Its primary flow of traffic was wandering peasants, moving along at an easy pace pushing a wheelbarrow or riding a mule. Now, this road belongs to the taxis, trucks and other four-wheeled manned vehicles shuttling the beautiful people to and from the secluded resorts of Playa La Ropa.

Numerous styles of music come booming my way from open-doored homes tucked into the dark green hillside; a little rock and roll here, a touch of salsa there, and *mucha música del mariachi*, cranked up by families enjoying a late-night meal gathered at tables in front yards and patios.

I dig into my Sabritas, ingest another salty paw's worth and sigh. Our time is just about through.

Soon I will be back in the fast lane, no more Eskimos, no more siestas, and, most certainly, no more majestic sunsets on which to end one's day. All these sights and sounds around me will become little more than pleasant memories, ready to be replayed on sleepless nights or dreamy rainy afternoons. What will I recall?

Of course, I'll recall the beaches, sunshine, and the warm water. But there is much more to the package.

I will remember the many good people who touched us on this journey, along with the Ugly Americans whose attitudes and expectations demonstrate how easy it is to be considered nothing more than a rude ass in the eyes of others.

I'll replay our many unique adventures; situations and special moments that mean little to anyone but those who happened to be there. For these chosen few, they will forever remain noteworthy.

I will think back to the many locals, who humbly exist within their modest means. These are people who, once they get to know you as a person instead of just another tourist, would go out of their way to make you a late-night meal or lend you the shirt off their backs should you need assistance, even though you have enough money back home to feed their entire family for many months.

They are people who, without knowing a stitch about what kind of person they are encountering, will offer you the comfort of their hammocks when you are wandering aimlessly about, deep in the evening without a place to end your day

This experience has been about heart and soul, pleasure and pain; shrewdness, patience, courage, and diligence as well as more than a jigger of grit--things you learn about yourself and whether you have them or you don't. Self-realization: are you a man or are you a Kid? Having this experience has allowed me discover a great deal about who I actually am.

Two middle-aged Señoras stand under a street lamp. They glance my direction as I pass, offering a smile and cheerful greeting, "*Buenos Noches. Como te llamas?*"

Another chance! Retribution! Just what I've been waiting for since my torta stand embarrassment several days ago. I know the right words this time. I am ready.

As I start to reply, a Sabrita fleck sticks in my throat and I suck the wayward crumb down into my windpipe. All I can do is wave in acknowledgment as I cough, cough, cough my way into the night. I'll get it right yet, I swear!

A truck slows up beside me, then stops. I tense up.

Back in the States it would not be unusual for someone to leap down from the cab, bash my brains into oatmeal, then hop back in and speed away.

Tonight, in Zihuatanejo, an elderly lady with more wrinkles than a well-worn shirt, steps down from the truck in slow motion, adjusts her shawl, then thanks the family of five stuffed into the cab for the short ride home.

The Sabritas are almost gone now. I have reached the top of the hill where the streetlights end and the starlight alone shall lead me along the path back to my mosquito-netted abode. As I leave the concrete for the short path back to our casa, there is one thing of which I am certain. On my walk back I have experienced a damn nice Grade-A epiphany. Boy it sure feels great…

In the distance, the ever-present rhythm of the waves continues pounding the shore, while closer by, waves of sound coming from the hillside Disco provide a completely different beat. Contrasts, contrasts, forever contrasts… I begin my descent back to La Ropa.

The sand is still warm beneath my huaraches, the temperature somewhere around seventy-five degrees. Not too shabby for 11 p.m.

So, dear reader, thanks for being patient. My epiphany has officially concluded. Still, this is what *it* is all about, at least the *it* I value. Sights, sounds, smells and feelings. Oceans, clean air, sunshine, sunshine, sunshine.

Thank you, Mexico, for everything you have given me and I hope I have given back nothing but positive energy.

Mexico--The sweetest wine this cowboy has ever tasted.

Thursday came and, for the third consecutive day, Western Union let me down. We stopped by the office at 10:30. No luck. Western Union man told me to check again later in the day as nothing had yet come across the wire. He assured me money could show up at any time of the day and that he would be in the office until 5 p.m.

His optimism boosted my spirit, enough so I made a return trip at 1 p.m. Sorry, same results. I even braved the scorching afternoon heat for a desperate round three, at 4:45, but the office was already closed. My ship had not yet come in. I contacted my brother, down at Larga Distancia, who confirmed he had sent the money shortly after my call Monday morning.

On our way back to TT one of my favorite moments of the entire trip occurred; a subtle unexpected moment we had no choice but to savor.

We were headed back through the side streets of Centro, where music blares from every shop preparing for the day ahead. Suddenly, from a small Pharmacia the sounds of a dobro emanated from the shop's transistor radio. It was Dire Straits. The song was 'Wild West End.' one of my very favorites the band has offered.

Without a word, Dave and I sat down upon the steps of the shop and listened:

Four minutes and forty-two seconds passed without a single word from either of us. Splendid. I missed my music but appreciated it ten times more than usual while it lasted. The final notes of Knopfler's guitar ended and up-tempo mariachi music took its place. We smiled at each other, stood up and made our way back to La Ropa.

Five hundred pesos was all that remained. Time to dig in; enjoy tonight's low budget feast of five taquitos and a Jugo de Pina; chewing slowly, savoring every bite. Who knows how long until, well, let's not even go there.

The sun bore down harshly for our Friday hike to town yet once there, the reward was sweet. As I opened the door, Western Union man saw me and smiled as he produced an envelope he eagerly slid my way. Our cash was here. Muy Bueno!

Off to the Banco to turn paper into pesos. A slight snag, as the teller asked for my passport or tourist visa. Uh-oh. I handed her the duplicate copy without the official stamp and she scrutinized me, top to bottom, then asked why there was no stamp. I did my best job to act as stupid as humanly possible.

She showed it to her supervisor and after a couple minutes of serious dialogue, she shoved it into her drawer, counted out a large pile of hundreds and handed them to me, all the while eyeing me suspiciously.

As I hastily headed out the door, I did a very subtle but sweet victory dance. This tense scenario was a reminder of Dangerous' adage that for every bit of pleasure you receive may require an ounce-worth of pain. The sweetest part of the Trifecta had yet to come.

Back at TT preparations were in high gear for Saturday night-- Daryl's yearly pig feed. It was hard to watch Bessie make the rounds from table to table, nosing the patrons affectionately. Hours from now, these same folks would be lifting knife and fork and help themselves to seconds of our porcine friend.

For the past few days, we have got to know this creature as one comes to know a dog, petting the back of its neck while feeding it chips, even carrying on one-way conversations, knowing full well Bessie understood nary a word of English.

As we prepared for our upcoming departure, we decided to take the high road and just have a safe and sane evening, as the buzz going on around headquarters was tomorrow night would be one for the ages.

After one of Adi's cheesy enchiladas, a plate of ceviche and fresh fiery salsa, I found a cozy chair away from the crew, laid back and let the ocean take me away.

29: Not Just Girls

Sunday Morning (the 'day after' blues)

I am still not quite sure what brought out the full-on party beast in me last night at Daryl's pig feed but the following detailed review of our soiree will surely provide the answer.

The fact Western Union had come through before the final grains of sand in my financial hour glass hit rock bottom certainly played a role in a high degree of giddiness I was experiencing. Couple that with the reality that this was to be our final fling as our departure from paradise was now less than a week away and the stage was set.

Other theories bandied about could include: inaugural pig feed participant syndrome, falling under mezcal's unholy spell, or, Dave's favored choice--turning into a lightweight after two months of having abandoned my normal winter pattern of excessive alcohol indulgence. When sorted out, there is a kernel of truth to each of the above.

And so, friends, pull up a chair and relive with me a night we shall call **Bessie's Demise**. Oh, what a night it was!!!

But this tale of last night's cheerful exuberance should appropriately begin with the following morning's initial rays of daybreak, as they made their presence known, rising just above the eastern hills of Zihuatanejo...

With a nod to mighty Lazarus, yours truly, thankfully began feeling my alcohol-satiated corpuscles creep back to life.

Slug-like, I test each limb, making sure they are still attached. I struggle against a mental mine field of dim-wit fog bearing down heavily upon my current state of existence. Man down! Man down!

But wait--do not panic! All surviving brain cells seem to be satisfactorily regrouping. Waking up on my back, mere yards from Casa 4 was a *choice*, not a *punishment*. I alone chose tie soft sand in lieu of navigating the fifty paces back to my mosquito-netted abode.

Both Daryl and Richard issued fair warning that every *Sabado Noche* under the Playa La Ropa palms has the potential to evolve into organized mayhem. Last night's festivities will go down as *Bessie's Demise* or, *Saturday Night Pig Feed*.

Bessie arrived on Tuesday and immediately became a favorite of the borders at The Toilet. Each day she wandered freely throughout our social area, the recipient of pets, scratches and other forms of affection more commonly associated with domesticate house pets, Sometimes, she charmed generous scraps and leftovers from each table she chose to visit.

Yesterday, right after breakfast, back behind the Toussaint Toilet kitchen, Bessie met her demise. The mournful squeals coming from behind the fence quickly had me contemplating the pros and cons of converting to vegetarianism, but Daryl looked up from his Cribbage board to assure me Bessie was not the first swine to meet its maker, nor the last. "By the way, didn't I see you chomping down on a huge plateful of bacon yesterday morning? And who was raving about Adi's ham and cheese omelet?"

The party began to gain momentum somewhere around 4 p.m.

Around 6:30 Steve and Adi emerge from the kitchen, bearing stacks of corn tortillas and bowls of salsa they then distributed to each card table, followed next by arms loaded down with heaping plates of shredded pig, cooked thoroughly to perfection. Add to this large mounds of rice and beans, alongside a huge plastic tub full potato salad and you have quite a sumptuous feast on hand.

Dangerous, myself, and a large contingent of fellow pork gobblers had a grand time, eating, reveling, singing, and drinking. Smoking, then drinking, then smoking and drinking even more.

Mezcal is a powerful libation whose signature is a smoky essence unlike any other consumable alcohol I have experienced. It is best drunk straight--no chasers, no frills; tip 'er up and down she goes.

I consider myself to be a moderate partier who favors Tequila as my go-to choice of spirits. Tonight, I have been invited by Richard to join he along with a handful of select regulars who would be *chasing the worm*, Mezcal's signature Cracker-Jack prize, which floats lazily at the bottom of each bottle.

He had returned late last evening from Oaxaca after spending a week on a Zapotec rug-and-blanket hunting expedition. While there, he acquired a footlocker's worth of the region's finest produced mezcal spirits, available at a price he could not turn down. Tonight, his purchase has become our good fortune.

The *chase* begins.

Shot glasses raise all around. *Salud*, then down the hatch. A reflexive shiver yields to a warm tingle which starts in the back of the throat, then travels on down to your toes like a runaway train.

Mezcal's trademark smoky essence greets you fully on first sip, before morphing into a sweet agave after-kiss to complete the rush. More chips, more salsa, more of generous Richard's mezcal. Salud.

From the kitchen side one of Santana's Latin-laced *Abraxas* jumps to life, heightening the surrealism as incredible food, drink, and music come together as one. As we feed off these positive vibes, the energy level begins to swell.

The waves continue to play out their role as tonight's backdrop, rolling in, then out; a never-ending rhythmic flow. This takes place less than fifty yards away, comes free of charge, and never takes a union break.

Salud! Warmth. Waves. Laughter. More pig. It just keeps getting better.

Glasses clink nonstop. Salud.

My ears have begun to tingle as if enveloped in large furry ear muffs. Santana fades away and The Grateful Dead at Barton Hall takes its place.

Around eight Dexter and Finn arrive, take out their acoustic Gibson's and the air around us suddenly fills with two voices meshed in near-perfect harmony.

Energy. Laughter. Warmth. *Bessie's Demise* has opened full throttle. So, this is Mexico. Salud.

The atmosphere could only be described as sublime, and the food exquisite--second to none Caught up fully in the festivities I feel a change in the air. Tonight, my claim of libation moderation begins to slip into excess

. As midnight approached, I failed to recognize the warning signs I was dangerously close to standing with both feet in the red zone.

Swept up by the festivities, I had let my guard down. Keeping track of shots had become irrelevant, influenced in large part by the continual passing of quality Mota traveling around the circle of muchachos I had become a part of.

As we closed in on the witching hour, less than a half inch of Reindo De Oaxaca, Richard's particular cactus beverage of choice, remain at the bottom of the final bottle and needed to be dispatched in order to bring finality to the proceedings.

After many years spent mastering the art of revelry, Lady Fortune has continually been on my side, granting me a streak of happy endings and soft landings. So far tonight she has not arrived to slap me in the head and send me back to number Four.

Saturday night does not fade easily in Zihuatanejo, and the denizens of Playa La Ropa came ready to give it their all. Well before midnight, our booze-fueled free-for-all had set the bar mighty high for pig roasts to come.

Those lacking the necessary measure of staying power packed it in early, before they ended up feeling worse than a harshly beaten dime-store Piñata. For those still standing, the party flowed long after the rooster crowed.

Midnight arrived. The next wave, those who did not adhere to the 'Can't leave until you've started to weave' mantra, began to dissipate.

Dexter, who had provided an evening's worth of sing-alongs, packed up his Gibson, then woke, Finn, snoring and drooling in the chair beside him.

Resurrected from his nocturnal state, Finn quickly hid his bloody red peepers behind Ray Bans, before jamming a golf ball-sized wad of sticky Moroccan Hash in his jean jacket pocket. Vertical yet wobbly, the duo headed back to Playa Madera.

Last of the non-in-house crew to say adios was Wales, he too suffering third-degree Crab Eye symptoms. Wales is a congenial weed farmer from Trinidad, California, a region known for stellar crystal-flecked prize-winning Indica bud--annually harvested and distributed up and down the entire west coast in abundant quantities.

Even in his oven-baked state, Wales was a true gentleman, the only soul considerate enough to assist Señora Adi in cleaning up the post pig-feed paper plate and cup carnage.

The hard-cores drew their chairs closer together, ready to party till the cows came home. Our focus turned to polishing off all remaining beverages, whether they be pints, fifths or half gallons still bearing spirits of varying flavor.

Finally, one hour past midnight, my toes officially crossed the line. Adept transformed into inept. Mezcal, just a short time ago my guide to the inner circle of chumminess, suddenly gave way to its dark side.

Terms of misfortune filled my whirling head. Time to find sanctuary; somewhere nearby preferred, where I can meditate and regroup

. Unfortunately, the terrain leading to Toussaint Toilet's baños had already become uncomfortably unstable as well as unfamiliar.

A sailor lost at sea. The party faded to black.

Sunday Morning (continued) Still lost in the sand

My legs are truly ablaze. The no-see-ums, obnoxious, tenacious microscopic creatures inhabiting the billions of grains of sand around me, have come upon good fortune this brand-new day.

I shift in my granular resting place, swooshing ineffectively at microbe-covered shins. The burning continues. These are hungry little bastards whose mandibles gnaw away ferociously upon my exposed flesh with no intention of calling off the dogs.

Still reeling from mezcal's potent spell, I rise, stumble, then regain my footing with the grace of a newly-born calf.

Daryl the Human Barrel, Richard's roommate, and self-proclaimed Minister of Mayhem at Toussaint Toilet, is already up and 'at em, playing solitaire and chain-smoking Winston's, his cancer stick of choice.

His red-rimmed peepers follow my wobbly gait. He smiles, saying, "Wakey wakey Mr. Bellingham! Looks like those no-see-ums got themselves one serious appetite this morning. God knows they beat the hell out of needing an alarm clock!"

Dangerous and I had only truly bonded with Daryl the past few days, yet he has been a major influence in our social activities during our week of residence here at TT.

.

The no-see-ums continued to gnaw. Daryl continued to badger.

"Last I saw of your carcass; the bell had rung and you were down for the count. Thought the boys were gonna have to dig a burial pit over on Las Gatos to throw your sorry ass in. I did have one weak moment though and rolled you over to sleep sunny-side up so you wouldn't pull a Hendrix on us. I need all the decent crib partners around here I can get."

"Looks like a good thing you chose your resting place where you did as I saw your partner swinging the door closed with that nasty little Dutch tart right on his tail." He grinned and inhaled, then pointed to our room. "Noise coming out of there last night sounded like a jungle full of monkeys fighting over a banana, if you catch my drift." I didn't but nodded anyway.

Daryl keeps an amused eye on my equilibrium-challenged battle with the no-see-ums, the other on his first-of-the-morning rum and Coke firmly in his grasp. Tall glass only.

It is just after 7:30 and he is well under way into his usual sunrise-greeting game of solitaire. He will continue this ritual; drinking, smoking, and beating himself game after game. He only gets up to pee, return to his room for a fresh pack of Winston's, or trek into Centro to replenish dwindling liquor supplies.

This is how Daryl passes his winters until the seasonal salmon runs commence. Then he pulls nets, sometimes in 18-hour shifts, humping it, until the abundant channels of Kings and Chinooks fade into a trickle. He says he pulls down enough coin to spend his winters here in paradise.

"Yank your feet out of the sand, Bellingham and you just might have a little blood left in those pistons of yours come breakfast time."

Even as I struggle to play post-revelry 'Piggies Pay', Mother Earth keeps spinning on its axis at an uncomfortable rate for me to come to grips with. Aside from this particular moment, life on the road has been incredible.

Just as I was preparing for a comeback of miraculous magnitude--to rise up out of this sand and greet another beautiful day in paradise--the smell of Señora Adi whipping up Daryl's daily dose of *huevos* in the bungalow kitchen, sends me back to the Tilt-A-Whirl for one more technicolor shout.

As I drop back down into the sand, the cribbage master released another billowing cloud of Winston-infused carcinogens and laughed heartily behind his wall of fog, urging me on to repent for my sins.

Bottom line, I am still alive. Back in my room after a night spent passed out on the sand, three sheets to the wind, under whirling stars, I intend to sequester myself here in good old Number Four— door closed, light off, answering to no one until Monday comes to town.

As mid-day arrived, Dangerous joined Ted and Doris and headed off to Las Brusas for some lip-blistering Camerones Diabla. With a stomach incapable of coping with such a potentially volcanic endeavor, I opted to pass.

Around 4 p.m. I decided to creep on out and give my nutrient-deprived body some sustenance. Having lived for nearly two months solely on traditional Mexican food I had the oddest desire to indulge in the guilty pleasure of eating American style at a gringo hangout, Harry's Hamburguesas.

I entered to what could only be an Mezcal delirium-induced hallucination. There before my bloodshot eyes sat four absolutely gorgeous female type individuals and two macho looking dudes, quite animated while intent on holding the ladies' attention.

I placed my order and as I waited, a tall red head, Mo, walked past, smiled and initiated conversation, asking where I was from. When I told her I was from Washington, all four girls started smiling and gestured for me to come join them. Imagine my surprise; they too were from back home; college students from University of Puget Sound who were attending school in, of all places, Morelia. Kaspar, oh Kaspar, you certainly were one magical mofo!!

The macho dudes were, of all things, Surf Nazis, from Galveston, Tex-ass. I thought back to our friend Señor Cognac and wondered if, perhaps, he had a surfer for a son.

The mustachioed-wiry dude doing all the talking introduced himself as Luscious Lew. Lew sported two snazzy earrings in each ear and a SURF OR DIE tattoo running the length of his right forearm.

I joined their table just as he was bragging he was a undercover US government agent who killed two guys in Puerto Escondido he caught trying to steal his Yamaha motorcycle.

My bullshit detector pegged deep into the red zone as I did my best to be a good listener. He spewed forth a non-stop stream of self-serving verbal caca. He had been riding high with their undivided attention until I arrived. Now the girls seemed to have lost interest in his cocky banter.

As he babbled on, the beautiful blonde, Marty, and I struck up a conversation regarding our Seattle Supersonics, currently the greatest team in the whole NBA universe.

As we discussed the merits of Jack Sikma's patented turnaround jump shot, The Luscious one finished explaining how he disposed of the bodies, "mere shark bait..." He gobbled up his fries, grabbed his silent but equally as cool partner and invited the girls to meet him at the hotel--9 a.m. sharp, then split.

As soon as they were out of sight, all four girls thanked me profusely for saving them from Lew's ramblings. Things just kept getting better for yours truly.

Marty was headed back to her room to crash, but before she left, I took the liberty to ask them if they would like to join us instead at Majahua for our last wave whompin' expedition. They enthusiastically accepted.

Mo said that the Surf Nazis had invited them to Ixtapa to watch Luscious Lew surf and to take pictures of him shooting the curl. He even told them he would cut their names in the waves. I was glad a simple day on the beach with a couple of casual well-tanned guys from home sounded more appealing.

Our embarrassed waitress explained that they had run out of buns and my hamburger was still about ten minutes away from being done. *No problemo*, tonight, my friend.

The three remaining students had not finished their meals and I asked them to stay, promising I would be back in two minutes. I needed witnesses to verify that this was not post-Mezcal hallucinations I was experiencing.

I played a hunch, and hustled over to the Cheeser's room. Sure enough, there was Dangerous and the Cheeser, hunkered down over a tray, busting down bud into a rollable commodity. They immediately picked up on my excited body language.

Both smirked but it was Cheeser that got in the first dig, "Whoa, we both thought you were dead, eh?"

"Girls--not just girls, *Beautiful Girls*!!!" They tried to play it low key but I could tell I had their attention. I gestured for them to follow me. They may have rolled their eyes but they both got in line and followed me down to Harry's.

Instead of taking them inside, we casually sauntered past. Dangerous glanced at Cheeser, Cheeser at me. By the look on their faces, it was apparent I had just hit a home run.

We reversed course and walked into Harry's where I introduced them to the remaining three ladies-- Mo, Lee, and Jill--all stunners. While small talk commenced, I went to work on my burger and fries, the first food I had partaken in since last night's plate full of Bessie.

Things were looking up. Positive energy abounded. As Dave spun tales about Majahua I whipped Mo in a quick game of backgammon, ending my long streak of crummy bones.

Marty's roommate Jill said goodbye but Mo, Lee and myself went cruising in search of cultural stimulus. We found an off-key baritone singing over the top of his Mariachi band at Valentino's, but Dave and Cheesehead were nowhere to be found. I suspected the whorehouse, but Dave didn't have enough money to get him in trouble so it was easy to assume they were back at Cheeser's room, bent over the rolling tray, busy getting sticky fingers and twisted minds.

I headed back to La Ropa, full of energy, revitalized by the irony of our time spent in the company of such a gorgeous and friendly first-class female crew in, of all places, a freaking hamburger shop.

In the morning, we would make another trek to Majahua for one last set of waves. Perhaps I should get in touch with secret agent Luscious Lew; see if he would walk the beaches to keep Smiler at bay.

On second thought, let him practice his cursive on the waves of Ixtapa while we entertain the ladies.

30: Marty

As we wing our way towards the finish line of this saga, a romantic interlude has found its way along our path. Welcome to the Harlequin Romance segment of my Mexican Madness.

Monday morning, during breakfast with the ladies, the subtle gesture of sharing a generous portion of my orange marmalade with Marty Lynn Riley set grand wheels into motion. They continued to roll smoothly as I let her know that this gesture did not mean we were now going steady. She laughed at that one.

The true sign things were going well came when she spied the six-pack of Heinekens on the shelf of the local groceria we had stopped at to pick up sunscreen and commented, "Hey look, Heinekens--next best thing to sex!" Who was I to argue? I took the time to convince the clerk to stash that last sixer in the cooler until our return from Majahua. No problemo.

From breakfast, we were off on our final calf burner to Majahua, Dangerous, Marty, Lee and our friend the Cheeser in the lead, Mo (the group's one true Spanish speaking wise cracker) and myself closely behind.

We paused to catch our breath at the summit, and watch our new friends do the inevitable oohing and aahing at their first glimpse of Majahua. We intentionally neglected to omit the saga of Smiler and the wrist rocket hailstorm, still Dangerous, Cheeser, and I each cast a cautious eye towards the jungle fringe the entire time, prepared to make a hasty retreat at the first sign of ballistic attack. Fortunately for us, Smiler had business elsewhere.

Everyone had an A-plus afternoon, throwing the Frisbee, body whompin,' swimming, and broiling in the sun. They all agreed Majahua was THE highlight of their brief midwinter's break.

During the afternoon, the chemistry between Marty and I kept on bubbling, helped along by a wealth of commonalities in our musical taste. While the Frisbee flew, we had deep conversations about musical artists we couldn't get enough of.

The Marshall Tucker Band, Jimmy Buffet, Jerry Jeff Walker, Pure Prairie League, and Elvin Bishop--she knew and dug them all. But when she lauded Barefoot Jerry, I knew this girl was special.

The ladies had an evening bus to catch, as school reconvened that Tuesday, so we made an early exit from sun and fun, in order to consume a farewell Eskimo, a very apropos 'one for the road'.

While our crew stopped at the Eskimo stand, Marty and I slipped off to grab our Heinekens.

Imagine our disappointment to find the gate to the *groceria* closed hours earlier than usual. An explanation hastily scrawled upon a brown grocery bag and left tacked to the door told the story: ILLNESS IN FAMILY, OPEN AGAIN TOMORROW. Where do we go from here?

Spontaneity, according to Marty, is her most prominent trait. I would be quick to add beautiful, intelligent, and humorous to that mix but right now let us focus on spontaneity. Slightly crestfallen, we headed back to her hotel for a melancholy farewell.

Once there, she made a decision I highly approved of--to stay for another night, be my guest for dinner, and then help consume the Heinekens the next day. She had no problem with catching the Tuesday evening bus back to Morelia, as her classes did not begin until mid-Wednesday.

Dangerous and I had not yet made plans for tomorrow, or for tonight, for that matter, so it was on! At that moment, neither Marty nor myself had the slightest inclination where this spontaneity was about to take us.

The plan was to rendezvous at Centro around 6:30, then have dinner at the Kon Tiki.

The Kon Tiki, had a reputation for being THE prime location to enjoy Zihuatanejo Bay's picture-perfect sunset. With a full load of Western Union pesos at hand I couldn't have scripted a better scenario.

Dangerous warned me not to be get too loose with our cash. I assured him things were under control.

We watched the local hoopsters and, for the first time, discussed plans for the trip home. With next week's rent due tomorrow, our newly-reorganized budget could not afford more than two days in Z-Wat. Our grand time had come to a close. We both agreed Western Union, Volume Two, was out of the question and we dare not return stateside with empty pockets.

As we spoke, Marty came around the corner, absolutely stunning in a long, flowered, silk dress that caught the eye of every male she passed. Her light scent of perfume made my knees wobble. She was struggling with a heavy suitcase. Could she have checked out of her hotel? Does this mean that she needs a place to stay??? Could this mean that--Wow!!!!!

Dangerous nudged me in the ribs. "Looks like we got ourselves a new roomy, mate. Don't just stand there, dummy, take the lady's bag."

32: Morelia

It's a glorious morning here in Morelia, capital of Michoacán, Marty and Moe's home court. It's a very modern up-tempo city in Mexico's interior with lots of hills and little pollution. Dangerous calls it the city of cathedrals and TV antennas.

Throughout our Mexican adventure, we have experienced an incredible variety of geographical contrasts and Morelia is no exception.

Short pants, T-shirts and sandals still work, but the evening's chilly breeze is a radical departure from muggy Z-Wat, therefore a sweatshirt or serape are mandatory.

We arrived yesterday at 6 a.m. after another all-night bus marathon and found an inexpensive room in the heart of the city. Dangerous launched into a firm diatribe about how crucial it was to practice frugality our two days in town. No more green beers or extravagant meals. Sometimes, he pointed out, intoxication by love proves more precarious than getting intoxicated by Dirty Mothers. Time to revert once more to living strictly within our means.

Our game plan/hasty exit from Z-Wat came about so swiftly we didn't bid a proper farewell to Cheeser, who had joined Daryl and Richard to do extensive early evening research at the whorehouse, but we did have a farewell lobster dinner, one last dose of financial frivolity, with Ted and Doris, before hopping aboard the Morelia Express with Miss Marty.

Quite early into this amorous endeavor I've found myself swept up in, I made a vow not to blather on about Marty this and Marty that, so I'll spare you, beloved reader, from the mushy stuff. But I must say, things were verrrry nice—right up there with the best this lad has ever experienced.

Mo came by and the M&M girls gave us the red-carpet treatment, payback for our killer day at Majahua. Part of their plan was to pick up the tab for a room for the boys at the San Jose, a plush hotel atop the hill overlooking the city. Go ahead, twist my arm.

After time spent in the Toussaint Toilet, Scorpion Heights, and every other place we have slept, the San Jose was the Taj Mahal.

Heavy wood furniture and comfortable beds with two pillows each provided bodacious lounging accessibility. Large colorful exotic Oaxacan rugs cover the shiny wooden floors and two brass lamps hanging down from the ceiling provide illumination the likes we have not experienced for quite some time. There is even a television, which we ignore, and a fireplace, complete with bundles of firewood and a can of kerosene-for quick ignition.

We haven't upgraded from solar-heated water but damn, we've got a tub as well as a shower! How do such road-weary gringo dogs rate such luxury?

I still feel slightly bummed about leaving Z-Wat two days earlier than planned, yet when I look out our large picture window, a pastoral potpourri of lush multi-colored flowers overrunning the garden helps to ease my slight bout with melancholy.

We are both fired up by the fact destiny landed us here in Morelia just in time to see what is bound to be another surefire highlight of our journey--a bullfight! Today of all days! Dave is pumped about this opportunity. Ole! This will adequately compensate for getting short changed by the cancellation of boxing matches in Z-Wat.

"Would the bulls be killed?" I asked.

"Most likely."

From all I've read, bullfights can be a rather harsh spectacle for those not prone to blood and gore.

"Look at it this way: A good, scary roller coaster often brings out the sissy in us all, yet when you're sitting beside a member of the female gender, you're forced to be cool--you can't piss your pants, throw up or pass out."

Reasonable logic. I nodded, he continued.

"Well, we'll take Mo and Marty along and if things get a bit *Clockwork Orangey* in the middle of the bull ring, we will let them do all the screaming. You and I can do the roller coaster thing, if you catch my drift."

.

Done with school by noon, Marty and Mo took us for a cultural expedition to the Morelia Zoo. The four of us hopped onto a one-peso northbound bus for the short ride away from downtown. Somewhere along the line, some scurrilous rascal seized the opportunity to rip off Marty's wallet, which included her passport and other invaluable articles. Momentarily freaked, she headed back to her room to regroup, and said she'd catch up.

Mo was the one who realized we had taken the wrong bus which left us at the opposite end of town. "Marty sometimes has a bit of trouble when it comes to navigating. I guess this keeps her streak alive." With no other bus in sight, time to use our huaraches to get to our destination.

Tromping along on Morelia's steep and sometimes challenging hillsides, we inquired with local passersby as to the location of the *Plaza del Toros* and, as usual, received a handful of contradictory directions.

For the next forty minutes, we walked three to maybe five miles in circles. Finally, we arrived at the zoo. It was closed--Mexican holiday. Our marathon hike was salvaged by the fact that the bus that could take us back to our hotel, materialized. We each paid our peso and got back on.

Dave and I crashed until three. The ladies arrived twenty minutes late, but compensated by bringing Dirty Mother Mix (requested by guess who?), tape player, and a poorly rolled but greatly appreciated joint, compliments of Marty.

I began to get the impression that Dangerous was growing fond of Miss Mo, as I noticed the Dirty Mother he concocted for her was far less lethal than the blockbuster dose of skinny-dipping-induced libations he had specially prepared for Cheeser.

We indulged in one, and postponed any further partying in lieu of the big event that was about to happen in the heart of Morelia; an honest to goodness bullfight.

We scurried down to the *Plaza del Toros* where a substantial-sized crowd was already milling about outside of the stadium. Admission was five pesos per person and our seats were first rate--ten rows up, dead center.

Today's program began with folk ballet, full of children in colorful costumes whirling about to pre-programmed music which went on well over a half hour, followed by twenty minutes of gunny sack races in which every child in Morelia seemed to participate. This seemed an unusual prelude to a traditional event, I mean, it's almost five o'clock and not a matador, let alone a bull, has made an appearance.

, Several groups of young people, dressed up in bullfighter costumes, danced around wildly as they sparred with others dressed as bulls as if they were -- bullfighting?

It was well after six. Two hours we had been sitting there in the grandstands, before we finally realized what was going on. Dave excused himself to visit the baños and came back with a poster he had peeled off a concrete pillar.

Today's much anticipated event being held at the *Plaza del Toros* was a Bullfight of the Niños. What a bunch of knuckle heads! Embarrassed but able to laugh at ourselves, we headed towards the exits. The locals sitting around us realized our folly and offered wide smiles and good-hearted ribbing as we departed. Time to get back to our room before all the ice melts.

We made short work of the remaining libations, then headed to the local cinema, currently showing the Spanish subtitled version of "Halloween." Funny how this movie is much more tolerable with a beautiful lady by your side, burying her head against your shoulder every time Michael Myers started whittling away on his teenage prey.

After all the victims had been hacked to smithereens, we went back to the San Jose where we put the kerosene to work to fire up a nice crackling blaze to end an amazing day.

The ladies laughed as we reminisced about Luscious Lew, Surf Nazi Extraordinaire, when a devilish brainstorm, let's call it 'Son of Vinnie Hercules,' came to fruition.

You may remember Vinnie-our imaginary friend: Defender of the poor, the weak and the common man, back in Barra. He was *the* man who sent Senior Cognac packing. Once again, we took to paper and pen for one more attempt at classic letter writing.

Mo excavated Luscious' address--a beer-soaked scrap of paper found at the bottom of her day pack. Dave and I went to work writing on a piece of stationary with an official looking letterhead Marty had snitched during a visit to the regional capital building in Mexico City a month ago. And the boys wrote on…

Dear Señor Lewis Bagwell:

Your alleged involvement in the deaths of Manuel Hernandez III and Julio Mendoza this past February in Puerto Escondido shall require you to appear in person before a court appointed board of inquest in Mexico City on April 21st, 1980.

Papers are being processed for your extradition as this letter is being composed, and shall be turned over to U S Federal agents should you not appear at the Mexico City Hall of Justice on or before April 21st, 1980.

Preliminary testimony by the prosecution shall begin at 1 pm of the afore-mentioned date. We feel that it would be in your best interest to begin preparing your defense statement at this time.

We will do our best to see that you have a fair and unprejudiced hearing.

Judge Manuel Hernandez II
Mexico City Central Hall of Justice

All those years spent stumbling around the Western Washington University journalism department have paid off! Mo argued it would look more professional if it was typed before sent, and we agreed. Marty still had two other blank pages of this same stationary, so Mo volunteered and promised to send it off the following day. Midnight was almost here. This being a school night, we saw them off, all participants sad this evening had come to an end.

Funds were dwindling, timing was crucial. This party's just about over. With great remorse, we decided to move on to Guadalajara. Tomorrow afternoon we must break the news to our friends. Any sense of melancholy was eased by the fact that in less than two months, school would end and they would be returning home to Tacoma.

If this wave of passion between me and Marty is meant to be, so be it. If the vibes stop here, I cannot imagine a grander conclusion to a journey which began with flies buzzing on a toilet seat back in that crusty little border town.

We had so much fun, we somehow spaced out on our three o'clock departure time. Our bus headed off to Guadalajara, leaving us behind. It took Mo's three years of upper-level Spanish to finally convince the stone-faced ticket master to exchange our now worthless boletos for a pair for tonight's 6 p.m. run.

At around 5 p.m. spontaneity played its last card. Dave and I made the decision to stay *just one more day*. This made everyone happy, except for the surly ticket master. With jaws grinding and eyes bulging ever so slightly, he executed this final exchange. We were on for the Friday afternoon *Tres Estrellas, primera classe*, to Guadalajara.

We renewed our room at the San Jose, the girls once again adamant about picking up the tab, so we broke out the kerosene and fired up the tape player for one last fandango. Ah, serendipity! Morelia was wonderful. We were in the best of company.

Outside a full moon provided all the light we needed. The thin burning alder crackled and snapped as Jimmy Buffett filled the room: "Wonder why you ever go home, yeah, you wonder why you ever go home…"

33: LAST LAP

Friday morning. Here we are, whirling down the highway once more; back towards Guadalajara with nearly a thousand miles of road before us, all the while wearing weary well-earned smiles on our well-tanned faces.

Many moons ago, way back when we first began heading south down icy I-5, Dangerous had gone into detail regarding his philosophy of the road; the Pain and Pleasure principal--that for all the good things which happen during a journey, an equal number of hardships, pain or adversity very well may come our way as well: A karmic balancing measure of sorts. For most of this trip, the scales have tipped heavily in pleasure's favor. Perhaps it's best to keep a wary eye on the miles ahead.

A sentimental goodbye breakfast with the ladies took place at a small Morelian coffee shop. There we caffeinated our systems with some of Mexico's finest-tasting beans while making one last glum assessment of our remaining finances.

After the cost of tickets for the train back to Nogales gets added in, we have a balance of only 600 pesos to get us to the border. Creative meal planning shall once again be necessary until we cross back over into Nogales, USA. No remorse whatsoever. This has been a fantastic week.

High noon--time to say our final farewell to the M&M girls from the Great Northwest. They have become special friends as well as fabulous hostesses.

Thursday at the San Jose had been Marty's treat, but our partying had taken its inevitable toll on her. She was stressed out and hung over, with too much to do and too little time to get it all done. A pile of neglected homework and a crucial Spanish test were foremost on her mind as we did the lovebird thing, hugging and smooching while waiting for our ride to arrive.

Boarding time; Dangerous and Mo pried us apart. Only thirty-two days of school remain, making our sad farewells much easier to accept.

Guadalajara bound *Tres Estrellas*, pulled out at three in the afternoon. Our friends held their noses as they waved adios, left behind in a familiar cloud of bluish gray monoxide as we pulled away from the depot. Goodbye Morelia, good bye beautiful friends.

Guadalajara. The train station. One more time. Back into the quagmire of pollution and squalor where, an eternity ago, I received my introduction to Mexican culture.

I remember marveling at the sight of watching Kid's face change from cheery pink to chalk white, there in the marketplace, as we passed the row boasting a dozen grinning pig heads impaled on sticks, dotted with flies and decaying in the sun.

Sometime during the next thirty-six hours of rail riding I will break out the paper, pencil, and a map of Mexico and begin the task of calculating the number of miles we have traveled by bus, plane, huarache, train, Mafia staff car, and taxicab. I'm certain the grand total will be quite staggering, even to the least impressionable of our circle of friends.

The leg from Morelia to Guadalajara was child's play, barely exceeding six-plus hours.

We expected the inevitable at the station, and the reader board confirmed our suspicions. Only one train per day follows the tracks northbound, Guadalajara to Nogales, and it leaves at 9 a.m., gate B.

We weighed other scheduled departures, yet none fit our needs. Just when we had gotten used to comfy beds and two pillows apiece, tonight we would return to down bags on cold concrete floor. Oh well, been there, done that.

We did have an ace in the hole to help make this evening pass by. Dave had a friend of a friend living here in Guadalajara, Mañuel, who we were to call once we arrived back in the city. Mañuel was the head of the Guadalajara Institute of Yoga, as well as a graduate of the University of Guadalajara. His family was of upper-class status, making him one of the fortunate young individuals capable of affording and receiving a level of education higher than the majority of his fellow countrymen.

Last fall, Mañuel and Dangerous had exchanged letters to discuss the possibility of a rendezvous in late February or early March and, by golly, here we were. Our timing could not have been better. As Dave began digging into his backpack to find Manuel's phone number, a cold, yet firm hand took hold of my bicep.

"Excuse me--are you the writers--from the land of the waters?"

A short misshapen Mexican woman, as wrinkled as she was ancient, suddenly was there beside us.

Her initial appearance was truly amazing.

Dressed in clothes most often associated with a common bag lady, she greeted us with a genuinely warm smile, as if we were old friends.

Her dress was a tattered gray over-sized hand-me-down with a stringy hem, well-worn from dragging on the floor. Florescent orange leg warmers were pulled up to her knees and a severely snagged green sweater, reeking of a week's worth of sweat suggested personal hygiene was low on her priority list.

She wore black wool gloves with the fingers cut off at the knuckles. A dark rim of grime lay beneath those fingernails and several strings of gaudy and mismatched beads dangled from her neck.

It appeared, as well, that several years have gone by without proper dental care. Most unusual of all, there below her dress, she was sporting high-top U.S. Keds, in excellent condition, although both shoe laces had been broken and retied.

Her question caught me totally off guard.

Yes, both Dangerous and I aspire to be writers, yet neither of us had said or done anything to let this ambition be known.

She picked up on my surprised expression, looked from one traveler to the other through blue eyes that shone brilliantly, then continued, "You know... Kosloski and O'Brien."

As she spoke, she waved her hand in front of her face, as if batting at flies or something else bothering her which neither of us could detect. Sorry, Kosloski and O' Brien we were not.

Still more than a bit exhausted following the trek from Morelia to Guadalajara, my ability to respond was too slow for her liking. She continued, "Does not matter, your train leaves at nine in the morning. This will be your gate, right here." She pointed at Gate B.

I glanced back up at the board to confirm. Sure enough, right on the money. Color me distracted, on a different wavelength, or just plain oblivious to her intent, something interesting was going on here, yet the punch line continued to elude me.

"Do you work here?" I asked.

She spat on the floor and grabbed a ragged broom which had been leaning against the wall.

"You could say I do. I clean the station. And help *travelers*-- those who seem to be seeking certain *pathways* in particular." She began moving the broom in circles on a floor that did not need sweeping. Very strange.

"How did you know that we were from the Northwest?"

She waved her hands in front of her face again, then stopped, probing intently into the depth of my eyes. "I see... tall snow-covered mountains... Sasquatch... Salmon leaping and diving through swift glacial waters..."

Impressive, but by what process was she obtaining this information? This went beyond the power of presumption. I asked her just that.

"Don't mind me; I'm nothing but an old Mexican pig." She continued to wave her hand before her, then spat once again onto the floor as she leaned the broom back up against the wall.

Three niños began to point at her and laugh rudely. She shooed them away with a wave of her hand and an angry growl. They ran off, laughing mischievously and continued to tease her from a distance until their parents stepped in, full of stern looks and an even sterner lecture.

While Dave excused himself to go look for a pay phone from which to call Mañuel, our new friend hung close by, inspecting the exterior of my backpack, as if she truly had nothing better to do.

I began hoping she would just wander off to sleep on a bench or to find others to pester. Unfortunately, that was far from her intention. She came closer, near enough for me to notice two hairy moles growing on her cheek. I was certain they were not there just ten minutes earlier.

"Do you consider yourselves to be men of knowledge?"

I assumed she was referring to our college education. "On a certain level that is true. My friend has graduated from college and I hope to have my degree in a year or so."

She seemed to be scanning me, her eyes gazing deeply into mine once again, same as when she pulled Sasquatch out of midair.

"When a man starts to learn, he is almost never clear about his true objectives. I see you have made great progress on your journey, yet there are many steps involved finding your true destination. Only you can unlock the freedom needed to follow that path."

I nodded, only half-listening to her prattle and sighed. Where the hell was Dave to bail me out of this one? "I do my best to try, but recently, I've been reading a book that tells me learning is a process of unending quest."

"Don Juan speaks the truth. You have begun to explore valuable avenues of understanding; ones you may choose to embrace. Just remember to follow that path with heart, as well as passion, as a path is only a path; if you feel you should not follow it, you must not stay with it under any conditions."

This all seemed so familiar, and wait--did she not literally just quote Don Juan? I asked where she acquired her wisdom and her eyes quickly averted mine. "I find some here, I listen there. Other times it comes from the sky--that is all, really." Once again, she started swatting at those invisible insects. "Do you seek power?"

The more she spoke, the more confused I found myself becoming. "What particular kind of power should I be seeking?"

Just then an extremely upset teenage girl interrupted. She spoke in English, bearing a strong French accent. "Excuse me, I do not mean to be a bother but do either of you speak English?" We both nodded.

"I am confused about which gate my train will be leaving from. Could you please assist me in finding my way?"

Before I could offer a suggestion, our bag lady stepped in and took over.

Mind-boggling as it may sound, she conversed with the young girl in fluent French. Dave had just returned and we both watched as they carried on a long, animated conversation. Then the girl was gone with a wave and a smile. Our host was a most talented individual.

It was now 8:15. Over twelve hours to go. Dave excused himself once more to attempt reaching Mañuel, as his last effort resulted in unanswered rings; no one home.

Our friend took an immediate interest in Dave's efforts to hook up. I explained the situation, but when I told her Mañuel was a college graduate, her face revealed disapproval. She squinted her eyes, then scowled ever so suspiciously. "Perhaps it is best this connection is not made. You need to spend your time here tonight." I asked for an explanation.

"Technology in Mexico does not always represent what is best for mankind. What appears to be progress inevitably results in greed alongside evil.

If progress continues to alter the Mexican way of existence, it shall only result in bringing my country to its knees." She started sweeping the spotless floor again, this time working off agitation, moving about the room, closer to the pay phones Dave was using.

"These people are trying to change the world in which we have happily existed for hundreds of years, and in many negative ways." I asked her for examples.

"Television is an evil. It exposes our niños and niñas to avarice and affluence; the type of life they will never have a chance to experience. The corrupt politicians use it to spin their web of deceit and false truths in order to control." She snapped her crooked fingers. "Just like that!"

I flashed back to those primitive huts we had passed on the road to Palenque, constructed of little more than Coke signs, mud and crooked sticks. She stood firmly against modern culture, ever finding opportunities to upgrade or refine their simple manner of existence.

I tried to visualize those impoverished village children, longing one day to be Charlie's Angels or Magnum PI instead of their inevitable destiny, of becoming anything greater than village housewives, baby makers, farmers, or craftsmen.

"Greed continues to take root and destroy our traditions. Already the family has begun to lose its importance. Our values are changing quickly and may soon be lost forever, for when a young person goes away to school they never come home." She sighed, then regrouped. As quickly as it had come her heavy look was gone.

"But don't mind me; I'm just an old Mexican pig." She smiled, set her broom down once again and took a seat on a bench next to a large overstuffed plastic bag, which, I assumed, were her belongings. This was a most unusual person, for sure.

I continued asking her questions about herself--did she have a family? Where did she live and how did she learn to master a variety of languages? She artfully dodged each question until I resigned myself to the fact that answers would not be forthcoming.

Dave returned with a pissed off look on his face. "I tried about five times but I could not get through. The lines were jammed and making all kinds of garbled noises. Didn't even get my five pesos back!" On the bench across from me, our omniscient bag lady smiled at me. Goosebumps rose from elbow to wrist along both arms.

From that point on, our affable conversation came to an end. She set up camp there on the bench across the way continuing to keep an eye on us, just in case we made another attempt to contact Mañuel.

I was dog-tired, mind focused on the long, back-busting, ass-throbbing thirty-six hours ahead. A numbness encased my cerebral cortex. Two months and however many thousands of miles of travel later, the gas was just about on empty in my tank. Add in a case of Marty withdrawal and you have the total picture.

We burned time playing backgammon, and even once asked a curious passerby to take a picture of us, there on the floor with our bones and our backpacks.

As time went on, our one-person welcoming party grew distant. Standoffish as she had become, she remained close by, spitting and coughing, her presence unwilling to be forgotten; all the while continuing to bat away at whatever invisible flies or insects she was at war with.

Through the night, curious niños drew close, watching the gringos play a game they were unfamiliar with. Each time they came too close for her liking, she would chase them off, with sharp, curt Spanish and waving arms. Each time, they would squeal and tease her as they scurried back to the safety of their parents. Once she had sent them packing, she would wrap herself back up in her shawl and pretend to sleep.

Dave attempted to call Mañuel several more times, yet the results were the same. Scrambled signal. He even went the length of the bus station to use a different phone to see if he could connect. No luck. Each time he returned, a pair of suspicious eyes shadowed him back to his seat. Once assured we were still there, she would feign sleep again. I assumed her intent was born of loneliness, that she enjoyed having two big guys for company to keep her from harm's way throughout the night.

Around eleven Dave wandered off to find a sleeping spot beneath the reader board to get some well-deserved rest before sunrise.

I remained on the bench, people watching, near the old lady, until I was sure she was asleep, and then grabbed the space to Dave's right. He was still awake when I got there.

"Well…"

"Well, what?"

"Whaddya think?"

"What do I think of *what*?"

"Meeting your first bruja."

A witch. Nah, just one more opportunity for my friend to mess with my mind.

"Think about it, Einstein--How many bag ladies do you know who can speak English one minute, as if they were born in Wisconsin, then flip the switch to start solving problems in fluent French?"

None came to mind.

"Do you think it was a coincidence she knew we were writers--or that we came from the Northwest? You don't have to be Sherlock Holmes to suss out what we're dealing with here."

Dave had certainly laid out food worthy for thought, but the best was yet to come. It appears my travel partner and I had some radical discrepancies when it came to her physical appearance.

Dave insisted she had gray frizzy hair. My bag lady's hair was jet black, filthy and shoulder-length. Dave says her dress was off-white and cotton, I say she wore a green stinky sweater made of silk. He says she wore brown knee-highs full of holes, I argued that they were florescent orange leg warmers. He didn't start laughing until I told him about the Keds. "No way--she was wearing sandals, no different than the ones you and I have on."

I urged him to go back over for another look but he declined. "She is going to appear however you choose to see her and, to me she will look just like whatever my vision of her happens to be as well. Chances are if you could find that French girl, she would tell you something completely different as well."

How could we come up with a significant way to prove who's right and who's out in left field?

Dave offered the most logical solution. "I guess we'll just have to wait until we get the pictures developed of us playing backgammon--that is half the reason I asked that guy to take our picture. I have always dreamed of having my picture taken with a witch."

The concept was mind-boggling, yet very possible. Why hadn't I seen it?

Her conversation was about as subtle as a flying mallet. Her talk about pathways, seeking power, men of knowledge, as well as her dislike for change were further indicators. Hadn't she even snuck Don Juan in there?

Some time, well after midnight, unable to go to sleep, I unzipped my bag and crawled out.

"Where are you going at this wee hour of the morning?" Dangerous inquired.

"I'm going back and ask her."

"Ask her what?"

"If she's really a witch." Sometimes I'll make an outlandish statement as such just to get a reaction, hoping the recipient will convince me my idea lacks credibility, but not tonight. I was going for it, baby.

"Have you thought of the negative ramifications?"

"Such as?"

What if she turns you into a toad?"

I thought for a moment and the answer was clear. "Then I'll expect you to pick me up, put me in your pack and get me safely back home."

"And just how do you expect me to pull that one off, with customs and all, and you--with no valid passport or tourist visa!"

Too late, I was off.

I returned to the benches where we had passed the evening. I was in luck, she was still there, sitting between the aisles in lotus position, rocking rhythmically as an incense burner she had set up on the ground beside her produced a weaving snake of odorless smoke. She seemed to be carrying on in a language quite different from the Spanish I had been exposed to.

I needed a good innocent opening line to jump start a conversation

"Ah, excuse me. I apologize for the interruption but I was wondering, did I leave my backgammon board around here somewhere? I can't seem to..."

"I thought you might be back." Still wrapped tightly in her tattered shawl, she motioned for me to join her.

"Look at you. You arrived in Mexico innocent, afraid, new to our ways and language. Now, miles later, you shall return home with a stronger and richer soul. You will be wiser for your journey ahead. You've spent your time embracing our warm oceans, hiking up and down many dusty roads, experiencing the chill of our mountain regions and the desert's often uncomfortable heat. Most of all you have respected our people, culture and values. I feel you truly understand what you and your friend have come to know The Manana Method. THAT alone is worth every mile you have traveled."

She turned her head and coughed the other way, spit on the floor, then put her weathered hand atop of mine. "Go now and join your friend in sleep. You have a long day or two ahead of you, amigo." She adjusted her shawl and dismissed me with a wave.

As I rose I glance one last time into her eyes. They gave me all I needed to know.

I returned, and crawled into my sleeping bag.

"Well, did ya get what you wanted?"

"She had one gray eye and one blue."

"That's it? No toad? Just as well, I didn't have any room in my pack to put you anyway."

34. Homeward

Loaded with enough incredible memories to make the miles pass by, our train ride from Guadalajara to Nogales clack-clacked along, as tediously as anticipated.

Sixty plus days ago, this journey began, way back at the Southern Arizona border. The thrill of the unknown had me charged up with energy, enthusiasm and a whopping dose of adrenaline. Now with thousands of miles behind us and hundreds of tales to tell I am sapped, shot, kaput. I am also damn close to broke.

There's only a handful of tales left that are worthy of sharing. Most of the time was spent replaying what had gone down the past two months, as we stood on the platform between cars watching the desert landscape pass by in a blur.

Occasionally, the conductor would come by and frown at us for not returning to our seats. This time, when they realized we weren't going back inside, they would merely shrug and move on. Damn gringos anyway. They always have a mind of their own.

I had to admit, not having The Kid along for the ride took away the element of *anything can happen* out of the grand scheme of things. We had come, we had partied. Now it was time to sleep, recharge, reflect, and enjoy the feeling of overwhelming accomplishment growing within me.

I had survived two months in a foreign country without a nervous breakdown, broken bone, or trauma of significance. Most important of all, I was going home with a new respect and adoration for a country other than my own. What a great feeling.

Cultural experiences aside, I had successfully learned how to count high enough to complete any transaction smoothly, learned the names of many foods, and could even carry on a wee bit of a conversation, no matter how primitive, with the locals along the way. Provided they spoke slowly.

I am going home determined to take a class or two in Spanish so my next visit will be more enjoyable. No more riding Dangerous Dave's coattails.

There is no doubt, if and when I take another journey, this time on my own, I will undoubtedly survive, be self-sufficient and more likely than not, even live to talk about it. A new door has swung open for me--one that will be revisited another time, perhaps, ever so hopefully, as soon as next winter.

The only Americans we spent quality time with on the train were Big Wes and his wife Honey, from Ironwood Michigan.

Big Wes and Dangerous carried on about their common passion for Harley Davidsons while Honey sat, listening patiently with the glow of a mother to be--eight months pregnant and ready to pop.

Three months earlier Honey had been playing bingo at the local Daughters of the American Revolution Bingo Parlor when Lady Luck came her way. Not only had she won the standard hundred-dollar prize, she was a Grand Prize Winner--accomplishing the rare feat of totally blacking out her card in the minimum number of calls possible.

Often, the grand prize would be a new Chevy pickup truck or a top of the line fully detailed snowmobile. That evening, the grand prize was an all-expenses paid trip for two, to Guadalajara. So why then was the lucky couple beside us taking the train back home?

Seems that on their third night in town they had befriended a young American couple, Morton and Denise Crabshaw, who were staying in the very same hotel, two floors above. That evening they ate dinner together and partied afterwards.

"We were having a good old time getting liquored up on mezcal in a small cantina the hotel people had recommended. Sometime around 1 a.m. we headed back to our room, considerably under the influence." Wes explained.

"They sure were nice. They helped me make it to my bed while Honey was busy fighting a late-night case of morning sickness in the community head.

When we woke up next morning our plane tickets, along with a large wad of Mexican money had mysteriously disappeared from our dresser. We checked at the desk to find that the Crabshaws had checked out quite hastily two hours earlier." Imagine that.

"Back home," Honey interjected, "Big Wes would've gone out to the airport with a baseball bat to wait for their asses and left them in a world of hurt, but in my condition (Wes pats her basketball-sized tummy) we decided to just live and learn and spend the rest of our meal money on the next train back home."

Big Wes pats her tummy again. "We've got to take care of the franchise. There are twin girls a' brewing down in momma's oven."

In the early evening, I borrowed Big Wes' atlas and commenced tallying up the many miles we had traveled. It was quite the challenge to convert kilometers to miles but when all was said and done, the total *from* Nogales heading south and back again *to* Nogales encompassed 5,323.2 total miles. Add another 1,770 miles from Bellingham to Nogales and you have a grand total of 7,093.2 miles. That's before we begin the drive back from the border to the Pacific Northwest. Toss that in and your grand total is 8,863.2. Round that puppy off to 9,000 miles and call it a day.

Early in the morning of the second day, we experienced an extended stop at a dot on the map called Benjamin Hill.
During our down-time we convinced Big Wes to step off the train with us and get Honey some nourishment from the local vendors on hand.

As Wes and I continued to vacillate over our many choices, Dangerous entered into a congenial conversation with one of our conductors who explained the long delay.

"The tracks split here, those rails head northwest to Sonora then on to Puerto Penesca while ours continue due north. We are going to be here about an hour while they take the last three cars off our train and link them to the Penesca bound engine."

Unfortunately, this handy bit of information did not get passed on to either Big Wes or me who were bartering vigorously with a señorita in regards to a plate stacked high with cheese-smothered enchiladas.

Just as he was exchanging pesos, the front half of the train lurched forward with a loud growl and a burst of stinky black diesel, and began pulling slowly ahead, before separating. Honey stood there in horror as her end of the train separated, which began moving due north, slowly away from us.

Dangerous and I momentarily bit on the separation and started to scurry back to our disappearing train car, but the conductor motioned for us to stay--this is only temporary. Our train car was moving ahead in order to add the other engine to the Northwest bound express.

Honey, stood at the back of the slow rolling train car, arms waving frantically as she screamed "Wesssssssly !!!!!"

Before we could clue him in on the process taking place, Big Wes, enchilada plate in one hand, burrito in the other, went sprinting down the treacherous rails, trying to catch up to his wailing wife. "Honnnney!!!!"

He had built up a considerable head of steam when the toe of his right boot met the edge of one of the protruding railroad ties. Big Wes went airborne.

If he had been willing to sacrifice either of the platefuls of food, he may have broken his fall. With his food a priority, Big Wes' forehead smacked down upon the center of one of the creosote ties with a god-awful thump.

At that moment, the front half of the train came to a halt. We quickly realized we had best remove Big Wes from the tracks, as ironically, he was lying exactly where the additional car was to be added.

We got our unsteady compadre to his feet and helped him weave a woozy path back down the tracks to where Honey stood shrieking and sobbing. His forehead sported a dandy knot the size of a tennis ball. Sticky black pitch mixed with a trickle of blood just above his left eyebrow. Miraculously the burrito and enchilada plate remained intact.

At first Big Wes did not know quite where he was or how he had got there but once Honey reached him and ran sobbing into his arms, everything came back into focus. It was a tender reunion as they sat there eating their goodies, watching as the two halves of the train successfully rejoined.

My last impressionable memory of the road was the Mexican *Reveille from Hell* performed shortly after sunrise on our last day.

Somewhere in the middle of the Sierra Madres, we made one of many brief stops.

While in the load/unload mode, a young boy no older than ten, hair slicked back and wearing his Sunday best, came aboard. His father stood alongside, wielding a well-worn, poorly tuned acoustic guitar with only five strings.

The boy smiled to anyone who would make eye contact, then made his way to the middle of our car where he stopped, and then began singing a Mexican ballad at the top of his lungs.

Did I say singing? This youngster's wretched warbling gave new meaning to the word slaughter. Not only was he out of key, he screeched like a coyote with his leg caught in a trap. What in heaven's name?

Ah but wait. There was a punch line to this devious joke.

It appeared the quickest way to rid ourselves of this racket was to throw a peso or two into a hat being passed down each aisle. The sooner the hat was filled, the sooner this rascal would move on to the next car. As short as we were on cash, it became imperative to put together enough pesos to rid ourselves of this off-key bandito

Once the hat had made the rounds, the boy smiled and they moved off into the next car where once again they began the same tortuous process, then again and again and again.

As we grew ever closer to Nogales and the good old *Estados Unidos*, Dave warned me to prepare myself for a potential dose of reverse culture shock. I asked him to elaborate to which he simply replied, "Just wait, you'll see."

Finding this response more than a little unsettling, I continued pursuing a broader definition. Finally, he relented with this insightful dissertation.

"You've just spent two months slowing your body and mind down; learning how to relax and to escape the fast-paced level in which we are forced to operate during everyday American life.

"You have managed to abandon your fast-food indulgences for cuisine of an entirely different nature. You have partaken in very little deep-fried entrees, let alone seen the golden arches, and, outside of Super Bowl Sunday, I cannot think of a single time you have plopped your glutes down to veg out in front of a television set for over sixty days. Let's see you keep that streak going once we get back to good old Bellingham!"

"Just think--you have not shifted a clutch, let alone driven an automobile for well over two months while averaging six miles per day to get where you needed to be. Let's hope that healthy habit will likely continue back on American soil."

"Most of all, once you step down off this train you will have little choice but to pick up the pace--to accelerate and readjust to the pace of life necessary. Put those siestas on hold. Step back into the fast lane."

"We were fortunate enough to be fed an enjoyable dose of music by our lady friends in Morelia, but outside of the appearance of Gruppo Shark, Beatles music in the Guadalajara market, a half-dozen off-key Mariachi bands, and four minutes of Dire Straits, you've been deprived of your favorite cultural delight--*Musica*."

"The leisure lifestyle--the very core of your existence these past two and a half decades--will once again be attainable. When that time comes, you will have to decide how much of your previous lifestyle is worth returning to, along with which aspects no longer appeal. Acclimatize and adjust wisely or you may find yourself quickly back in the very same rut you were mired in before we left."

"This sounds corny as hell but let this trip be the springboard for the rest of your life. Why not use the Mañana Method to your advantage?

You have become a part of it; Embrace everything you've done and accomplished. Bring *it* back--make it be a part of what you are and always shall be." He paused, then smiled as he added "What a load of shit, eh?"

I wish I had stashed a a profound witticism--a real Mohammed Ali uppercut--with which to end this journey; one guaranteed to grab you, inspire you, perhaps make you laugh and to have you walk away from this tale longing for more. Alas, amigos, both pockets and pen are empty.

I stepped down off the train in Nogales, Arizona torn between relief and melancholy. We had done it! Having been away for such an extended time my first concern was to call home, to make sure all was well and no surprises would be there to greet me around the bend. Out of cash that call would have to wait.

During my Western Union conversation with my brother's girlfriend, she assured me that my family was well; that no major catastrophes of any significance had taken place among our circle of friends. No rock stars or well-known personalities had left the earth, nor were any politicians assassinated. Neither had any natural disasters worth mentioning.

Across the street, a large Safeway beckoned. Time to step inside and get my first true jolt of culture shock. It was a doozy.

I walked through the self-opening doors into air-conditioned comfort only to be greeted by loud Muzak pouring from surround-sound systems. Brilliant neon lighting made my eyes ache. Slowly I shuffled down row after row of shrewdly-merchandised processed food products. I felt as if I had wandered into another world.

I stood before the frozen foods, transfixed by the multi-colored tantalizing packaging. It is downright amazing how damn good Swanson can make those frozen dinners appear: lasagna, thick as a brick and oozing with hot sticky cheese; roast beef and mashed potatoes slathered in a generous layer of succulent brown gravy; fried chicken stacked atop a generous bed of buttered corn-they were all there, stacked high, ready to be reheated in one's oven.

As intended, these subliminally delicious-looking images made my stomach start to growl. I looked about, hoping to find those little old ladies with plastic hairnets who hand out free samples on Saturdays. Sadly, this was Sunday.

An aisle away, a pillar of chunky-style soup cans rose taller than a downtown Seattle skyscraper. We located the soda section. No Yoli, dammit! After an absurd amount of deliberation, a can of Mountain Dew was chosen. Off to the checkout stand where our eyes fell upon the bookrack full of tabloids as we waited in line.

Current editions teased amazing headlines about strange transmissions from Russia coming through Ronald Reagan's dentures and that Elvis recently made love to a Sasquatch.

As I pondered these headlines, the checker asked us to hand over forty-five cents. In English. Second phase of culture shock was officially underway.

With our packs once again molded to our backs and the Dew opened and passed between us, it was time to consider our options.

We were fifteen miles from Linda's house. We could either a) hitch a ride; b) take a cab and spend every last cent we had left; c) walk the distance and roast in the hundred-degree sun, or, option d) find the local bus station and spend *almost* every last cent we had. We attempted the first.

I have never had a knack for the art of hitchhiking and it showed. Car after car treated us as lepers or prison escapees, zooming by without as much as a glance our way. Two discouraging hours later, we cashed in our pesos traveling by bus then finished the last two miles by cab.

Arriving at Linda's, we found ourselves two dollars and twenty-four cents in the red with our cab driver. No problem, Linda would loan us the meager coinage so Dangerous hurried up to her door. Problem: Linda was still at work. A note left inside the milk box apologized for the later than usual hours.

We were penniless; officially and unequivocally broke.

We explained our predicament to our driver, and, in doing so, revealed where we had been the last two months.

"Sounds like a great one. Wish I could have been with you." He stuck out his hand and we each shook it. "This one's on me."

As we walked away, he hollered, waving for us to come back. Damn, did he have a change of heart?

"Hey would you guys write down the name of that town, Barra whatever, for me? I got three weeks paid vacay coming up in the fall. Always looking for a new place to go and do nothing, ya know?"

Yeah, we knew.

Dangerous was privy to the location of Linda's stashed keys and we were inside in no time.

It was early afternoon yet a hasty decision needed to be made. Do we hang around until she returns or do we hit the road for a marathon sprint northward bound? Running strong on adrenaline, sugar and caffeine (thank you, Mountain Dew), we decided to get while the gettin's good. Back to Bellingham; *muy rapido*.

Dave spent twenty minutes jotting down a thoughtful thank you, before doing what I had dared not consider; casing out her refrigerator for what he termed "essential *propulsion* for the many miles ahead."

Starved banditos we plundered various leftovers in a manner which would have made Poncho Villa proud.

Dave's *propulsion* happened to be a bowl containing a dozen leftover meatballs the size of tennis balls. He stabbed one with a fork, examined it as if it were the first he had ever encountered, then stuffed the entire circumference into his mouth.

"Damn tasty!" He handed the fork over to me. I stabbed one heavily soaked in a coat of greasy meatball gravy and down the hatch it went. Damn tasty was right.

We considered the possibilities. Warm them up or eat them cold. Heating them up would require time. Patience. Screw that! Even at refrigerator temperature, all eight of the greasy gravy-covered burger balls were devoured with neither conscience nor remorse. It was good to be home.

Outside, my Datsun sat waiting, ready to roll. The doors were unlocked, the key slid easily into the ignition and, with one turn of my wrist, the motor turned over and started. Smooth and easy, just like an Eskimo on a hot Zihuatanejo afternoon.

The wheels rolled and we were back on the road.

With a full tank of gas, we drove on through the night in long, exhausting shifts, truck driver-approved twangy redneck music blaring on the AM dial.

We kept on moving, stopping only for gasoline (thanks to the gas card left beneath the driver's mat!) and an occasional potty break.

North of Eugene, the first band of dark gray clouds, our uninvited, yet anticipated welcoming committee, appeared and with it, reality fell upon us.

In Portland, the windshield wipers came on, first on intermittent, then high speed, for the remaining one hundred eighty miles. Without a word we turned to each other, smiled, and then gave each other a resounding high five as well as one of those fancy hippie handshakes. It had been one helluva run.

Andy Clark, Official Voyager

29. EPILOGUE

Thanksgiving 2016

"You've got to be effing kidding me!!"

My daughter, Molly, was more than a bit put out when informed that neither a Costco or Walmart existed within driving distance of the coastal village town of Melaque.

Everyone loves a good surprise, so, as the four Clarks gathered over our annual Turkey Day feast, my wife presented our children, Max, 28 and Molly, 24 with their early Christmas present.

Mary had just booked seven days in Melaque during the upcoming holiday season, Christmas included, for a family adventure.

After two decades of the same old routine—waking up, opening presents for ten minutes, then pecking at a variety of finger foods while watching either "It's a Wonderful Life" or "Christmas Story" until the holiday dinner hit the table, it was time to switch gears. While some folks enjoy a White Christmas, folks in Kirkland, Washington annually celebrate a Wet Christmas. Not this year. The idea was this: To bask in as much sun as they could handle, swim all day in the warm Pacific, chow down on fresh seafood at criminally modest prices, all while imbibing as many cheap margaritas as they cared to indulge in.

Thirty-six years have passed since Dangerous Dave and I lived our dream in Barra/Melaque, so when Mary came to me with her family vacation concept, it was a no brainer. Game on.

Flights were booked and a house was ours for $300 for seven days.

More likely than not our kids would have preferred Cancun, Puerto Vallarta or Mazatlán, more prominent Mexico destinations. Still, they had certainly heard enough stories over the years to be intrigued to step out of their comfort zones, be good sports, and go with the flow. The next half month, I found myself getting considerably jazzed for what lay ahead.

Memories came surging back. Dangerous and I have spent many hours rehashing that road from Nogales, back when we were truly road warriors, built to spill. Now we have become middle-aged mortals, although Dave begs to differ.

As we near the close of this tale, let us tie up loose ends; fill in the blanks, verify lessons learned as well as sum up the legacy those many miles still etched upon on my soul.

In the years that followed, I have ventured below the borderline five more times--four to Zihuatanejo, once to Barra. Wonderful and beneficial as each one was, they paled in comparison to the epic journey of '79

Dangerous passed on one truism which holds great merit for those returning to destinations they possess fond memories of: Don't waste energy trying to relive previous experiences. No Two Trips Shall Ever Be the Same.

I returned to Zihuatanejo in 1981, 1983, and again in 1987. I brought my family for one last hurrah during Christmas 2005. Sleepy little fishing village no more, Z-Wat was now home to over one hundred thousand people--ten times in size since we casually cruised its cobblestone Calles on foot, looking for a friendly street vendor to fend off late-night munchies.

Each time I made that journey my priority was to take along a newbie, someone unfamiliar with the nuances, trials, and tribulations which await. Each one of those experiences reinforced Dangerous' adage.

I paid another visit to Palenque, via Isla Mujeres, the following year, '81. It's still there and remains absolutely breathtaking and awe-inspiring, peyote or no peyote.

One truly magical moment occurred just north of Palenque, as we headed towards the closest airport in Villahermosa.

An hour outside of Palenque, our Suburban transporter began to overheat. Fortunately, we happened upon a remote village with a Pemex gas station, identifiable only by one rusted-out pump standing amidst foot-tall weeds. Our rig limped onto the premises, hoping to purchase a can of Stop Leak, a wad of bubble gum or whatever it would take in order to complete the final hundred miles or so to Villahermosa.

While J P, this visit's traveling companion, and the attendant contemplated the task at hand, I headed to the restroom to relieve myself of an afternoon's worth of Tecates. As I came out, I noticed two familiar short men, dressed completely in white, wearing rubber boots and sporting Beatle-style haircuts standing by the roadside. What a stroke of luck had come our way!

Our overheated engine had brought me face to face with the same bow and arrow salesmen Dangerous Dave and I had met in San Cristobal last February!

They were carrying several sets of bows and arrows, exactly the same as Dave had purchased before absent-mindedly leaving them on the bus in Palenque.

I did not squabble over the inflated price--they had gone up 200 pesos in less than one year. Today that was irrelevant. I quickly purchased a replacement set of this fine primitive hand-crafted weaponry for my friend. This time they stayed close by my side.

You should have seen the look on Dangerous' mug when he met us at the airport and I handed him the sheath of arrows. Seizing the opportunity to mess with him for a change, I told him I found them still stashed on the overhead rack of a bus at the Palenque bus station. Even though he quickly dismissed this fictitious line of whoopee, he was one happy amigo.

From Palenque, we returned to Z-Wat, where we spent a week and a half embracing the delightful sunshine on La Ropa at the good old Toussaint Toilets. Daryl and Richard were on hand to add their special flair to the affair. They did a great job of leading me into ten solid days of debauchery and misadventure. Some things never change.

I spent the winter of '82 stuck in Bellingham, making a trade out: cutting firewood for a woods-dwelling biologist friend in exchange for basic bone-head Spanish lessons. Even though winter would be chilly purgatory the result was worth it.

In exchange for cutting and stacking twenty cords of Douglas fir I absorbed a wealth of verbs, adjectives, and enough helpful phrases to get through almost any situation encountered.

Winter of '83 I took a young lady, Mary, who two years later ended up becoming my wife, on a journey in which she more than proved her mettle.

We flew to Puerto Vallarta and grabbed the first bus for Barra to spend New Year's Eve. Outside of the fact Scorpion Heights had been, renovated into a mish-mash of ugly apartments Barra remained very much the same.

After finding suitable quarters elsewhere, we learned that the outdoor theater was gone as well. What a shame. No more Hercules, British comedies, or shark movies for the locals come Saturday nights.

Hotel Guadalajara still served pancakes with sticky syrup and rock-hard butter and Poncho's *Camerones Diabla* was still the best Barra offered. Frank's pad was vacant; one of the locals said he was back in the Bay area, taking care of business, and even though the Swordfish Festival still took place, sponsored by Sauza, Señor Cognac had not returned to participate in the past two year's event.

And what became of others met along the way?
Remember the mysterious Elaine we met in those chilly foothills of San Cristobal?
One night, shortly after we had returned, I tried to reach her and express our gratitude for those peyote buttons which made our Palenque experience so extraordinary.
I dialed the very legible phone number she had given me that afternoon in her hotel room. Even though I punched in the correct digits, the person answering said he had the number I called was his and his alone for over four years and had never shared it with anyone named Elaine. I then checked Eugene information which yielded the same result. There was no Elaine McCrary, either listed or unlisted in Eugene or in any of the outlying areas.
So, Elaine, if you do exist, Dangerous and I thank you from the bottom of our pie-eyed souls for providing the propellant which led us to the high level of consciousness achieved there in the Palenque wonderland. Your generosity was crucial and will long be remembered.

A month or so after we returned, Dave got in contact with Mañuel who insists he was at home that night, we reached out from the train depot, awaiting our call. He says his phone was in perfect operating condition and how sorry he was he could not have been our host for a tumultuous going away bash in Guadalajara. Which bring us back to our other host that peculiar evening.
Dangerous still sticks by his vision of our lady of the depot— her attire as well as well as the color of her eyes, just as I shall always stick by mine. The only way this impasse could logically be solved lay in the two pictures we asked a passerby to take of us, hamming it up while hunched over the backgammon board, our bruja present in the background. That possibility ended in disappointment.
Picture number one found her millimeters out of the top left-hand corner and the other? We will never know. Of the seven rolls of

film we had developed, only one picture did not turn out. You will never guess which one that was. Strange indeed.

I reread *The Teaching of Don Juan* many years later, and then looked back at the notes of my conversation with our mysterious bus station welcome committee.

She had asked many questions in regards to challenges Don Juan had placed before Castaneda. Even though a slight correlation exists between the two, we traveled very different paths. Don Juan was seeking power, we were not, yet she had asked if that was what we had come for.

She said I had the freedom to follow *the path*, which I interpreted to be *the road*. Don Juan's freedom to follow a path led him towards his goal of becoming a man of knowledge, not to finding a room in Zihuatanejo.

When Dave first ventured off to call Mañuel, our bruja asked if we were men of knowledge. Thinking she meant educated individuals I nodded. Don Juan's Man of Knowledge required a level of attainment neither of us were ready for or had considered seeking.

Were her phrases relative, even though within themselves our journeys bore little comparison? What is the blue eye, gray eye connection between the mongrel dog on my blanket, Enrique, Kaspar and the Bruja, or, as Smokey Robinson asked, was it just my imagination, running away with me?

Years from now, if asked about this mysterious lady, my opinion shall remain steadfast. I stand by what I saw, on four separate occasions. There you have it; it is what it is.

Then there's Marty—or shall we say was. To this day, I have never experienced such chemistry in such a short period of time with any member of the female persuasion. I had been truly, quickly, and fully smitten by *Marty mania.*

Back home in Bellingham, I received either a postcard or letter from my special friend in Morelia every other day. Each reinforced my giddiness as she continually expressed how excited she was to be coming home, May 12th, to be exact. The stage was set.

I had my own bachelor pad, lava lamp, and comfy couch, along with a trio of Teddy Pendergrass albums I purchased at the used record store in anticipation of May 13th.

The day arrived. My phone never rang. No sweat; probably jet lag, delays along the road, time needed to be spent with immediate family. What's a day or two longer?

Five days later her call finally came. It was a positive exchange yet unusually brief, ending with Marty asking if I would drive down to Seattle the next day and have lunch with her. Lunch??????

Right there in the Bellevue Country Club lounge she broke the bad news to me, just as lunch arrived at our table. Her flight home experienced an unexpected layover in Los Angeles. While there, she had a *chance* meeting with an old flame and, yes, a romantic fire, long put out, had been magically rekindled. Such is life.

Remember our Amiga, or rather Amig**o** Kid? By the grace of God, he made his way to the Acapulco *Air Puerta*--I mean *Air Puerto*, where he miraculously managed to catch that flight back to the states. Six years and thousands of dollars later he earned a degree from the University of Washington. His chosen field? Psychology. You figure it out.

And the mummified bat, wedged deeply into the bottom of his backpack? Here I must disappoint you as much as Dangerous and I have been these past thirty-odd years.

You see, even though we've both envisioned the look on Kid's face as he came upon this special souvenir, to this day he has *never* mentioned coming across our special surprise. Dave and I have agreed to remain tight-lipped ourselves. Let it forever remain a mystery as to how mummy bat got there. Kid's refusal to acknowledge our gift continues.

There is one thing worthy of pointing out.

Some time, toward the end of that summer, according to Dangerous' parents, who were also Kid's next-door neighbors, something strange happened. It seems that Kid's parents spent several hundred dollars with Ralph's Bug Busters & Fumigation Service, trying to rid their attic of a radical infestation of microscopic black insects--millions of the little buggers. Both Kid's dad as well as the head fumigator were scratching their heads as to where the heck this strange species of vermin could have possibly originated from.

And the infamous Dangerous one? He's semi-grounded in the real world, earning his money as CEO of a mental health institute in Oakland. Oh yes, he is still a creature of the road.

The bulk of his adventures are restricted to long distance motorcycle trips, an occasional South Sea adventure and our annual rendezvous at Phish Concerts held against the gorgeous canyon-filled backdrop of eastern Washington at The Gorge, Washington.

Last week a postcard arrived in the mail. On the front, four natives in grass skirts stood over a pit, cooking large white fish on sticks over a fire. In the background, four shrunken heads could be seen hanging outside a large thatched hut.

On the back, in his trademark nearly-unreadable cursive: *"Hola amigo. Snorkeled yesterday with a school of baby sharks and barracudas. This is it--The Cook Islands--My New Z-Wat. Get ready; I'm bringing you back a shrunken head and a sack of Kava Root which we'll discuss later. Gotta go, there's a Tiki fest happening three palapas down the beach. One of the local natives promised me I might even get a chance to walk across a bed of glowing coals. Wish you were here...Dangerous Dave."*

And how did it go for the Clark family in Melaque?

Our $300 per week house was a steal. No *rattatas*, you could flush your toilet paper, we even had our own *Agua Purificada,* although one had to be on their toes and hurry out into the road and flag down the water man as he worked his way down the dusty excuse of an unpaved side street. Once you got his attention, and paid thirty-two pesos, a fresh jug of water was yours.

Barra sat around the bend and the first time I glanced in that direction I was itching to board the local bus and reacquaint myself with my old haunts.

The kids turned up their noses at the second-class clunker chugging by that charged eight pesos to take you into town, choosing instead to partake in the shifting sand and mile-long beach walk necessary to get there.

When thirty years pass by it is inevitable things change. Progress marches on. Barra proved to be no exception.

The most shocking aspect was that our beautiful uninhabited lagoon out past the spit's end, the place where we would get stoned silly then sit and stare peacefully at the lush green vegetation across the way, was no longer uninhabited.

 Land developers had fired up their diggers and loaders. The result? Welcome to the 199 room Grand Bay Hotel. Standard rooms go for $225 per night during summer, $275 in prime tourist season. There is also a golf course attached where duffers pay in excess of $100 for 27 holes of fun. There goes the neighborhood.

Ponchos closed its doors many years back, as hurricane season after hurricane season took their toll. A large modern hotel overlooks the water where once we ate pancakes and *Milanesa De Res* at the Hotel Guadalajara.

As I wandered down side streets, many small shops and storefronts remained the same, selling blankets, watches, and a multitude of odds and ends. It seemed like each store sold the same commodities as their next-door neighbor, which must have made for interesting relationships.

Beachside restaurants are abundant, Contemporary hip-hop now blasts from their systems, having replaced the mariachi music once so prevalent, an essential ingredient of our experience.

One Karmic coincidence was worth mentioning. On our day trip to town, we rented a twenty-peso-per-day beach umbrella. From there we spent several hours swimming in the bay which had become non-swimmer friendly.

The slope of the bank leading down to the water had changed, due to the hurricanes and the extension of the spit, created by Grand Bay Hotel, which altered the eco-flow and the direction the currents reached the shore. This quickly recalled how our bruja lashed out against advancing technology and the pitfalls of modern ways.

After returning from a liquado run with Max, I took off my sandals and plunged enthusiastically into the bay. Unfortunately, I had left my wallet in my swim trunks' back pocket. When I returned to the shore the wallet did not come back with me.

While giving myself a tongue-lashing for being a freakin' idiot, I suddenly realized this very location was where I had my wallet and tourist visa stolen way back when. Could this be an actual dip-shit vortex? Does any such thing exist?

Vacation 2016 came to a successful close. We opted to pass on the spendy airport shuttle option. Instead, we cut a deal our last night with our cab driver, Luis, who promised to get us back to the airport in Manzanillo for less than half price.

We left Melaque at midday, just as the sun started kicking into overdrive. It was Sunday and outside of a few niños playing wall soccer while their older sisters braided each other's hair in the shade, our departure was unceremonious, played out before empty streets with little to no sign of activity.

Our cab arrived with an hour to spare—No stress, no mess. Luis was not there to greet us, "Hangover" his young nephew Alejandro told us. The 90-degree sun has him sweating profusely as he fit our bags into the trunk. He pushed his shades up the bridge of his nose, and smiled, revealing several gold fillings which made his mouth sparkle. "Let's get this road on the show!" he exclaimed as he clicked his seatbelt. And we did.

While the kids became transfixed with their electronic apparatus and my wife calmly took in the palm trees passing by, Alejandro and I chatted.

I told him we had been there seven days, far too little time to fully appreciate the experience.

"Ah, The Mañana Method, no? Longer is better, si; but while the world which you exist in keeps moving faster and faster, you have found some time to come back here--to appreciate what the art of doing little of nothing is all about, si?"

I told him our trip was primarily for the young ones in the backseat; to expose them to the less commercial side Mexico had to offer them. I told him that I had already found my groove.

"And did they see that while here in Melaque? Do you think they had enough time to feel Mexico's true heartbeat?"

"We did our best to move slow, catch every sunset until long after the stars take the stage, and to respect the culture around them as well as for those who make it their home. That is a pretty good start, don't you think?"

"Do you practice what you have learned while here when you return home?"

"Undeniably." I could only summon up one example, that of waiting in long lines in the local supermarket.

As the poor fool at the front of the line fumbles with his cash card and the basic process of swiping it correctly, those in front of me twitch and roll their eyes impatiently. Two minutes pass. The transaction continues to falter. The dude just ahead of me sighs, rolls his eyes then, from the corner of his mouth, "Can you believe this shit?" I pause for a second, a picture of calm repose, then respond. "No big deal. Not nearly as excruciating as spending eight hours on a cold bus station floor in Guadalajara waiting for the morning bus. I guess I have an extra couple minute to spare."

Alejandro nodded his head. "Then, you have done well, my friend. It is exactly what I have come to expect from you."

I assumed something may have got lost in translation so I nodded, smiled, and joined my wife, trying to appreciate one last time the final miles of jungle terrain we were leaving behind.

Around the bend, Manzanillo airport suddenly stood before us. We were an hour and a half early. Crumple up any lingering airport arrival stress and let's check in.

Alejandro unloaded the trunk and accepted my two hundred pesos with a firm handshake. As the others headed off the scorching asphalt he added.

"Once again it is sad to see you go, amigo, as sad as you are feeling to leave, no doubt. Each visit you continue to choose the right path, looking at each deliberately, as you would say, to make sure that path has a beating heart. As always, you are forever welcome to share what is ours. May we see you yet another day."

Alejandro gave me one last golden-tooth grin, offered me a solid soul handshake, then removed his sunglasses so I could look once again into those eyes.

July, 2017

Ye Olde Acknowledgments

It has taken over three decades for this work to arrive ready for publication. After twenty-plus years of revisions, two wonderful, constructive, and stickler-for-detail editors stepped forth to help push The Mañana Method over the finish line.

Thank you very much Sara Samson and Lynne Pearson for your insight, patience, and assistance in completing that task.

The first edition was a self-published test pilot which found its way into the hands of 250 readers. Thanks to their feedback I was made aware of several typos and other 'warts' which I felt necessary to eradicate in order to provide a *smoother/more professional* read that you, the reader, deserve. Henceforth welcome to **THE SECOND EDITION** version of this tale.

Thanks go out to Mad Science Institute author, Sechin Tower, for providing me with the Valerian sword necessary to hack my way through the self-publishing process brambles, as well as to my lifelong friend and artist extraordinaire Kim Lamb, for his ability to take a Sunset Magazine-style photo and fulfill my vision of a *psychedelically-tinged* cover delivered in Dali-esque grandeur. And a special shout out to my good friend and mentor, the late Allen Johnson for his feedback, painful at times, yet truthful that it was along the way.

Thanks to John Love whose technical know-how, friendship and patience was beyond valuable in solving the production quirks and headaches before me during the layout process.

Kudos to Randy Bass, whose keen eye spotted previously undetected flaws which were swiftly eradicated in the name of professionalism.

And a special thanks to you, the reader, for traveling along with us down those many miles. I hope more than a smile or two has graced your face along that path. If you would like to share comments, hellos, or even order personalized copies, feel free to reach me at mimamoma.nav@comcast.net

Finally, there's Dave Damschen, Droogie Supreme, who badgered, motivated, and reassured me that this adventure was worth telling. Without his encouragement, The Manana Method would never have graced the light of day. Gracias, Dangerous…

Michael Dean Navalinski

www.ingramcontent.com/pod-product-compliance
Lightning Source LLC
Chambersburg PA
CBHW030432010526
44118CB00011B/600